中国故事丛书
Understanding Modern China Series
（Editor-in-Chief: Feng Jun）

冯 俊◎主编

中国农业与农村发展

China's Agriculture and Rural Development
in the Post-Reform Era
By Feng Jun, Wang Youming, Hu Yunchao, Yu Ji

冯 俊　王友明　胡云超　余 佶◎著

人 民 出 版 社

总　序

　　中国国家的制度安排是怎样的？中国共产党为什么能够长期执政并带领全中国人民不断从胜利走向胜利？中国共产党执政的"秘诀"有哪些？中国的发展道路是什么？中国现阶段有哪些重大战略？中国下一步发展向何处去？中国经济为什么能够快速发展？诸如此类的问题，都是国际社会尤其是外国政党政要来华访问时思考和询问的问题。为了回答这些问题，让读者了解一个真实的中国和中国共产党，我们组织编写了《"中国故事"丛书》（以下简称《丛书》），作为介绍中国共产党，介绍中国发展道路、发展理论和发展经验的基本材料。

　　《丛书》以党的十八大以来习近平总书记提出的治国理政新理念新思想新战略为指导，着力体现"中国梦"的发展愿景和"两个一百年"的奋斗目标，着力体现协调推进"五位一体"的总体布局和统筹推进"四个全面"的战略布局，着力体现把握、适应和引领中国经济发展的新常态和贯彻落实"五大发展理念"，着力体现"一带一路"、京津冀协调发展、长江经济带等三大经济发展战略，在占有大量鲜活案例和经验的基础上,讲好中国故事,传播中国声音,分析中国问题,提供中国方案。

在编写过程中,《丛书》还努力注意把握好以下四个方面:一是在全面介绍中国改革开放以来取得的成就经验的基础上,注重阐释党的十八大以来全面深化改革的新举措、经济发展的新思路、对外工作的新理念等;二是在展示中国经济社会发展成果的同时,着重分析取得这些成果的原因、背后的运行逻辑、演进的过程;三是坚持问题导向、需求导向,不求大而全,不求系统完整,从国外受众需求出发,有针对性地释疑解惑;四是既讲中国"从何处来",更讲中国"向何处去",一方面引导读者了解认识中国历史发展进程,另一方面注重讲清楚中国如何把握过去、现在和未来的有机统一,继承与创新的有机结合,规划设计未来发展走向。

《丛书》在中共中央对外联络部的指导下,由中国浦东干部学院组织编写。

中共中央对外联络部(简称中联部)是中国共产党负责对外工作的职能部门。目前,中国共产党同世界上160多个国家和地区的600多个政党和政治组织有着不同形式的联系和交往,其中既有左翼政党,也有右翼政党;既有执政党,也有在野党。中国共产党的对外工作是党的事业的一条重要战线,也是国家总体外交的重要组成部分,其工作目标是通过政党交往促进国家与国家、人民与人民之间的了解与沟通。

中国浦东干部学院(CELAP)是中国国家级干部学院,作为中国开展国际合作培训交流的窗口,自2005年3月创立以来,坚持国际性、时代性、开放性的办学特色,大力开展国际合作培训,培训对象包括外国政党政要、企业高管、高级专家等各类国际领导人才。截至2015年年底,已经培训了来自130个国家和地区的学员6000余名,获得了培训国家和地区以及参训学员的广泛认可和普遍好评。

基于国外学员学习的需要,中国浦东干部学院于2012年年初启动《丛书》编写工作，历经 4 年的打磨精炼，数易其稿，于 2015 年年底定稿。《丛书》首批推出 10 册，分别是《中国治理新方略》、《中国共产党党的建设》、《中国经济改革与开发区建设》、《中国政府架构与基本公共服务》、《中国城镇化》、《中国农业与农村发展》、《中国外交与和平发展》、《中国干部选拔任用》、《中国干部教育》、《中国改革开放的"排头兵"——上海》。丛书的作者主要来自中国浦东干部学院，此外还有上海市政府发展研究中心、上海国际问题研究院、杭州城市学研究中心的领导和专家。

《丛书》以中英文对照方式出版，英文翻译主要由上海外国语大学的资深教授主持，深致谢忱！人民出版社对《丛书》的出版予以大力支持，在编写和翻译过程中提出了诸多建设性意见，一并表示感谢！

编写供国外学员学习培训的系列化教材，在国内尚属首次。作为一种新的探索和尝试，难免有所疏漏、错谬，敬请指正。

《中国故事丛书》编写委员会

2016 年 9 月

中国故事
Modern China

目 录

导　言

（一）本书目标

从 20 世纪 70 年代末开始,中国率先在农村开启了改革开放的大门。从此,农业生产和农村面貌发生了翻天覆地的变化,粮食、油料、蔬菜、水果、肉类、禽蛋和水产品等产量连续多年居世界第一,创造了用世界 9% 左右的耕地养活世界近 20% 的人口的奇迹;农村经济协调发展,农林牧渔业全面发展,优质化生产、区域化布局、产业化经营、标准化管理的现代农业格局初步形成。农村第二、第三产业快速发展,带动了农村就业结构的变革和小城镇的发展;农民生活显著改善,农民收入大幅度增长,全国已由温饱不足发展到向全面小康迈进的阶段,中国成为第一个实现联合国千年发展目标要求的使贫困人口比例减半的国家;农村教育、医疗、社会保障制度等公共服务水平全面提升。

中国农业、农村所经历的波澜壮阔的改革发展,为中国成功实现经济体制转轨积累了宝贵的经验,也引起了全世界的瞩目。和世界上其他国家交流发展农业农村的经验,分享富有成效的做法,共同面对资源环境挑战,让人类生活得更美好,不仅是我们的愿望,也顺应了全球化的召唤。正如联合国粮农组织在其发布的《2012年世界粮食不安全状况》中指出,在我们生活的地球上还有8.68亿人长期营养不良,大量人群还处于饥饿状态,而他们中约8.5亿人就生活在发展中国家的农村。唯其如此,我们越感觉到这种交流、分享和共同努力的必要性。出于此目的,本书以介绍中国农村基本制度为主线,分篇章阐述中国如何立足于人多地少、资源紧缺的基本国情,因地制宜地推进现代农业发展、建设新农村、帮助农民实现增收致富的政策措施,并穿插部分实践案例配合阐释。

我们希望国外读者,特别是来中国浦东干部学院进行交流研讨的外国官员、专家和研究人员,通过阅读本书,能够了解中国农业农村发展的历史过程,找到他们感兴趣问题的答案,如中国如何保障粮食安全?如何减贫?如何促进农村建设?如何帮助农民致富?等等。如果能在学习、交流、分享中,为其他发展中国家农业农村的发展提供有益启示和思路,则更是编者的意外之喜了。

（二）框 架 结 构

全书由四章组成。就逻辑结构而言,第一章是背景知识,总体论述中国农业农村农民的基本情况和制度,这有助于读者全面了解改革开放以来中国农业农村发展的历程、制度变迁和当前状况。第二、第三、第四章则分别围绕农业现代化、农村建设、农民增收三个主题进行阐述。

具体而言,第一章概括性介绍中国农业农村农民的基本情况和经济、组织制度,包括家庭承包制、农村土地制度、乡镇企业发展、乡村治理机制等。首先,第一节概述中国农业农村农民的基本情况。第二节总览中国农村改革的背景和历程,梳理出三步重要改革,分别是20世纪 70 年代末开始的建立以家庭承包经营为基础的统分结合的双层经营体制改革;20 世纪 80 年代中期开始推进的农产品流通体制改革和农村经济市场化改革;以及 21 世纪初开始的统筹城乡经济社会发展的基本方略。然后,第三节就农村集体所有制基础上的农村土地制度和以家庭承包经营为基础、统分结合的农业双层经营体制这两项基本经济制度作了详细阐述。第四节则描述中国乡镇企业兴起推动农村第二、第三产业发展及其今后发展走向。第五节介绍中国农村的治理结构,即国家在乡镇设置最低一级政府,代表国家对乡村进行管理;在村一级则实行村民自治。

第二章聚焦于中国如何推进农业现代化发展。在简要回顾农业生产取得的长足进步后,分别从五个方面详细介绍做法。第一节首先强调稳定发展粮食生产的举措。这是从保障中国国家粮食安全出发,任何时刻也不能放松的战略。第二节指出推进农业结构战略性调整的方向。结构调整的目的是提高农业经济效益。第三节从科技为农业生产提供动力角度,指出如何加快农业科技创新和技术推广。第四节和第五节则分别从改善农业设施装备条件和提高农业生产经营组织化程度两方面,提出推进农业现代化的政策措施。

第三章集中论述 2005 年以来中国社会主义新农村建设的情况。在介绍中国提出新农村建设的背景后,具体讨论其建设进展和措施。第一节围绕农村饮水、电力、清洁能源、农村公路、住房、扶贫开发和水库移民后期扶持等方面提出加强农村基础设施建设。第二节从改善农村教育、医疗卫生体系建设、文化体育事业、就业服务工作等方面指出加快发展农村社会服务。第三节则介绍中国按照"保基本、广覆盖、多层次、有弹性、可持续"的要求,健全农村养老、医疗、社会救助制度,提高农村社会保障水平,逐步解除农民后顾之忧。第四节从发展农业循环经济、改善农村生产生活环境角度简要介绍推进农村环境综合整治。第五节从不断推进农村改革和制度创新角度,提出健全农村经济体制机制的各项制度。

第四章探讨如何缩小城乡收入差距,帮助农民增加收入。农民收入构成主要包括农业经营收入和工资性、转移性收入等。第一节探讨了通过农业产业化发展实现增值，通过发展休闲农业等拓展农业功能，以及发挥比较优势培育专业村镇来挖掘农业内部增收潜力。第二节从发展农产品加工业、提升乡镇企业发展水平和发展农村生产及生活性服务业等方面，指出通过发展农村第二、第三产业增加农民收入。第三节从转移农村劳动力向非农产业和城镇转移角度，提出发展壮大县域经济。第四节则关注如何帮助农民转移就业，包括提供培训、信息服务、鼓励创业、劳动权益保护等。第五节是努力增加农民转移性收入，介绍中国政府推行的减税、补贴、社会保障等政策支持体系和扶贫政策。

（三）重点难点

本书的重点在于通过阐释框架性的制度概念和技术性的政策操作，使得国外读者了解30多年来中国农业农村发展的路径和采取的政策工具。本书的难点在于将中国农业农村发展置于整个中国改革发展的宏大背景下，结合中国基本国情和政治经济制度理解其发展历程。

（四）使用要求

建议读者在使用本书时，首先，在阅读顺序上，认真通读第一章，全面了解中国农业农村的基本情况和经济、组织制度，这有助于读者理解后续篇章中各项政策工具。其次，在阅读过程中，请结合书中所提的思考题，有意识地带着问题寻找答案。最后，如果要深入研究相关问题，请参阅相关参考文献。

由于本书试图用简短篇幅对中国农业、农村、农民进行系统分析和科学总结，难免存在挂一漏万。因此，读者如果能在阅读学习过程中，结合所附案例，开展实地走访，我们认为会加深其对中国农业、农村的感性和理性认识，了解田野里辛勤劳作的农民和他们曾经和正在为过上幸福生活所付出的努力。

（一）农业、农村和农民的基本情况

中国是一个发展中大国，有 13.47 亿人口（2011 年），近半数生活在农村。人多地少是基本国情，提高农业综合生产能力、确保粮食安全、增加农民收入始终是中国经济发展的首要任务。党中央、国务院历来高度重视农业，坚持把农业放在国民经济发展的首要位置，强调把农业、农村、农民工作作为全部工作的重中之重。特别是 2012 年 11 月召开的中国共产党第十八次全国代表大会明确提出，到 2020 年实现全面建成小康社会的宏伟目标中，农业现代化和社会主义新农村建设必须成效显著。经过长期的艰苦奋斗，中国实现了粮食等主要农产品供给由长期短缺到总量基本平衡到有余的历史性转变，农民生活从温饱向小康的历史性跨越，中国以占世界不到 9% 的耕地解决了全球近

20%人口吃穿的问题,不仅为中国改革发展奠定了稳定的基础,也为人类的发展做出了巨大贡献。

2003年以来的10多年,是中国农业农村发展最快、农民得实惠最多的10多年。粮食连年增产,年总产量从2003年的43070万吨增长到2012年的58957万吨,年均增产350多亿斤。农业科技进步贡献率达到54.5%;农机总动力突破10亿千瓦,耕种收综合机械化水平达到57%;主要粮食品种良种覆盖率达到96%以上,亩产首次达700斤以上,单产提高对粮食增产的贡献率达80.5%。与此同时,农业农村经济各业发展势头良好,乡镇企业总产值突破60万亿元人民币;农产品加工业产值超过15万亿元;农垦生产总值突破5000亿元;农产品进出口贸易总额超过1700亿美元,其中出口达650亿美元,再创历史新高。

农民人均纯收入连年较快增长,从2003年的2622元提高到2012年的7917元,年均增收540多元,尤其是近几年连续出现了农民人均纯收入增幅高于城镇居民人均可支配收入增幅的可喜局面,城乡居民的收入差距由此有所缩小。同时,农民进城务工经商乃至举家外出到城镇定居的种种束缚正在加快解除。到2011年年底,全国农民工数量已突破2.5亿人,其中举家外出的农民工数量已突破3000万人,农民工已经成为中国诸多行业产业工人中的主体力量。农村劳动力的大规模流动和进城务工经商,不仅为城镇和工商业的发展带来了新生力量,加强了城乡之间经济社会的交融,更为发展现代农业和促进农民收入较快增长开辟了新的空间。与2002年相比,中国农业劳动力的数量减少了7000多万人,乡村中从事农业的劳动力比重降低了12个百分点以上,平均每个农业劳动力实际经营的耕地面积由此扩大了20%以上。2011年,全国农民人均纯收入中的工资性收入达2963.4元,占人均纯收入总额的42.5%。与2000年相比,农民人均工资性收入增加了2261.1元,在人均纯收入中的比重提高了11.3个百分点;同期农民人均家庭经营的收入增加了1794.7元,在人均纯收入中的比重下降了17.2个百分点。工资性收入已经成为21世纪以来中国农民收入增长的重要支柱。

这10多年来,中国农业农村的发展和农民的增收,主要得益于一系列强农、惠农、富农政策的密集出台。从彻底免除农业税到推进乡镇机构改革,从实行对种粮农民生产的直接补贴到建立粮食最低收购价制度,从提出把国家基础设施建设和社会事业发展的重点放到农村,到农村义务教育经费保障制度、新型农村合作医疗制度、农村最低生活保障制度、新型农村社会养老保险制度的建立,从全面推进集体林权制度改革到明确农村土地承包关系要保持稳定并长久不变,从大幅度提高农村扶贫标准到分类指导城镇户籍制度改革政策的出台等,广大农民多年的期盼开始得到实现,这使得蕴藏在亿万农民群众中最丰厚的发展动力得到了极大调动,由此也就造就了中国农业农村发展的新的黄金时期。

(二)农村体制改革历程

1. 农村体制改革背景

1949年10月,中华人民共和国成立后,如何在一个经济基础非常落后的国家上建设社会主义成为摆在新中国缔造者面前的一个全新课题。从新中国成立初期到1978年这30年间,中国曾借鉴苏联模式建立起高度集中的计划经济体制,利用10年时间建立了独立的比较完整的工业体系和国民经济体系。但是,随着经济的进一步发展,这套高度集中的计划经济体制越来越不适应生产力发展状况,严重地束缚和影响了人民群众的积极性、主动性、创造性,使社会主义经济在很大程度上失去了活力。而这一系列的制度与生产力发展之间的矛盾集中爆发在中国的农村,集中体现在中国的农业问题上,人民公社时期的吃"大锅饭"现象,严重影响了农民的生产积极性。要从根本上解决这些问题,解放生产力,就必须启动农村制度的改革。

1978年12月18—22日,中国共产党召开第十一届中央委员会第三次全体会议。大会科学地分析了国内状况和世界大势,总结中国及其他社会主义国家建设的经验教训,决定把全党全国的工作重心转移到社会主义现代化建设上来。大会作出改革开放的伟大决策,从此开辟了建设社会主义的新路。农村改革的序幕也就此拉开,包括恢复和扩大农村社队的自主权,恢复自留地、家庭副业、集体副业和集市贸易,逐步实行各种形式联产计酬的生产责任制,同时提高了粮食和其他部分农产品的收购价格,随后又解决了多种经营的方针问题,从而使农业面貌很快发生显著变化。

2. 农村体制改革历程

中国农村改革经历了 30 多年不断的探索和发展,既有中央农业政策的逐步放宽,也有地方试点与全面推行的不断政策试验。总体来看,中国农村进行了三个阶段的重要改革。

第一阶段改革是 20 世纪 70 年代末开始的以家庭承包经营为核心的农村经营体制改革,通过这一改革,中国在农村建立了基本的经济制度,保障了农民生产经营的自主权,奠定了农村市场经济的基础。第二阶段改革是 20 世纪 80 年代中期开始推进的市场化改革。当时主要从两条线展开:一条线是农产品流通体制改革,即放开农产品的价格和经营;另一条线是在所有制方面的突破。农村多种经济成分的发展,特别是乡镇企业由原来的人民公社、生产大队所有,发展为包括了个体、联户所有的形式,再后来发展为个体、私营等非公有制经济。市场化改革极大地促进了农业和农村经济的发展。而第三阶段改革则是 21 世纪初开始明确统筹城乡经济社会发展的基本方略。一是从 2000 年逐步展开的农村税费改革。税费改革一开始是规范税费管理、实行税费合一,在这个基础上逐步降低农业税,到 2006 年完全取消了农业四税(农业税、屠宰税、牧业税、农林特产税),之后又对国有农场税费实行与农村并轨,共减轻农民负担 1335 亿元。在这个基础上,实行增加对农民的直接补贴,包括种粮直补、良种补贴、购置农机具补贴和农资综合直补,到 2011 年补贴额达到 1406 亿元。从而结束了 2600 年来农民种田纳税的历史,开辟了对农民补贴的时代。二是改革农产品进出口贸易体制,从 2001 年年底中国加入世界贸易组织后,农业全面对外开放。三是推进以乡镇机构、农村义务教育和县乡财政管理体制改革为主要内容的综合改革。四是按照统筹城乡发展的要求,全面推进新农村建设和新型城镇化发展。

在农村改革的推动下,农业和农村发展的体制和机制发生了彻底改变,从计划经济转变为市场经济,市场机制在农业和农村发展中扮演着日益重要的作用;农业和农村发展的手段和环境发生了彻底改变,农业和农村需要依靠现代科技和新型农民,发展现代农业,积极参与国际竞争,提高农业竞争力;农业和农村发展已经进入新的阶段,建设社会主义新农村和全面建成小康社会成为首要目标。

表 1-1　中国农村改革的政策措施

阶段	重要措施	政策效应
1978—1984	家庭联产承包责任制 提高农产品价格 农村土地承包期 15 年不变	农业超常规增长 粮食产量达到历史顶点 农民收入增长迅速
1985—1999	改革农产品统派购制度 发育农产品市场 调整农村产业结构 发展乡镇企业 宏观经济治理整顿 粮食提价和深化流通体制改革 农产品市场体系建设 延长土地承包期 30 年不变 乡镇企业迅速崛起 户籍制度松动与"民工潮"出现	农业增长减速 农产品市场调节范围扩大 农业生产结构多元化 农村经济结构多元化 农民收入增速减缓 农业生产增速加快 农产品供求格局变化 非农产业比重大幅度上升 非农就业比重大幅度上升 农民收入较快增长
2000—至今	全面改革农村税费制度 粮食流通体制改革取得重大进展 加入世界贸易组织 统筹城乡发展 农村综合改革和新农村建设	农业进入无税时代 农业全面对外开放 农民收入恢复性增长 农村社会经济全面发展 城乡经济联动与协调发展

资料来源:宋洪远主编:《中国农村改革三十年》,中国农业出版社 2008 年版,第 2 页。

（三）农村土地制度与农村基本经营制度

1. 农村土地制度

根据《中华人民共和国土地管理法》第二条第一款规定："中华人民共和国实行土地的社会主义公有制,即全民所有制和劳动群众集体所有制。"根据这一规定,中国的土地所有制有两种基本形式:一种是全民所有制土地即国家所有土地,另一种是劳动群众集体所有制土地即农民集体所有土地。该法第八条明确规定,城市市区的土地属于国家所有。农村和城市郊区的土地,除由法律规定属于国家所有的以外,属于农民集体所有;宅基地和自留地、自留山,属于农民集体所有。

土地制度是农村的基础制度。它不仅对土地资源配置及其效率具有重大影响,而且对农村社会稳定和社会公平正义具有重大影响。改革开放以来,中国在明确界定和保护农民土地权利上取得巨大进展,市场机制在土地资源配置中发挥着越来越重要的作用,国家对耕地的保护政策和措施不断强化,政府对土地利用的调控能力不断提高,土地的法律框架也逐步完善。但是,从贯彻落实科学发展观以及构建新型工农关系、城乡关系的要求看,农村土地制度还需要进一步改革和完善。2008 年,中国共产党第十七届三中全会《中共中央关于推进农村改革发展若干重大问题的决定》(本章中以下简称《决定》)提出,"按照产权明晰、用途管制、节约集约、严格管理的原则,进一步完善农村土地管理制度。"这为今后推进农村土地制度改革指明了方向。

（1）建立健全耕地保护制度和节约用地制度

坚持最严格的耕地保护制度。中国是世界上人地矛盾最紧张的国家之一。近年来,国家出台了强化对耕地保护的政策,非农建设占用耕地的规模逐步下降,城镇和园区等各类建设大量圈占土地的势头得到初步遏制。但土地农转非的速度仍然太快,城乡建设用地规模仍然过大,耕地保护的利益补偿等长效机制还不健全,违规违法占地现象依然严重。坚决守住 18 亿亩耕地红线,应进一步强化用途管制,进一步落实最严格的耕地保护制度。一是层层落实责任,增强保护耕地的法定性和强制性。地方各级政府主要负责人应对本行政区域内的耕地和基本农田保护面积负总责。二是完善占补平衡等制度。耕地实行先补后占,不得跨省区市进行占补平衡,要防止只占不补、先占后补、占多补少、占优补劣的现象发生。三是在全国范围划定永久基本农田,确保基本农田总量不减少、用途不改变、质量有提高。对承担耕地保护任务重、基本农田保护数量多的粮食主产区,由国家探索建立补偿机制,注重采用经济手段调动地方政府特别是广大农民保护耕地的积极性。

名词解释:基本农田保护

基本农田保护是指根据一定时期人口和国民经济发展对农产品的需求,以及对建设用地的预测,而对长期不得占用的耕地,依法实行保护的一项土地行政措施。基本农田保护的对象是:国务院有关主管部门和县级以上地方人民政府批准确定的粮、棉、油和名、优、特、新农产品生产基地;高产、稳产田和有良好的水利与水土保持设施的耕地以及经过治理、改造和正在实施改造计划的中低产田;大中城市蔬菜生产基地;农业科研、教学试验田;省级以上人民政府确定的其他农业生产基地。

《中华人民共和国土地管理法》、《基本农田保护条例》和国土资源部制定的有关规章对基本农田保护制度作了规定。这些制度概括起来主要有以下几个方面:

(一)基本农田保护规划制度。各级人民政府在编制土地利用总体规划时,应当将基本农田保护作为规划的一项内容,明确基本农田保护的布局安排、数量指标和质量要求。

(二)基本农田保护区制度。县级和乡(镇)土地利用总体规划应当确定基本农田保护区,保护区以乡(镇)为单位划区定界,由县级人民政府设立保护标志,予以公告。

（三）占用基本农田审批制度。基本农田保护区经依法划定后，任何单位和个人不得改变或者占用。国家能源、交通、水利、军事设施等重点建设项目选址确实无法避开基本农田保护区，需要占用基本农田，涉及农用地转用或者征用土地的，必须经国务院批准。严禁通过调整各级土地利用总体规划变相占用基本农田。

（四）基本农田占补平衡制度。

（五）禁止破坏和闲置、荒芜基本农田制度。禁止任何单位和个人在基本农田保护区内建窑、建房、建坟、挖砂、采石、采矿、取土、堆放固体废弃物或者进行其他破坏基本农田的活动。禁止任何单位和个人占用基本农田发展林果业和挖塘养鱼。禁止任何单位和个人闲置、荒芜基本农田。

（六）基本农田保护责任制度。并作为考核领导干部政绩的重要内容。

（七）基本农田监督检查制度。县级以上地方人民政府应定期组织土地行政主管部门、农业行政主管部门以及其他有关部门对基本农田保护情况进行检查，发现问题及时处理或向上级人民政府报告。

（八）基本农田地力建设和环境保护制度。地方各级人民政府农业行政主管部门和基本农田承包经营者，要采取措施，培肥地力，防止基本农田污染。

2012 年 10 月 11 日，国土资源部召开加快推进高标准基本农田示范县建设工动员部署视频会议，要求加快建设 500 个高标准基本农田示范县，"十二五"期间（2011—2015 年），在划定的基本农田保护区范围内，建成不少于 2 亿亩集中连片、设施配套、高产稳产、生态良好、抗灾能力强、与现代农业生产和经营方式相适应的高标准基本农田，确保完成全国 4 亿亩高标准基本农田建设任务。

实行最严格的节约用地制度。目前，无论城市还是乡村，土地资源利用的粗放和闲置浪费现象仍较为突出。据调查，中国人均城市建设用地达 130 多平方米，超过发达国家 82.2 平方米和发展中国家 83.3

平方米的水平;工业用地平均产出率远低于发达国家水平,农村建设用地利用效率也普遍较低。解决保护耕地和保障必要建设用地矛盾的根本办法,就是节约集约利用建设用地,加快由外延扩张向内涵挖潜、由粗放低效向集约高效转变。一是严格控制新增建设用地规模。二是积极盘活存量建设用地。加强城镇闲散用地整合,鼓励低效用地增容改造和深度开发。积极推行节地型城镇更新改造,重点加快城中村改造,推广各类建设节地技术和模式。三是积极拓展建设用地新空间。加强规划统筹和政策引导,在不破坏生态环境的前提下,优先开发未利用地和废弃地,积极引导城乡建设向地上、地下发展。

(2)强化农民土地承包经营权,健全土地承包经营权流转市场

完善土地承包经营权权能。家庭承包制的推行,实现了集体土地所有权与使用权的分离。《决定》明确提出现有土地承包关系保持稳定并长久不变,夯实了党的农村土地承包政策基础。农民对稳定土地产权关系的愿望非常强烈,必须依法保障农户享有的对承包土地的占有、使用、收益等权利,完善土地承包权权能,赋予农民更加充分而有保障的土地承包经营权。这有利于减少现行农村土地产权关系中内含的不确定性,使农民形成长期的预期。

规范土地承包经营权流转。农村改革以来,国家一直实行允许农村土地承包经营权合理流转的政策,各种形式的土地流转有了一定发展。在总结实践中正反两方面经验的基础上,国家逐步完善农村土地承包经营权流转的政策和法律,明确土地承包经营权流转必须坚持"依法、自愿、有偿"的基本原则,并在不同时期对承包地使用权流转提出了一些具体的政策要求。《决定》关于土地承包经营权流转的政策与过去一脉相承,明确提出允许农民以转包、出租、互换、转让、股份合作等形式流转土地承包经营权,有条件的地方可以发展以专业大户、家庭农场、农民专业合作社等为主体的多种形式的适度规模经营。《决定》还提出土地承包经营权流转的"三个不得":不得改变土地集体所有性质,不得改变土地用途,不得损害农民土地承包权益。按照这一要求,必须禁止擅自通过承包地流转、"村改居"等方式将农民集体所有

土地转为国有,确需转为国有的必须履行法定程序;必须坚持农地农用的原则,农户和农村集体经济组织不得非法出让、出租集体农用地用于非农业建设;必须保证农户的承包权益,土地承包经营权流转收益归承包方所有,任何组织和个人不得侵占、截留;必须防止采用行政命令去推进土地流转,积极培育土地流转中介服务组织,加强土地承包经营权流转的管理和服务。

2014年11月,中共中央办公厅、国务院办公厅印发了《关于引导农村土地经营权有序流转发展农业适度规模经营的意见》,指出:伴随我国工业化、信息化、城镇化和农业现代化进程,农村劳动力大量转移,农业物质技术装备水平不断提高,农户承包土地的经营权流转明显加快,发展适度规模经营已成为必然趋势。实践证明,土地流转和适度规模经营是发展现代农业的必由之路,有利于优化土地资源配置和提高劳动生产率,有利于保障粮食安全和主要农产品供给,有利于促进农业技术推广应用和农业增效、农民增收,应从我国人多地少、农村情况千差万别的实际出发,积极稳妥地推进。

为引导农村土地(指承包耕地)经营权有序流转、发展农业适度规模经营,按照加快构建以农户家庭经营为基础、合作与联合为纽带、社会化服务为支撑的立体式复合型现代农业经营体系和走生产技术先进、经营规模适度、市场竞争力强、生态环境可持续的中国特色新型农业现代化道路的要求,以保障国家粮食安全、促进农业增效和农民增收为目标,坚持农村土地集体所有,实现所有权、承包权、经营权三权分置,引导土地经营权有序流转,坚持家庭经营的基础性地位,积极培育新型经营主体,发展多种形式的适度规模经营,巩固和完善农村基本经营制度。使农业适度规模经营发展与城镇化进程和农村劳动力转移规模相适应,与农业科技进步和生产手段改进程度相适应,与农业社会化服务水平提高相适应,让农民成为土地流转和规模经营的积极参与者和真正受益者,避免走弯路。

具体措施上,通过健全土地承包经营权登记制度,推进土地承包经营权确权登记颁证工作来稳定完善农村土地承包关系;通过创新土地流转形式,规范土地流转行为,加强土地流转管理和服务,合理确定土地经营规模,扶持粮食规模化生产,加强土地流转用途管制来规范引导农村土地经营权有序流转;通过发挥家庭经营的基础作用,探索新的集体经营范式,加快发展农户间的合作经营,鼓励发展适合企业化经营的现代种养业,加大对新型农业经营主体的扶持力度,加强对工商业企业租赁农户承包地的监管和风险防范来加快培育新型农业经营主体;通过培育多元社会化服务组织,开展新型职业农民教育培训,发挥供销合作社的优势和作用来建立健全农业社会化服务体系。

(3)推进土地征收制度改革

近年来,中国各地推进征地制度改革,在征地安置补偿和规范征地程序方面取得了明显进展。但征地制度仍然存在亟待解决的矛盾和问题:土地征占规模过大,失地农民越来越多;对失地农民的补偿偏低,失地农民就业和社会保障是很大的难题。在加快工业化和城镇化进程中,土地征用应当有利于富裕农民,而不是造成大批农民失地失业;应当有利于缩小城乡差距,而不是扩大社会不公。《决定》对深化征地制度改革提出了明确要求。

严格界定公益性和经营性建设用地。中国宪法明确规定,国家为了公共利益的需要,可依照法律规定对土地实行征收或者征用并给予补偿。但《土地管理法》等相关法律并未对公共利益作出明确界定,征地中公益性和经营性建设用地不分,征地范围模糊不清,大量商业性用地也打着公共利益的名义进行征地。按照《决定》要求,今后征地制度改革的重要方向是明确界定"公共利益",缩小强制性征地的范围。在土地利用规划确定的城镇建设用地范围外,经批准占用农村集体土地建设非公益项目,将允许农民依法通过多种方式参与开发经营并保证农民合法权益。

合理确定征地补偿标准。《土地管理法》规定的征收土地补偿费、劳动力安置补助费都是按照被征收土地前3年的平均年产值计算的,而与被征地的区位、经济社会发展水平、土地供求状况等地价因素以及土地征用后的用途和市场价值无关,造成对农民的补偿偏低。《决定》

对完善征地补偿机制提出了新要求,即"依法征收农村集体土地,按照同地同价原则及时足额给农村集体组织和农民合理补偿"。在规划划定的相同区片内,征地应采取统一标准补偿农民,征地补偿标准不应随项目性质不同而不同。在征地过程中,要维护被征地农民的知情权、参与权、监督权和申诉权,逐步建立和完善征地补偿争议的协调裁决机制,为被征地农民提供法律援助。

解决好被征地农民就业、住房和社会保障问题。加强对失地农民的就业培训,多渠道促进失地农民就业,在贷款、税收、场地等方面对自谋职业和自主创业的失地农民提供优惠政策。被征地农民的社会保障费用,按有关规定应纳入征地补偿安置费用,不足部分由当地政府从国有土地有偿使用收入中解决,社会保障费用不落实的不得批准征地。对土地征用面积超过一定数量的村,可以在征地以后给农民留下一定面积的居住地、经营地,由村集体按照统一规划开发经营项目,使农民有长期稳定的收入。

(4)完善农村宅基地制度

农村宅基地是指农村居民因居住生活而建造房屋等建筑物所占用的土地,包括住房、辅助用房与房前屋后庭院用地等。中国农村宅基地分布广、占地面积大,且近年来呈不断增长之势。《决定》对完善农村宅基地制度提出了明确要求。

严格宅基地管理。严格执行农村一户一宅政策,控制超标准建房。农村宅基地节约集约利用潜力大,开展农村宅基地整理,使农村居住由零乱分散变为集中有序、由自然形态变为规划形态、由土地零散使用变为集约使用,有利于基础设施和公共服务设施配套。应在坚持尊重农民意愿、保障农民权益的原则下,合理引导农民住宅相对集中建设,加强对"空心村"用地的改造,盘活用好农村现有宅基地。农村宅基地和村庄整理所节约的土地首先要复垦为耕地,调剂为建设用地的必须符合土地利用规划、纳入年度建设用地计划,并优先安排满足集体建设用地需要。

保障农户宅基地的用益物权。农村宅基地作为一种重要土地资源,是国家为保护农民的利益和基本生活居住权利而实施的一种特殊制度安排。农民期望享有对宅基地更明确的财产权利。《物权法》明确了宅基地的用益物权性质。《决定》提出"依法保障农户宅基地用益物权",就是要保障农户宅基地依法取得、使用和收益的权利。当农户宅基地被征用时,对失去宅基地的农民应给予合理补偿。同时,要防止以扩大城镇非农建设用地来源为目的强行收回农民宅基地,损害农民宅基地权益。

(5)改革农村集体建设用地制度

农村集体建设用地是指农民从事第二、第三产业及其居住生活的空间承载地,包括农村居住用地、农村公共服务及基础设施用地、村办及乡镇企业用地等。总体上看,中国土地要素市场还不完善,在城乡之间发展不平衡、不统一,特别是集体建设用地基本被排斥在土地市场之外。《决定》提出,逐步建立城乡统一的建设用地市场。这是农村集体建设用地使用制度改革的重大政策导向。推动农村集体建设用地在符合规划的前提下进入市场,与国有建设用地享有平等权益,有利于形成反映市场供求关系的土地价格,建立与城镇地价体系相衔接的集体建设用地地价体系,促进土地在竞争性使用中实现更合理的配置。

建立城乡统一的建设用地市场,是规范土地市场的需要。由于缺乏规划指导和法律规范,大量农村集体建设用地自发、盲目进入土地市场,造成违规项目不断出现,规划指标屡遭突破,建设用地供应总量很难有效控制,正常的土地市场秩序受到干扰。规范集体建设用地交易行为已成为今后加强农村土地管理工作的重要任务。《决定》明确提出:"对依法取得的农村集体经营性建设用地,必须通过统一有形的土地市场、以公开规范的方式转让土地使用权,在符合规划的前提下与国有土地享有平等权益。"随着工业化、城镇化的发展,农村集体建设用地的资产价值已经充分显现出来。以公开规范的方式转让农村集体建设用地土地使用权,可以防止以权力扭曲集体土地的流转价格,有利于充分挖掘集体建设用地的巨大潜力,形成统一开放竞争有序的城乡建设用地市场体系。

2. 农村基本经营制度

(1)农业双层经营体制的确立与演变

始于 20 世纪 70 年代末期的农村改革,确立了以家庭承包经营为基础、统分结合的双层经营体制,这是中国改革开放最重要的突破和最重大的成果。1982 年,中央在"一号文件"中肯定了联产承包的基本原则。1983 年,中央"一号文件"《当前农村经济政策的若干问题》进一步把联产承包责任制概括为集体统一经营与家庭分散经营相结合的双层经营体制。1993 年,八届全国人大二次会议将以家庭承包责任制为主的责任制和统分结合的双层经营体制载入了《宪法》。同年 7 月,又将其载入了《农业法》。2002 年,《农村土地承包法》正式颁布,农村家庭承包经营制度进一步巩固。2007 年通过的《物权法》,明确赋予了土地承包经营权的物权属性,强化了对农民土地承包经营权的权利界定。在 30 多年的实践中,农村经营制度不断得到巩固强化。

中国农村以家庭承包经营为基础、统分结合的双层经营体制的内涵可以概括为三个方面:一是坚持农村土地等主要生产资料的公有制。农村和城市郊区的土地,除由法律规定属于国家所有的以外,其余属于集体所有;宅基地和自留地、自留山,也属于集体所有。集体土地所有权归农民集体,由该农民集体全体成员共同行使或农村集体组织在法律规定的范围内行使对土地的占有、使用、收益、处分的权利。二是以家庭承包经营为基础。《农村土地承包法》明确指出,国家实行农村土地承包经营制度。农村土地承包采取农村集体经济组织内部的家庭承包方式,不宜采取家庭承包方式的荒山、荒沟、荒丘、荒滩等农村土地,可以采取招标、拍卖、公开协商等方式承包。三是实行统分结合的双层经营体制。农业集体经济组织实行统一经营和家庭分散经营两个经营层次,集体经济组织用合同的形式确立划分为两个经营层次的经济内容,以责权利体现两个经营层次的统分结合。

(2)稳定完善农村基本经营制度

在改革开放 30 多年的实践探索中,在坚持基本经营制度的前提下,很多地方还结合实际积极创新和完善农村经营体制的有效途径,丰富和完善了农村双层经营体制的内涵。一是推进农业产业化经营。从20世纪90年代中期开始,适应市场经济和农业增长方式转变的要求,在家庭承包经营基础上又创造了农业产业化经营方式,找到了一条对接小农户与大市场的有效途径。截至2012年9月,全国各类农业产业化组织总数达28万多个,带动农户1.1亿户,农户从事产业化经营年户均增收2400多元。二是发展农民专业合作经济组织。作为农民组织起来共同面对市场风险的重要形式,从20世纪80年代中后期开始,各种形式的农民专业合作经济组织开始产生。2007年,《农民专业合作社法》的正式实施,为农民专业合作社自主发展开辟了广阔道路。据统计,到2008年年底全国农民专业合作经济组织有15万多个,成员总数达到3870多万户,占全国农户总数的13.8%,带动非成员农户5512万户。综合有关数据,每个农民专业合作经济组织平均吸纳农户在250多个,一般吸纳农户在100—200户左右,加入专业合作经济组织的农户一般年均增收20%左右,增幅比普通农户高出一倍。三是建设农业社会化服务体系。不断健全农业社会化服务体系,通过社会化服务来解决市场经济条件下一家一户办不了、办不好、办起来不划算的事情。目前,中国的农业社会化服务体系已由改革开放之初政府主导的模式逐步发展为政府相关部门、涉农企业、农民合作经济组织等多元主体参与,公益型、互助型、经营型等多种类型并重,产前、产中、产后等多个环节兼顾的农业社会化服务体系。四是创新农业经营形式。除传统的农户自己从事生产之外,随着农村劳动力的转移和农业社会化服务体系的健全,还出现了种养大户流转土地从事规模经营、农田作业委托、股份合作制经营等多样化的农业经营方式,丰富了家庭承包经营的体制内涵和实现形式。

总体看来,以家庭承包为基础、统分结合的双层经营体制在实践中凸显出普遍的适应性和旺盛的生命力,取得了举世瞩目的成效。

一是保障了农业生产持续稳定发展。农村双层经营体制再造了农村经济微观主体,调动了广大农民群众的生产积极性,解决了人民公社体制下农业生产长期难以解决的激励机制问题,推动了农业生产持续发展,满足了经济社会发展对农产品日益增长的需求。1978 年以来的 30 多年间,中国农业总产值年均增长 10% 以上,粮食和其他主要农产品大幅度增长,创造了用不到世界 9% 的耕地养活世界近 20% 人口的奇迹。从 1978 年到 2011 年,粮食产量由 30477 万吨增加至 57121 万吨,棉花产量由 217 万吨增加到 659 万吨。中国粮食、油料、蔬菜、水果、肉类、禽蛋和水产品等产量连续多年居世界第一,人均主要农产品占有量超过了世界平均水平。

二是推动了农民就业结构不断优化。统分结合的双层经营体制赋予了农民生产经营自主权,使农民获得了自由支配劳动力的权利。随着改革开放后乡镇企业和第二、第三产业的发展,大量的农村劳动力开始向城镇和非农产业转移,使农民的就业结构发生了重大变化,兼业成为普遍现象。农业生产劳动力不仅占社会劳动力的比例在下降,绝对数量也呈减少趋势。2012 年,全国农民工总量为 26261 万人,比上年增长 3.9%。其中,外出农民工 16336 万人,增长 3.0%;本地农民工 9925 万人,增长 5.4%。

三是促进了农民生活条件持续改善。在家庭承包经营制度下,农民获得了独立的生产经营主体地位,奠定了农民持续增收的制度基础。改革开放以来,农民收入保持了持续较快增长,生活水平得到极大改善。1978—2012 年,农民人均纯收入由 134 元增加到 7917 元。特别是 2004 年以来,农民收入连年增长幅度在 8% 以上。中国提前实现了联合国千年发展目标提出的使贫困人口减半的目标,为全球减贫事业做出重大贡献。全国农村已由温饱不足进入到总体小康向全面小康迈进的阶段。

四是推动了改革开放不断深入发展。中国的改革开放首先从农村取得突破,农村改革又首先从经营体制开始取得突破。以家庭承包经营为基础、统分结合的双层经营体制的确立,突破了高度集中的人民公社体制,不仅引领和推动了农村改革,极大地解放和发展了农村生产力,促进了农村经济社会快速发展,有力支撑了经济社会持续进步,而且还吹响了全面改革的号角,为国家经济体制改革探索了路子,积累了宝贵经验,推动了社会主义市场经济体制的形成。

(四) 乡镇企业发展

1. 乡镇企业的兴起

中国乡镇企业的前身是 20 世纪 50 年代中后期出现的社队企业。改革开放以前,为了配合实施重工业优先发展战略,国家采取抑制社队企业发展的政策,规定社队企业只能"就地取材、就地加工、就地销售",不允许社队企业从事商品运输和流通等产业,严禁私人创办农村企业,中国的社队企业发展十分缓慢。1978 年全国社队两级企业共有 152 万个,平均 1924 个农村人口才拥有一个社队企业;社队企业安置农村劳动力 2827 万人,占农村劳动力总量的 9.2%;社队企业的社会总产值 491 亿元,占全社会总产值的比重为 7.17%,占农村社会总产值的比重为 24.10%。

改革开放初期,尽管政府已经认识到社队企业对农村经济发展的重要作用(1979 年 9 月党的十一届四中全会发表的《中共中央关于加快农业发展若干问题的决定》),但受计划管制体制的影响,对社队企业的约束仍然比较大,主要表现在仍然只允许办集体企业,对社队企业生产的产品在流通、价格等方面作出很多限制,社队企业缺乏经营决策、招工用人和利润分配等方面的自主权,甚至一些地方随意关停社队企业。与 1978 年相比,1983 年社队企业总数反而减少到 134.64 万个。

乡镇企业"异军突起"是发生在 1984 年以后。1983 年全国普遍推行了家庭联产承包责任制,农业生产效率明显提高,大量农业剩余劳动力显现。改革开放后农副产品价格几次大幅度提高,部分农民初具投资能力。农民创办企业的积极性高涨,通过挂靠社队企业或创办合资经营企业拓展增收途径,发展农村经济。1984 年年末乡镇企业数量猛增到 606.52 万家,较上年净增 471.88 万家,其中乡村办企业净增

51.66万家,私营企业和个体企业开始涌现。1985年乡镇企业发展势头不减,年末全国乡镇企业数量增加到1222.5万家,比上年翻了一番多,其中农民个体企业达1012.3万家。

2. 乡镇企业的发展

为了与1983年废除农村人民公社体制相适应,经国务院批准,1984年3月中共中央转发了原农牧渔业部及部党组起草的《开创社队企业新局面的报告》,正式将社队企业易名为乡镇企业,并扩大包括社员联营的合作企业、私营企业和个体企业,原有的社队企业归入全乡(镇)或全村农民所有,农民兴办企业同样受到鼓励。

尽管随后几年中乡镇企业数量增长趋缓,但增幅仍然较大,一直持续到1988年,是中国乡镇企业发展最辉煌的时期。乡镇企业突破了所有制形式和经营行业的限制,由过去的社办、队办转变为乡办、村办、联户办和户办同时发展,由农副产品加工为主的产业结构拓展为农业、工业、商业、运输业、建筑业和服务业同时并举的产业格局。1988年,乡镇企业总产值占全国社会总产值的比重达到了24%,占农村社会总产值达58%,年末在乡镇企业就业的劳动力占到农村劳动力总数的23.8%,1986—1988年农民净增收入中有一半以上来自乡镇企业。乡镇企业成了农村经济的"半壁江山"。然而,20世纪80年代中后期中国出现了比较严重的通货膨胀,经济秩序比较混乱。乡镇企业的高速增长,也带来了一系列问题。1989年年初全国乡镇企业在中国农业银行和农村信用社的贷款余额达847.86亿元,比1984年年初增加近5倍,加大了国家的信贷压力。乡镇企业由于技术落后,原材料和能够消耗过高,粗放式增长比较突出。

从1989年开始,国家开始对国民经济进行治理整顿,乡镇企业受到很大冲击,大批乡镇企业关停并转,大量乡镇企业职工回流到农业。1989—1991年乡镇企业发展基本停滞,甚至倒退。

1992年以后,在宏观经济发展环境和经济体制改革影响下,乡镇企业全面发展。针对乡村集体企业存在的产权不清、体制不顺问题,各地通过改革产权制度,完善了乡镇企业的经营机制。针对乡镇企业存在的技术落后、产品质量差、成本高和经济效益低的问题,乡镇企业通过加强科技和人才队伍建设,提高自身素质。针对乡镇企业发展区域的不平衡问题,国家实施了东西合作工程,加快中西部地区乡镇企业的发展。针对乡镇企业高度分散、"遍地开花"的弊端,通过建设工业小区和小城镇,引导乡镇企业集中连片发展。

1992—1996年为乡镇企业发展的第二个高速增长时期。1996年的乡镇企业总数达2336万家,是1991年的1.2倍;吸纳的劳动力达1.35亿,是1991年的1.4倍;在乡镇企业就业的劳动力已经占到农村劳动力总数的29.8%,比1991年上升了7.8个百分点;完成增加值17659亿元,是1991年的5.9倍。乡镇企业已经成为中国农村的主体力量。

为了扶持和引导乡镇企业持续健康发展,1997年1月1日起正式施行《中华人民共和国乡镇企业法》。标志着乡镇企业进入了依法经营、依法管理的新阶段。1998年以后,乡镇企业面临的经营环境发生了很多的变化。长期以来,中国经济商品短缺是企业面临的主要经营环境。1998年以后,中国经济进入新阶段,商品过剩成为企业面临的主要经营环境。在这种环境下,乡镇企业市场竞争力不高的弊端逐渐暴露出来。针对乡镇企业在发展中突出存在的规模偏小、竞争能力比较弱、经营管理水平比较低,以及一些企业破坏资源和污染环境相当严重等问题,自1998年以后乡镇企业进入到结构调整和体制创新的新阶段,主要表现:增长方式由外延扩张型向内涵提高型转变;个体私营企业迅猛发展,乡镇企业的产权主体呈现出多元化趋势;乡镇企业融入现代工业体系的进程加快。

中国乡镇企业的发展深刻地改变了农村经济单纯依靠农业发展的格局。1978年,社队企业总产值只相当于当年农业总产值的37%左右。到1987年,暨乡镇企业发展的第一个"黄金时期",乡镇企业中第二、第三产业产值合计增加到4854亿元,这相当于农业总产值的104%,首次超过了农业总产值。这是中国农村经济发展史上的一个里程碑,它标志着中国农村经济已经进入了一个新的历史时期。到 2007 年,乡镇企业增加值已占农村社会增加值的 68.68%,成为支撑农村经济最坚实的支柱。

乡镇企业的出现和发展革命性地开创了农民在农村就地就近就业的新路子。到 2011 年,乡镇企业从业人员达 241.6 万人,极大地缓解了我国的就业压力,优化了农村劳动力结构,同时为农业适度规模经营、提高劳动生产率创造了条件。继联产承包解决温饱之后,乡镇企业成为实现农村小康生活的另一把钥匙。到 2011 年乡镇企业支付职工工资达 590 亿元,农民人均从乡镇企业获得年收入 24420 元,大大加快了农民致富奔小康的进程。

但是,也必须看到由于乡镇企业地处农村,一些企业产权改革不彻底,管理和技术人才严重缺乏,技术装备水平低,融资困难,规模小,中西部乡镇企业发展水平不高。所以,改革乡镇企业产权,使产权的内部关系明晰化,加快乡镇企业技术改造,大胆引进各类人才,改进企业经营管理,促进乡镇企业向重点小城镇集中,扩大企业规模,组建企业集团,保持农村优美环境,使其成为农村经济的最重要支柱,是未来乡镇企业发展的重要方向。

(五) 乡村治理结构

1. 改革以来的"乡政村治"

中国农村实行家庭联产承包责任制之后,农民获得了土地的经营自主权,土地经营从集中到分散,从而瓦解了建立在土地集中经营基础之上的人民公社制度,"乡政村治"成为农村的基本政治格局。

所谓"乡政村治",包含乡政和村治两个层面的内容,乡政即国家在乡镇设置最低一级政府,代表国家对乡村进行管理;村治即村民自治,在农村成立自治组织,实行民主选举、民主决策、民主管理和民主监督。乡政体现的是国家权力,而村治则是社会权力的化身,乡政是主导力量,村治是基础。乡政和村治在权力的来源和性质、权力的结构、权力的运作方式、权力的职能目的等方面表现出诸多不同。

从权力的来源和性质来看,乡政和村治分享相同的权力来源,但表现出不同的权力性质。中国宪法规定,国家一切权力属于人民,决定了乡政所代表的国家权力和村治所代表的自治权力都来源于人民。虽然来源相同,但二者性质迥异,乡政是国家权力在基层的代表和延伸,而村治则代表社会权力的勃兴,乡政与村治之间的关系就是国家权力和社会权力在基层的关系,这也是乡政村治格局与全能化人民公社体制的重要区别。

从权力的结构来看,乡政作为最低一级政府,其权力机构是乡镇人民代表大会,权力的执行机构是乡镇政府,乡镇党委则对乡镇人大和乡镇政府实行一元化领导。村治是基层农民群众的自治,其权力决策机构是村民会议或村民代表会议,权力的执行机构是村民委员会,村党支部是基层的领导核心,凸显党的一元化领导。

从权力的运作方式来看,乡政体现的是国家权力,代表国家依法对基层施行管理和治理,作为最低一级政府,乡政要贯彻落实国家对基层的方针政策,其权力运作方式强调自上而下的行政命令。而村治则要求实现村民的民主选举、民主决策、民主管理和民主监督,村委会主任、副主任及其成员等都应由村民选举产生,村内公共事务应由村民共同商议决定,村规民约应由村民参与制定。村民自治权力的运作,处处决定于权力对象的意志。

从权力的职能目的来看,乡政身处国家行政序列的末梢,国家对基层的方针政策,通过层层分解传导,最终落实在乡政身上,乡政权力的职能目的更多地是为完成国家下达的任务指标,其责任向度更多体现为对上负责。村治并非隶属国家的行政序列,实行村民自治的目的,是为了实现村民自我管理、自我服务、自我教育,通过直接民主的方式,实现村民当家作主,其责任向度更多体现为对下负责。

"乡政村治"作为治理乡村过程中形成的一种新的政治模式,是中国特色社会主义的上层建筑活动并为社会主义经济基础服务的。乡政以国家强制力为后盾,具有高度的行政性和一定的集权性;村治则以村规民约、村民舆论为后盾,具有高度的自治性和民主性。就村治对乡政的作用而言,村治是乡政的基石。"乡政村治"是中国特色的农村政治。

2. 探索新型乡村治理机制

在新的历史时期,中国乡村治理也进入了一个新的发展阶段。必须通过完善乡村治理机制,进一步健全乡村治理法制,理顺乡村治理主体之间的关系,明确乡村治理主体的权限和职责范围,充分发挥乡村主体多元治理的合力,以促进农村和谐发展。

一是要通过完善法制建设,依法处理乡镇政府与村委会的关系。《村民委员会组织法》已经以法律的形式将乡镇政府与村民委员会的"指导与被指导"关系确定下来,在此基础上要进一步完善相关法律制度,进一步明确界定乡镇政府与村民各自的治理权限,进一步规范乡镇指导村委会的内容、方式以及村委会协助乡镇的事项范围。

二是要进一步健全村民自治机制,提高村委会自治能力。村民自治是实现乡村有效治理的关键一环。村委会作为村民自我管理、自我教育、自我服务的基层群众性自治组织,是激发基层活力的主要载体。健全村民自治机制的关键是明确规范村党支部与村委会的具体职责和工作程序,正确处理和加强党的领导与扩大农村基层民主的关系,使村党组织领导与村民自治协调起来。

三是要积极推进乡镇政府改革,切实转变乡镇政府职能。适应乡村治理变迁的需要,推进乡镇政府改革,转变政府职能是完善新农村乡村治理机制的重要一环,即由管制型政府转变为服务型政府,将乡镇政府工作的重心转移到促进社会事业发展和建设和谐社会上来,重点是加强社会管理和公共服务职能。乡镇原有的经营性、社区性、社会化服务性职能转移给社会组织承担。在社会管理和公共服务的方式上,乡镇政府可采取招投标制、合同承包制、出租制、凭单制、付费制等市场方式,鼓励民间组织参与社会管理和公共服务。

四是积极发展农村新型社会服务组织。农村社会组织是乡村治理的重要力量。长期以来,中国农村社会组织发育不良,农民组织化程度低,制度化参与乡村治理空间狭小,除少数人当选为党代表、人大代表或村民代表能在有限的范围内参与乡村公共事务决策外,广大群众很少有参与乡村治理的渠道。在经济发展落后的地区,乡村企业组织的整体实力薄弱,并导致其难以承担发展乡村经济的职能,这反过来又形成应由乡镇行政机构来承担经济发展职能的错觉。因此,随着农业产业化和市场经济的发展,农民越来越需要组织起来,并且通过各种社会组织来表达利益诉求,共同抵御市场风险,实现农民"自我管理、自我教育、自我服务"的自治目标,使农民真正成为乡村治理主体。

中国农村有 58.9 万个村委会 98%以上实行直接选举

2013 年 3 月 13 日,十二届全国人大一次会议新闻中心在梅地亚中心多功能厅召开记者会。

民政部副部长姜力在回答记者提问时指出,民主选举已经是我国农村广大农民参与中国特色的社会主义政治建设最广泛的实践形式。现在我们国家农村有 58.9 万个村委会,其中有 98%以上都是实行直接选举,大部分省份到目前为止已经开展了 8—9 轮的村委会换届选举,村民平均参选率达到了 95%以上。最近一届的村委会选举是在 2011年开始,到今年结束,全国将有 6 亿农民参加直接选举,这是世界上涉及人数最多的直接选举。现在的村委会选举广泛的采取了无记名投票、公开计票和普遍设置秘密写票处,农民可以按照自己的意愿,选举自己的当家人。民主选举已经成为了我国农村基层民主政治建设的一个重要内容,当然不是全部内容,村民自治还包括民主决策、民主监督、民主管理。这四个民主都实现了,就是我们农村的基层民主政治制度就实现了。

思考题

1. 如何理解中国农村基本经营制度,包括土地制度、家庭经营基础上的统分结合的双层经营体制?

2. 中国乡镇企业的发展对当地农村工业化起到了推动作用,请谈谈如何处理好农村工业化与农业现代化的关系?

参考文献

1. 陈锡文、赵阳、陈剑波、罗丹:《中国农村制度变迁60年》,北京:人民出版社,2009年。

2. 陈锡文、赵阳、罗丹:《中国农村改革30年回顾与展望》,北京:人民出版社,2008年。

3. 宋洪远:《中国农村改革三十年》,北京:中国农业出版社,2008年。

4. 农业部农村经济研究中心:《中国农村改革:过去与未来》,北京:中国农业出版社,2008年。

5. [美]约翰逊著,林毅夫等编译:《经济发展中的农业、农村、农民问题》,北京:商务印书馆,2004年。

6. 林毅夫:《制度、技术与中国农业发展》,北京:格致出版社,2014年。

二、中国农业现代化如何推进

中国是一个人均农业自然资源很不丰富的国家。人均耕地拥有量 1.38 亩,约占世界人均水平的 2/5;淡水人均拥有量 2134 立方米(2007 年),约占世界人均水平的 1/3;森林蓄积量人均拥有 10.2 平方米(2012 年),约占世界人均水平的 1/9;草地人均拥有量为世界平均水平的 1/3。

1978 年以来,随着以家庭承包经营为核心的农村改革的全面推开,社会主义市场经济体制的确立和完善以及对外开放程度的加深,中国农业资源配置效率不断提高,生产结构不断优化,农业综合生产能力大幅度提高,总产出快速增长,粮食总产先后迈上 4 亿吨和 5 亿吨的台阶,基本解决了全国人民的吃饭问题,扭转了多年来粮食供不应求的局面,实现了供求基本平衡,农业发展进入新阶段。主要体现在现代农业建设取得重大进展,生产方式发生了阶段性变化。10 年来中国农业设施装备条件、良种良法推广应用、生产经营管理等方面都有长足进步。主要粮食品种良种覆盖率达到 96% 以上,单产提高对粮食增产的贡献率超过 80%。2012 年,农业科技进步贡献率达到 54.5%,比 2006 年提高 6.5 个百分点,科技已成为农业发展的主要支撑。农业机械化水平达到 57%,比 2006 年提高 19 个百分点,标志着农业生产方式实现了由千百年来以人力畜力为主向以机械作业为主的重大转变。

表 2-1 中国主要农产品产量   单位(万吨)

年份	粮食产量(主要指谷物、豆类、薯类)	油料	棉花	水果	肉类总产量	奶类	水产品总量
2001	45263.7	2864.9	532.4	6658.0	6013.9	1122.9	3795.9
2002	45705.8	2897.2	491.6	6952.0	6105.8	1400.4	3954.9
2003	43069.5	2811	486.0	14517.4	6443.3	1848.6	4077.0
2004	46947.0	3065.9	632.4	15340.9	6608.7	2368.4	4246.6
2005	48402.2	3077.1	571.4	16120.1	6938.9	2864.8	4419.9
2006	49803.9	3059.4	674.6	17239.9	7089.0	3302.5	4583.6
2007	50160.0	2461.0	760.0	18136.3	6865.7	3633.4	4747.5
2008	52871.0	2952.8	749.2	19220.0	7278.7	3781.5	4895.6
2009	53082.0	3154.3	637.7	20395.5	7649.9	3677.7	5116.4
2010	54647.7	3230.1	596.1	21401.4	7925.8	3748.0	5373.0
2011	57120.8	3306.8	658.9	22768.2	7957.8	3810.7	5603.2

资料来源:《中国统计年鉴 2012》,中国统计出版社 2012 年版。

表 2-2 中国农业主要产品产量居世界的位次

项目	1978	1980	1990	2000	2007	2008	2009	2010
谷物	2	1	1	1	1	1	1	1
肉类①	3	3	1	1	1	1	1	1
籽棉	3	2	1	1	1	1	1	1
大豆	3	3	3	4	4	4	4	4

项目	1978	1980	1990	2000	2007	2008	2009	2010
花生	2	2	2	1	1	1	1	1
油菜籽	2	2	1	1	1	2	1	1
甘蔗	7	9	4	3	3	3	3	3
茶叶	2	2	2	2	1	1	1	1
水果②	9	10	4	1	1	1	1	1

注:①1990 年以前为猪、牛、羊肉产量的位次。②不包括瓜类。
资料来源:联合国 FAO 数据库。

中国粮食总产量实现"十一连增"(2003—2014)

新华社北京 2014 年 12 月 4 日电(记者王宇、王希)国家统计局 4 日发布公告,2014 年全国粮食总产量达到 60709.9 万吨(12142 亿斤),比 2013 年增加 516 万吨(103.2 亿斤),增长 0.9%。我国粮食总产量实现"十一连增"。

根据公告,2014 年全国谷物总产量 55726.9 万吨(11145.4 亿斤),比 2013 年增加 457.7 万吨(91.5 亿斤)增长 0.8%。谷物主要包括玉米、稻谷、小麦、大麦、高粱、荞麦、燕麦等。

据国家统计局对全国 31 个省(区、市)农业生产经营户的抽样调查和农业生产经营单位的全面统计,2014 年全国粮食播种面积为 112738.3 千公顷(169107.4 万亩),比上年增加 0.7%。粮食单位面积产量 5385 公斤/公顷(359 公斤/亩),比上年提高 0.2%。

资料来源:农民日报—中国农业新闻网,2014 年 12 月 10 日,http://www.farmer.com.cn/newzt/sylz/gz/201412/t20141210_1000395.htm。

但市场需求、资源环境对中国农业生产的约束明显增强,转变农业发展方式、促进现代农业建设成为新时期农业发展的要求。在工业化、信息化、城镇化深入发展中同步推进农业现代化,是中国"十二五"时期(2011—2015 年)的一项重大任务。加快发展现代农业,既是转变经济发展方式、全面建设小康社会的重要内容,也是提高农业综合生产能力、增加农民收入、建设社会主义新农村的必然要求。

（一）确保国家粮食安全

2013 年 12 月，中共中央总书记、国家主席、中央军委主席习近平在中央农村工作会议上发表重要讲话，他从国家经济社会长远发展大局出发阐述了推进农村改革发展若干具有方向性和战略性的重大问题，同时提出明确要求。会议强调，小康不小康，关键看老乡。一定要看到，农业还是"四化同步"的短腿，农村还是全面建成小康社会的短板。中国要强，农业必须强；中国要美，农村必须美；中国要富，农民必须富。必须坚持把解决好"三农"问题作为全党工作重中之重，坚持工业反哺农业、城市支持农村和多予少取放活方针，不断加大强农惠农富农政策力度，始终把"三农"工作牢牢抓住、紧紧抓好。

关于确保国家粮食安全，会议指出，中国是个人口众多的大国，解决好吃饭问题始终是治国理政的头等大事。要坚持以我为主、立足国内、确保产能、适度进口、科技支撑的国家粮食安全战略。中国人的饭碗任何时候都要牢牢端在自己手上，中国人的饭碗应该主要装中国粮，一个国家只有立足粮食基本自给，才能掌握粮食安全主动权，进而才能掌控经济社会发展这个大局。要进一步明确粮食安全的工作重点，确保谷物基本自给、口粮绝对安全。耕地红线要严防死守，18 亿亩耕地红线仍然必须坚守，同时现有耕地面积必须保持基本稳定。调动和保护好"两个积极性"，要让农民种粮有利可图、让主产区抓粮有积极性。搞好粮食储备调节。中央和地方要共同负责，中央承担首要责任，各级地方政府要树立大局意识，增加粮食生产投入。善于用好两个市场、两种资源，适当增加进口和加快农业走出去步伐。高度重视节约粮食，让节约粮食在全社会蔚然成风。

中央明确提出确保"谷物基本自给、口粮绝对安全"的底线。要集中力量保重点，这是由中国的资源禀赋决定的。同时，靠国际市场解决中国人的吃饭问题也是不现实的。近年来，中国的粮食进口量有所增加，但是总量并不是很大，主要是因为国际市场上的粮价比国内市场低,同时也为了满足国内多样化的消费需求,适当进口一些优良的品种进行调剂。2013 年水稻、小麦、玉米这三大谷物的进口量仅占国内产量的 2.4%,今后可能还要适当进口一些国内短缺品种,但是谷物进口不会大幅增加。中国不会到国际市场上过多地采购谷物,因为中国粮食安全战略就是保证基本自给,而且还要考虑到本国农民的就业和增收。

中国增加粮食产量的主要做法有如下方面。

第一,稳定粮食播种面积。坚持最严格的耕地保护制度,严格控制非农建设占用耕地,加大土地整理复垦开发补充耕地力度,确保 18 亿亩耕地面积不减少、质量有提高。全面完成基本农田划定工作并落实到地块,确保基本农田保有量不低于 15.6 亿亩,其中水田面积保持在 4.75 亿亩左右。抓紧划定一批基础条件好、生产水平高的粮食生产区域,实行永久保护。提高粮食复种指数,确保全国粮食播种面积稳定在 16 亿亩以上,其中谷物播种面积稳定在 12.6 亿亩以上。

第二,优化粮食品种结构。积极发展南方地区双季稻生产,因地制宜扩大东北优质粳稻生产,稳步推进江淮等粳稻生产适宜地区"籼改粳"。大力发展优质专用小麦。扩大玉米播种面积,加快发展优质专用玉米。积极发展高油高蛋白大豆,力争稳定大豆自给水平。积极发展小杂粮,扩大优质专用薯类生产。

第三,提高粮食单产水平。积极选育高产优质粮食新品种,加快新品种繁育和推广,提高粮食作物良种普及率。改进耕作方式,推行水稻大棚和工厂化育秧、土壤深松深翻、免耕播种、测土配方施肥等高产栽培技术和模式,推进粮食生产全程机械化、专业化和标准化。加大高产创建力度,因地制宜实施整乡整县整建制推进,促进大面积均衡增产。

随着工业化、城镇化快速推进,包括农业资源的高强度利用,对耕地污染带来的环境问题也是比较突出的。中国农业部门对此高度重视,正在采取一系列措施解决这些问题,全力加强耕地质量保护与提升,总体目标主要是"两提一改"。即:提高田间设施水平,主要是建设高标准农田;提高耕地基础地力,力争到 2020 年耕地地力提升 0.5 个等级,土壤有机质含量提高 0.5 个百分点;改善耕地质量,使耕地酸化、盐渍化、重金属污染等问题得到有效控制。在路径上突出"四字"要领,就是"改、培、保、控"。改良土壤,培肥地力保水保肥,控制化肥和农药的施用量、控制重金属和有机物对土壤的污染。围绕这些目标,主要抓四件事:一是制定分区耕地改良的实施方案;二是制定耕地质量等级标准;三是制定《耕地保护条例》,依法保护耕地;四是抓好永久基本农田的划定。

一粒小小的种子改变了世界

2005 年年底,联合国世界粮食计划署在北京正式宣布从 2006 年起停止对华粮食援助。这标志着中国 26 年的粮食受捐赠历史画上了句号,并开始成为一个重要的援助捐赠国。中国以占世界不到 10% 的耕地养活了占世界 20% 多的人口,其中杂交水稻立下了汗马功劳。

袁隆平,这位"杂交水稻之父",在 1973 年率领科研团队开启了杂交水稻王国的大门,在数年的时间内就解决了十多亿人的吃饭问题,有力回答了世界"谁来养活中国"的疑问。

1973 年 10 月,在全国杂交水稻会议上,袁隆平发表论文《利用"野败"选育"三系"的进展》,正式宣告中国籼型杂交水稻"三系"配套成功。

1976 年,杂交水稻开始进行大面积推广,全国达到 208 万亩,增产全部在 20% 以上。

1981 年,袁隆平被授予新中国第一个国家特等发明奖。

1982 年,国际水稻研究所学术会首次公认:中国科学家袁隆平为世界"杂交水稻之父"。

1986 年,他提出了杂交水稻育种方法从"三系"向"两系"再向"一系"迈进的战略设想。1987 年,"两系法"杂交水稻研究被列为国家"863"计划项目,袁隆平出任责任专家,主持全国 16 个单位协作攻关。1995 年,"两系法"杂交水稻大面积生产,平均产量比"三系"增长了 5%—10%。

当全国农业界的兴奋还没有离开"两系法",袁隆平又提出超级杂交稻分阶段实施的战略目标:把塑造优良的株叶型与杂种优势有机结合起来,提出了旨在提高光合作用效率的超高产杂交水稻选育技术路线。

2000 年,超级杂交水稻亩产 700 公斤目标实现;2004 年, 800 公斤目标实现;2005年,超级稻第三期小片试验田达到900公斤。

杂交水稻不仅解决了中国人的吃饭问题,也对世界减少饥饿做出了卓越的贡献。从亚洲到美洲,再到非洲、欧洲,增产优势明显的杂交水稻被冠以"东方魔稻"、"巨人稻"、"瀑布稻"等美称,甚至将之与中国古代四大发明相媲美。

包括"拯救饥饿奖"、联合国粮农组织"世界粮食安全保障奖"、"世界粮食奖"、入选美国科学院外籍院士等多个世界奖项和荣誉,是对袁隆平为全人类做出伟大贡献的肯定。

资料来源:新华网,2009年8月25日,http://news.sina.com.cn/c/2009-08-25/175918508894.shtml。

中国杂交水稻之父:袁隆平

袁隆平,1930年9月7日生于北京,江西德安县人,无党派人士,现居湖南长沙。中国杂交水稻育种专家,被称为中国的"杂交水稻之父",中国工程院院士。2006年4月当选美国国家科学院外籍院士。2010年荣获澳门科技大学荣誉博士学位。2011年获得马哈蒂尔科学奖。

现任政协十二届全国委员会常务委员,湖南省政协副主席,湖南省科协副主席。国家杂交水稻工程技术研究中心主任暨湖南杂交水稻研究中心主任、西南大学农学与生物科技学院名誉院长、

图2-1 "中国杂交水稻之父"袁隆平
(新华社记者陆波岸摄)

湖南农业大学教授、中国农业大学客座教授、怀化职业技术学院名誉院

长、湖南生物机电职业技术学院名誉院长、联合国粮农组织首席顾问、世界华人健康饮食协会荣誉主席。

第四,加强粮食主产区建设。产粮大省、大市、大县,是保障国家粮食安全的中坚力量。中国 13 个粮食主产省的产量占全国的 75%、商品量占 80%、调出量占 90%,全国超 10 亿斤的产粮大县有 400 多个、产量占全国的 54%,全国超 100 亿斤的产粮大市(地)有 33 个、产量占全国的 43%。抓住了这一块,粮食安全就有了重要的保障。

全国确定 800 个产粮大县作为新增千亿斤粮食生产能力的规划重点,加大投入力度,加快实施进度,尽快形成新的生产能力,将粮食生产核心区和非主产区的产粮大县建成国家级商品粮生产基地。在保护生态环境的前提下,根据全国粮食供求状况,适时、适度开发粮食生产后备资源。

吉林省榆树市:粮食主产区的规划建设

吉林省榆树市是中国重要的商品粮生产基地,被誉为"天下第一粮仓"。2010 年,吉林省榆树市被列为中国首批 50 个现代农业示范区之一。

2011 年,全市农作物种植面积达到 37.9 万公顷,其中粮食 34.7 万公顷。2011 年,全市粮食总产量达到 62 亿斤,创历史最高水平,连续八年夺得全国粮食生产标兵县(市)的光荣称号。榆树市围绕百万亩高标准良田、全程

图 2-2 吉林:天下粮仓再创丰收奇迹
(新华社记者王昊飞摄)

农机化、蔬菜生产基地、牧业生产基地建设以及农业产业化等方面,对示范区建设进行了科学规划。

1. 规模化经营,在土地所有制不变的情况下,大力推进土地规模化经营,2011年全市土地流转面积达到87万亩,共发展种粮大户500户,培养农民企业家436人,组建农民经济合作组织330个。

2. 机械化耕种,大量引进先进设备,全市拖拉机保有量28510台,其中大型拖拉机13493台,全市农业机械化水平在全国名列前茅。

3. 水利化保障,在粮食增产方面,新增加10万亩节水灌溉工程,实现玉米密植种植,可增产30%。

4. 科技化支撑,把农业项目资金打捆使用,集中建设高标准良田,投资4500万元,建设高产示范田41万亩。集成推广了测土配方施肥、保护性耕作、玉米宽窄行休闲种植等科技增产措施,农田灭鼠、赤眼蜂防治玉米螟实现了全覆盖。

5. 继续加大中国北方冬季蔬菜生产基地建设,新建蔬菜园区26个,建成日光温室1440栋、大棚1560栋,总数达到44000栋,蔬菜产值实现18亿元,争取在10年内基本实现户均一栋大棚,把榆树市建成"东北的寿光"。

第五,完善粮食生产的激励机制。建立健全粮食主产区利益补偿机制,支持粮食生产的政策措施向主产区倾斜。完善产粮大县奖励政策,将财政支持与粮食播种面积、产量、商品量以及粮食调出量挂钩。逐步取消产粮大县农业基本建设项目县级配套。完善粮食补贴机制,研究制定将粮食直接补贴与粮食播种面积、产量和交售商品粮数量挂钩的操作办法,切实发挥补贴对粮食生产的激励作用,使种粮农民能够获得较多收益。

为了鼓励农村流转土地用于粮食生产,2014年11月发布的《关于引导农村土地经营权有序流转发展农业适度规模经营的意见》明确提出:一是新增补贴向粮食生产规模经营主体倾斜。二是通过粮食主产区、粮食生产功能区、高产创建项目实施区的产业规划和相关的农业生产扶持政策,引导经营主体生产粮食。三是合理引导土地流转价格,以降低粮食生产成本,稳定粮食种植面积。

(二)推进农业结构战略性调整

1.优化农业区域布局

从规划层面,中国因地制宜,发挥优势,鼓励和支持粮食、棉花、油料、糖料等大宗农产品向优势产区集中,加强蔬菜、水果、茶叶、花卉、蚕茧等园艺产品基地建设,发展各具特色的优势畜产品和水产品产区。加快构建以东北平原、黄淮海平原、长江流域、汾渭平原、河套灌区、华南和甘肃新疆等农业主产区为主体,以其他农业地区为重要组成的"七区二十三带"农业战略格局。

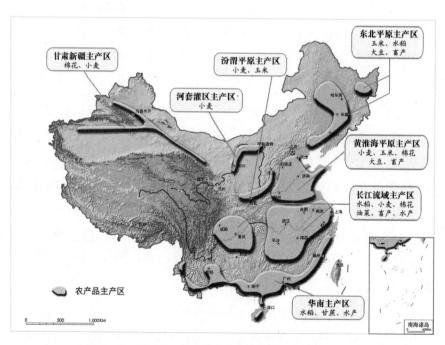

图2-3 "七区二十三带"农业战略格局(新华社发)

中国设定"七区二十三带"农业战略核心区域

根据中国国务院于 2010 年年底印发的《全国主体功能区规划》,中国将构建"七区二十三带"为主体的农业战略格局。

七区二十三带是指包括七大农业主产区和小麦、玉米、棉花等总计二十三个农产品名称。构建以东北平原、黄淮海平原、长江流域、汾渭平原、河套灌区、华南和甘肃新疆等农产品主产区为主体,以基本农田为基础,以其他农业地区为重要组成的农业战略格局。

东北平原农产品主产区,要建设优质水稻、专用玉米、大豆和畜产品产业带;黄淮海平原农产品主产区,要建设优质专用小麦、优质棉花、专用玉米、大豆和畜产品产业带。

长江流域农产品主产区,要建设优质水稻、优质专用小麦、优质棉花、油菜、畜产品和水产品产业带。

汾渭平原农产品主产区,要建设优质专用小麦和专用玉米产业带。

河套灌区农产品主产区,要建设优质专用小麦产业带。

华南农产品主产区,要建设优质水稻、甘蔗和水产品产业带。

甘肃新疆农产品主产区,要建设优质专用小麦和优质棉花产业带。

在重点建设好农产品主产区的同时,积极支持其他农业地区和其他优势特色农产品的发展,根据农产品的不同品种,国家给予必要的政策引导和支持。主要包括:西南和东北的小麦产业带,西南和东南的玉米产业带,南方的高蛋白及菜用大豆产业带,北方的油菜产业带,东北、华北、西北、西南和南方的马铃薯产业带,广西、云南、广东、海南的甘蔗产业带,海南、云南和广东的天然橡胶产业带,海南的热带农产品产业带,沿海的生猪产业带,西北的肉牛、肉羊产业带,京津沪郊区和西北的奶牛产业带,黄渤海的水产品产业带,等等。

2. 大力发展养殖业

做大做强畜牧业,加强品种改良和疫病防控,推进畜禽养殖规模化、标准化、集约化和现代化。促进生猪生产平稳健康发展,积极支持生猪标准化规模养殖场(小区)建设,改善饲养、防疫和粪污处理条件,切实加强生猪疫病公共防控体系建设,完善生猪饲养补贴制度、良种繁育政策,进一步强化信贷和保险对生猪生产的支持,继续实施生猪调出大县(农场)奖励政策。加快转变奶业发展方式,努力保障乳制品质量安全,促进奶业持续健康发展。加快发展肉牛、肉羊生产,稳定发展禽肉、禽蛋生产,鼓励发展特种养殖。促进水产业健康发展,推广水产生态养殖模式,扶持和壮大远洋渔业。

3.加快发展资源节约型农业

积极推广渠道防渗、管道输水、喷灌滴灌等农业节水技术,大力发展高效节水灌溉,新增5000万亩高效节水灌溉面积。采用地膜覆盖、集雨补灌、保护性耕作等技术,积极发展旱作农业,加快建设旱作农业示范基地。提倡精耕细作,发展间作套种,推广立体种植,提高土地利用率。积极推广节种、节肥、节药、节能等技术措施,提高农业投入品使用效率。

干旱地区发展旱作农业

甘肃省位于中国西北部,年平均降雨量只有300多毫米,多集中在7—9月,蒸发量大,全省旱地面积3600万亩,占耕地面积的70%。甘肃自然条件严酷,农业灾害频发,但是近几年,全省粮食生产连年丰收,产量屡创新高。

产量屡创新高是科技推动的结果。全膜双垄沟播技术攻克了提高降水利用效率的难题,将宝贵的降水留在土里滋润农作物生长也成为可能。全膜双垄沟播技术是指:地上起大小双垄,再覆上一层地膜,一来全膜覆盖可以减少水分蒸发,二来将平作改为起垄,可以将春季无效降水通过集雨面汇集到播种沟,将种子播在沟里,便可充分吸收水分。这项技术能让天然降水的利用率提高1倍。据统计,在正常年景下,全膜双垄沟播玉米可较半膜玉米平均增产35%以上,马铃薯比露地栽培平均增产30%以上。

实现粮食稳产增产，选择"种什么"很关键。随着全膜双垄沟播技术的推广，甘肃旱作农业区采取"压夏扩秋"的办法，扩大玉米、马铃薯等高产秋季作物的种植面积，减少冬小麦种植面积，科学调整了农业结构。据统计，全省玉米面积已由 2000 年的 697 万亩扩大到 2010 年的 1274 万亩；马铃薯面积由 626 万亩扩大到近 1000 万亩；夏秋作物比例由 51∶49 调整为 38∶62，玉米、马铃薯成为甘肃粮食稳产、增产的重要支撑。

图 2-4　地膜铺就旱塬上的"希望工程"（新华社记者张锰摄）

广河县齐家镇周家子村 70 岁的老人马少元介绍，"去年我家玉米打了 26000 斤，卖了好价钱。大量的秸秆拿来喂牛，产生的有机肥再还田。牛有吃的了，庄稼也长得好。"现在，甘肃玉米种植面积超过了 1000 万亩，在增加粮食产量的同时，也为草食畜牧业发展提供了原料。广河等地正在探索"旱作农业—玉米秸秆—养殖牛羊—能源沼气—有机肥料—粮食增产"的循环农业模式。2010 年，草食畜在甘肃畜牧业中的比重上升到 45%，比 2000 年提高了 7 个百分点。

4.积极发展都市型农业。发挥城市科技、人才和市场等优势,加强农业深度开发,不断拓展农业功能,大力发展科技农业、设施农业、生态农业、精品农业和观光农业。加强大中城市周边"菜篮子"产品生产基地建设,提高大中城市蔬菜等生鲜食品自给能力。

上海:都市现代农业的领跑者

对于农业资源和农业产值占 GDP 的比重而言,上海是一个标准的农业小市;对于农业发达程度和单位面积效益而言,它又是一个不折不扣的农业强市。

尽管上海耕地资源稀缺,但科技、人才、资金、信息和市场优势明显,都市现代农业发展走在全国前列。上海农业总产值仅占全市经济总量的 0.6%,但与市民生活密切相关的蔬菜等农产品的供应却多年来保持少有的稳定,蔬菜价格指数在全国 50 多个城市对比中稳居 30 名开外,尤其是市民生活不可或缺的绿叶菜 90%靠自己解决;尽管从事农业劳动的人数不多,但各种现代化的农业园区惊艳全国,高科技农业服务、辐射全国,农业创新理念、实践引领全国;农村第一、第二、第三产业有机交融,农业不再是弱质产业,耕地亩均效益接近 5000 元,远高于全国平均水平;尽管农田总量不多,但 160 万亩粮田成为城市天然的季节性人工湿地,构成城市一道绿色生态屏障;种类丰富的农业旅游如火如荼,郊区农村已成市民周末休闲度假、科普体验、寓教于乐的首选。

20 多年来,上海历经不同农业发展阶段,都市现代农业先行先试,农业发展一脉相承,在我国大城市中具有典型性,见证了都市现代农业发展的轨迹。

20 世纪 80 年代中期,上海从乡村农业步入城郊农业。农业功能仅限于为城市提供鲜活和初级加工农产品,农业发展依靠自身,实力赢弱。90 年代初期,市民消费需求趋于多元化,城市对农业发展提出了更高要求。上海市"九五"计划提出"要走出一条具有生态平衡、观光休闲、科技示范、出口创汇等多种功能的都市农业发展新路"。上海都市农业开始起步。从 90 年代后期开始,上海都市农业逐渐转变为都市现代农业,城郊融合开始提速,郊区农村成为城市重要组成部分,以财政、金融、科技为主要内容的农业支持体系日臻完善。现代化温室、喷灌、滴灌等设施和技术得到普遍应用,并成为市民参观和游览的重要景观。

2007年,时任上海市委书记的习近平同志在上海市第九次党代会上指出,依托特大型城市综合优势,着力发展高效生态农业,全面提升农业的经济功能、生态功能和服务功能。

上海农业发展"十二五"规划(2011—2015)明确指出,大力发展都市高效生态农业,强化农业的经济功能、生态功能和服务功能,确保地产农产品有效供给和质量安全,把拓展农业多种功能作为现代农业发展新的生长点。

上海的农业形态正由传统单一的农业生产功能向经济功能、生态功能、科技示范功能、服务功能等多位一体的都市现代农业功能转变。上海农业占全市GDP的比重今后还会降低,但农业的组织化程度却在显著提高,都市现代农业变得更为高效,"拳头效应"更加显现。

资料来源:农民日报—中国农业新闻网,2012年4月23日,http://www.farmer.com.cn/jjpd/hyyw/201204/t20120423_713100.htm。

5.发展林业产业

加强优质苗木和珍贵树种培育,搞好工业原料林、用材林等木材战略储备生产基地建设,加快发展森林旅游、竹产业、花卉苗木、野生动植物繁育利用产业和沙产业,大力发展油茶、核桃等木本粮油和特色经济林产业,加快发展林下经济。

6.保障农产品质量安全

加强宣传引导,增强农产品生产经营者质量安全意识,落实质量安全责任。以农业投入品安全使用、农兽药残留限量、种养殖规范等为重点,完善农产品质量安全标准体系,大力推行农业标准化生产。切实强化农业生产投入品和产地环境监管,从源头上确保农产品质量安全。建立农产品质量安全可追溯制度,加大农产品注册商标和地理标志保护力度,积极发展无公害农产品、绿色食品、有机农产品和地理标志农产品。加强农产品质量安全检验检测体系建设,搞好农产品质量安全例行监测和监督抽查工作。加大监管力度,强化农产品生产、收购、储运、加工、销售全程监管,严禁使用违禁药物、非法化学物和其他可能危害人体健康的农业投入品。大力开展农产品质量安全风险评估,提高风险防范能力。

(三)加快农业科技创新和技术推广

1.提高农业科技创新能力

立足中国基本国情,面向产业需求,大力推进现代农业产业技术体系建设。加大国家各类科技计划向农业领域倾斜支持力度,支持发展农业科技创新基金,推进国家农业高新技术产业示范区和国家农业科技园建设,改善农业科技创新条件。深化农业科研院所改革,完善农业科研立项和科研评价机制,积极培育以企业为主导的农业产业技术创新战略联盟,支持企业加强技术研发和升级,鼓励企业承担国家各类科技项目,不断完善农业科技创新机制。加强农业教育科技培训,加快培养农业科技人才和创新团队。

2.突破农业科技重大基础理论与关键技术

加强农业基础研究,在农业生物基因调控与分子育种、农林动植物抗逆机理、农田资源高效利用、农林生态修复、有害生物控制、生物安全和农产品安全等方面突破一批重大基础理论和方法。加快推进前沿技术研究,在农业生物技术、新材料技术、先进制造技术、精准农业技术等方面取得一批重大自主创新成果。加强农业节本降耗、节水灌溉、农机装备、新型肥料、疫病防控、加工贮运、循环农业、海洋农业、农村民生等领域的技术创新、集成与应用。提高农业生产经营信息化水平,在信息采集、管理信息、资源调查、气象预测和灾害预警等领域实现新突破。

3. 做大做强种业

加大种业基础性、公益性研究投入,加强种质资源收集、保护、鉴定,创新育种理论方法和技术,创制改良育种材料,实施转基因生物新品种培育重大科技专项,加快培育一批突破性新品种。继续做好常规育种研究。深化种业体制改革,构建以产业为主导、企业为主体、基地为依托、产学研结合、育繁推一体化的现代种业体系。整合种业资源,优化资源配置,提高市场准入门槛,推动种子企业兼并重组,加快培育具有核心竞争力的大型优势种子企业。加大生物育种产业重大创新发展工程、动植物良种工程实施力度,加强优势种子繁育基地建设,在粮棉油生产大县建设新品种引进示范场。加强种子市场监管,完善品种审定、保护、退出制度,强化种子生产经营行政许可管理。

中国紧凑型杂交玉米之父——李登海

李登海,1949 年 9 月出生,山东省莱州市人。他被誉为"中国紧凑型杂交玉米之父",与"杂交水稻之父"袁隆平齐名,共享"南袁北李"的美誉。

30 多年来,李登海研究的玉米品种 7 次刷新我国夏玉米高产纪录,2005 年创下亩产 1402.86 公斤的世界夏玉米高产纪录并保持至今,使我国土地由每亩养活 1 个人提升到养活 4.5 个人。他开创了我国紧凑型玉米育种先河,有 52 个品种通过国家和有关省市审定。他培育的玉米高产品种在全国累计推广 10 亿亩,实现经济效益 1000 亿元。

1972 年,初中毕业的李登海当上了村农科队队长。一则材料深深地震撼了他:美国先锋种业春玉米亩产 1250 公斤。李登海立志"培育良种,赶超美国"。1974 年,李登海被推荐到莱阳农校(今青岛农业大学)培训。老师刘恩训送给他 20 粒珍贵的杂交品种"XL80"。玉米育种家于伊又给了他点拨："现在的玉米是平展型的。要高产,就要培育一种叶片上冲、适于密植的紧凑型玉米。"

1979 年,李登海用"XL80"中分离出的"掖 107"为父本,首次在海南收获 7.2 斤珍贵的杂交种子,亩产达 776.6 公斤,首创我国夏玉米单产最高纪录,这就是"掖单 2 号"。随后掖单 6 号、7 号……12 号,亩产 824.9 公斤、953 公斤、962 公斤……李登海用中国的玉米种刷新着夏玉米亩产纪录。1989 年 10 月,李登海以"掖单 13 号"最高单产 1096.29 公斤,创造了新的夏玉米世界纪录! 2004 年,"掖单 13 号"荣获国家科技进步一等奖。2005 年 10 月 17 日,超级玉米新品种"登海超试一号"亩产达到了 1402.86 公斤。时隔 16 年后,他再次刷新了世界夏玉米高产纪录。

图 2-5　玉米专家李登海(新华社发)

连续 38 年高产攻关,7 次刷新中国夏玉米高产纪录、2 次刷新世界夏玉米高产纪录。李登海开创了我国紧凑型杂交玉米育种先河,被称之为"中国紧凑型杂交玉米之父"。

4. 提升农业技术推广能力

切实加强基层农技推广服务能力建设,普遍健全乡镇或区域性农业技术推广、动植物疫病防控、农产品质量监管等公共服务机构,明确公益性定位,完善管理体制、人员聘用和考评制度。切实落实"一个衔接、两个覆盖"要求,提高基层农技推广人员待遇,改善工作条件,改进服务手段。加快把基层农技推广机构的经营性职能分离出去,按市场化方式运作,探索公益性服务多种实现形式。推动高等学校、科研院所同基层农技推广机构、农民专业合作社、龙头企业、农户开展多种形式的合作,实现科技创新与农业生产经营的有效对接。鼓励高等学校、科研院所建立农业试验示范基地,集成、熟化、推广农业技术成果。建立健全农业技术交易市场,培育多元化的市场主体,完善农业技术市场交易法规和从业规章制度,加大农业知识产权保护力度,维护好农业技术市场秩序。

(四)改善农业设施装备条件

1. 大兴农田水利建设

加快大型灌区、重点中型灌区续建配套和节水改造,在水土资源条件具备的地区,新建一批灌区,增加农田有效灌溉面积。实施大中型灌溉排水泵站更新改造,加强重点涝区治理,完善灌排体系。充分发挥现有灌溉工程作用,力争完成70%以上的大型灌区和50%以上的重点中型灌区骨干工程续建配套与节水改造任务。加快推进小型农田水利重点县建设,加强灌区田间工程配套。因地制宜兴建中小型水利设施,支持山丘区小水窖、小水池、小塘坝、小泵站、小水渠等"五小水利"工程建设。稳步发展牧区水利,建设节水高效灌溉饲草料地。

2. 大规模建设旱涝保收高标准农田

加快中低产田改造,按照灌排顺畅、田地平整、土壤肥沃、路林配套的要求,突出重点地区和关键措施,以完善农田灌排体系为重点,配套实施土地平整、土壤改良、培肥地力、机耕道路、农田林网等田间工程,力争再建成4亿亩旱涝保收高标准农田。建立健全农田设施管护机制,确保农田设施长期发挥效益。

3.加快推进农业机械化

支持农机工业技术改造,加强农机关键零部件和重点产品研发,提高产品适用性、便捷性、安全性。着力解决水稻机插和玉米、油菜、甘蔗、棉花机收等突出难题,加快推进粮食生产全程机械化,大力推进棉油糖等经济作物生产机械化,协调推进养殖业、林果业、农产品初加工机械化。大力发展设施农业、畜牧水产养殖等机械装备。积极推广土地深松、精量播种、化肥深施、保护性耕作和农作物秸秆粉碎还田等农业机械化技术。促进农机农艺融合,推广适合机械化作业的种植模式。支持农用工业发展,提高化肥、农药、农膜等农资生产水平。

4.加强农业防灾减灾能力建设

继续加强大江大河大湖治理,加快中小河流治理和病险水库除险加固,以及易灾地区生态综合治理,提高江河防洪及山洪地质灾害防治能力,基本建成工程措施与非工程措施相结合的大江大河综合防洪减灾体系,基本完成重点中小河流(包括大江大河支流、独流入海、内陆河流)重点河段治理。搞好抗旱水源工程建设,抓紧解决工程性缺水问题。加强气象基础设施和服务体系建设,做好农业灾害预报工作,提高农业气象灾害监测预警的准确率和精细化水平,强化人工影响天气基础设施和科技能力建设,科学开发利用空中云水资源,增强农业应对气候变化能力。加强灾情监测、预警和调度工作,搞好应急救援物资储备,完善农业重大突发事件信息报告和发布制度,提高对农业灾害和突发事件等的应急反应能力,最大限度地减少灾害损失。加强动植物疫源疫病监测和防控体系建设,开展主要农作物和森林病虫害、草原鼠虫害专业化统防统治。建立饲草料储备制度,提高牧区防灾减灾能力。加强渔港建设,加快渔船标准化改造,提高渔业安全生产能力。

（五）提高农业生产经营组织化程度

1. 推进农业产业化经营

完善扶持农业产业化经营的政策措施,加大财政、金融、税收、信息等支持力度,构建生产、加工、销售有机结合的农业产业体系,不断延长农业产业链条。扶持壮大成长性好、辐射面广、带动力强的农业产业化龙头企业,支持龙头企业开展技术创新、产品升级和品牌创建。依托龙头企业建设专业化、标准化、规模化生产基地,大力发展龙头企业联结农民专业合作社、带动农户的组织模式。

江苏省培育"龙头",壮大新型农业经营主体

江苏省政府办公厅 2013 年 2 月发文,成立由省农委、省发改委、省财政厅等 8 个部门参加的农业产业化工作联席会议。这是江苏近期连续以政府名义出台的第三个加快推进农业产业化发展的政策文件,为培育"龙头",壮大新型农业经营主体助力加油。

近年来,江苏农业产业化水平不断提升,农业龙头企业群体不断发展壮大,在推进农业现代化进程中发挥了越来越重要的作用。2013 年 1 月,省农委公布的全省农业龙头企业总数达到 5447 家,比上年增加 470 家。龙头企业运行质量稳步提升。截至 2012 年年底,全省 443 家省级以上农业龙头企业实现销售 4955 亿元,实现纯利 152.57 亿元,分别增长 25.86%、10.17%,带动农户 953 万户,同比增长 10.22%。销售额超过百亿元的达 11 家,约占全国的 1/3。2012 年,443 家省级以上农业龙头企业带动农户 953 万户。

"加快推进农业产业化,壮大新型农业经营主体,关键是提升农业龙头企业运行质量。"江苏省农委副主任徐惠中说。近年来,江苏在全国率先提出开展"农业龙头企业运行质量提升年"活动,积极鼓励农业

龙头企业通过自建、共建、订单收购等方式,建立稳定的农产品原料生产基地,形成稳定购销关系,实现企业带动农民共同致富;同时以省政府名义出台了《关于进一步扶持农业产业化龙头企业发展的实施意见》,从加大财政扶持、强化金融服务、增强企业内力等方面扶持农业龙头企业做大做强。

为强化项目扶持,金融助推,江苏设立省级农业产业化发展专项资金,对带动能力强的省级以上龙头企业和成长型龙头企业给予扶持,2012年省级财政投入达2.3亿元,扶持了240家龙头企业。与省农行签署了"金融支持龙头企业、助推现代农业发展"全面战略合作框架协议,已累计授信132亿元。支持南京雨润集团等5家企业共同出资1亿元注册成立江苏汇隆投资担保公司,为农业企业提供融资担保。市县农业产业化主管部门按照"五个一"示范创建部署要求,制订方案,明确目标,分解责任,采取有效措施扎实推进。农业龙头企业积极参与创建活动,充分发挥技术、市场、信息优势,带头创办、领办农民专业合作组织,强化与种养大户、合作组织的紧密联结,突出有机、生态、原产地等特色,积极打造名牌产品,不断提高企业市场竞争能力。

在新的一年里,如何进一步推进农业产业化工作再上新台阶?省农委产业化指导处处长潘长胜介绍了五项举措:深入开展龙头企业示范创建行动,确保实现省级以上龙头企业年销售额、带动农户数分别增10%和8%以上;加快建设优势特色产业基地,推动优势产业向优势产区集中,加快形成功能互补、分工协作的现代农业产业体系;积极扶持农产品加工集中区建设,引导龙头企业入驻集中区,推动集群集聚发展;着力构建农产品现代流通体系,力争10%的农业龙头企业全年网络销售额突破100亿元目标;有效提升行政服务指导能力,重点支持企业或基地(园区)的科技研发、产品检验检测以及信息网络建设。对2012年年底的382家省级龙头企业实行动态监测,优胜劣汰。

资料来源:农民日报—中国农业新闻网,2013年2月28日,http://www.farmer.com.cn/xwpd/jjsn/201302/t20130228_813663.htm。

一家农业产业化龙头企业的发展

2003年的一天,一位叫陈世贵的湖北宜都市王家畈村农民创办了一家叫"土老憨"的生态农业开发有限公司。陈世贵把农民视为野草的农副产品花钱收购过来,进行深加工和精心包装,然后送到城里的大超市去卖,城里人视之如珍宝。短短几年时间,"土老憨"从一个乡村小作坊到省级重点龙头企业,"土老憨"在宜昌、全省乃至全国创造了一个农字号品牌的神话。

"土老憨"立足于山乡农村传统的家庭食品,以市场的喜好来开发产品,严把产品质量关,在每个生产环节都一丝不苟,保证产品无公害、纯天然,很快形成14个大类35个品种的特色食品。

2006年4月,陈世贵的湖北土老憨生态农业开发有限公司加入到宜都市红花套柑橘产业合作社,将宜都市农字号两大品牌,即"土老憨"与"宜都蜜柑"成功嫁接,整合资源,实现优势互补,依托柑橘产业合作社的载体,陈世贵和他的红花套柑橘专业合作社经过充分协商,联合宜都市10家柑橘专业合作社,组建起了宜都蜜柑集团合作社。推广柑橘标准化生产,在生产把关上狠抓产品质量,在销售环节上注重市场营销,在产品研发上注重科技投入,借助"土老憨"的品牌,宜都蜜橘的产业越做越大。

企业已形成三大类主导产品,精品宜都蜜柑及深加工产品系列;调味品类(蜜橘调味醋系列、鱼鲜酱油系列、豆豉酱系列);休闲食品类(清江野渔系列、陈皮蜜饯系列)。产品先后被评为三峡十大特产,湖北省消费者满意商品和湖北名牌产品,畅销沃尔玛、家乐福、中百集团、武商集团、上海百联等国内外知名超市以及北京、上海、武汉、宜昌等20多个大中城市和农产品市场,精品宜都蜜柑连续四年销进北京中南海,优质宜都蜜柑出口到俄罗斯、中欧、东欧、香港等国家和地区。2012年集团实现产值15亿元,创造利税7800万元。

集团位于宜都市绿色产品创业园(红花套镇),占地面积700余亩,建有23350平方米的农副产品综合交易市场,标准厂房55000平方米,柑橘商品化处理中心面积11000平方米。现有员工2000余人,专业技术人员105人,其中大学本科学历186人,研究生学历9人,博士生学历2人。

2. 大力发展农民专业合作社

全面贯彻落实《农民专业合作社法》,加快发展农民专业合作社,扶持专业合作社做大做强,提高市场竞争力。创新合作社发展形式,鼓励在生产经营各个环节组建专业合作社。拓展合作社服务领域,完善合作社服务功能,支持有条件的专业合作社开展信用、土地流转等合作。增强供销合作社对农民专业合作社的带动力。支持农民专业合作社兴办农产品加工企业或参股龙头企业。鼓励有条件的地方成立农产品行业协会。

农民专业合作社能否破解农产品"小生产大市场"困局

目前,农民专业合作社已经成为农村继个体工商户、私营企业、各类有限责任公司之后的第四大市场主体。最近出版的《中国农民专业合作社发展报告(2006—2010年)》提供的数据显示,目前"全国入社农户的收入普遍比非成员同业农户高出20%以上"。然而,我国农民专业合作社依然处于发展的初级阶段,在走向"引领农民参与国内外市场竞争的现代农业经营组织"之路上依然面临多重困难。

"我们也想学电子商务,在网上动动手指卖蔬菜,但是晚上从地里回来后才有时间研究,只会些简单操作。"55岁的周忠朝说。从2007年开始,陕西省大荔县农民周忠朝联合村里的蔬菜种植户,建立起以自己名字命名的"忠朝蔬菜专业合作社"。几年来,加入合作社的蔬菜种植户统一品种、统一管理、统一销售,规模越做越大,目前已经有800多名社员。"组织合作社前,一斤辣椒只能卖10元,现在统一品种、统一管理,质量和口碑都上去了,一斤能卖到20元。"周忠朝说,目前加入合作社的社员种植蔬菜,每亩能赚7000元至8000元。

农业部农村合作经济经营管理总站副站长赵铁桥指出,"缺人"和"缺钱"正成为制约农民专业合作社发展的两大瓶颈。目前农村外出务工的青壮年劳动力较多,具有较强市场经济意识和经营管理能力的带头人比较缺乏。为解决人才匮乏难题,今年农业部门将在全国培训19万名合作社理事长,未来10年还要培养15000名合作社人才,同时大力支持农村青年和大学生村官参与领办、创办合作社。

在资金支持方面,农业部联合相关部门出台了合作社销售成员的产品视同农户自产自销、合作社向成员提供农资免征增值税、对合作社给予"先评级后授信再用信"解决贷款难等相关财税、金融政策支持。

解决销售难题也是今后合作社攻坚的方向。业内专家表示,除了推动"农超对接"、"农校对接"拓展销售渠道外,合作社还应该积极参加展销会、农交会、团购会等各类推介促销活动。"单个小规模合作社与其他市场主体对接时可能有些力不从心,这种情况下可采取多种方式联合合作,如建立各类专业社联合社等方式,从更大规模、更高层次上引导农民、引导合作社参与市场竞争。"赵铁桥说。

同时,各类合作社还可逐步探索在城市社区、公益性农贸市场建立直销店、连锁店或代销店等,实现农产品从"土地"到"餐桌"的无缝对接。

赵铁桥认为:"农民专业合作社是弱者的联合,产业是弱势的农业,成员是贫困的农民,所在地是落后的农村,必须有相应政策扶持。"但是,政府的扶持只是一种导向,合作社的发展不能完全躺在政府怀抱里吃财政,关键还是广大成员规范办社、民主管理,建立健全成员大会、理事会、监事会"三会"制度和分配制度,不断增强合作社的凝聚力。

资料来源:新华网,2011年10月30日,http://news.xinhuanet.com/fortune/2011-10/30/c_111133437.htm。

3.建立新型农业社会化服务体系

加快构建以公共服务机构为依托、合作经济组织为基础、龙头企业为骨干、其他社会力量为补充,公益性服务和经营性服务相结合、专项服务和综合服务相协调的新型农业社会化服务体系。培育和发展多元化的农业社会化服务组织,扶持农民专业合作社、供销合作社、专业技术协会、农民用水合作组织、涉农企业等社会力量广泛参与农业产前、产中、产后服务。增强农村集体组织对农户生产经营的服务能力。

4. 发展农产品现代流通方式

健全农产品市场体系,推进农产品批发市场建设和升级改造,加快形成布局合理、设施先进、功能齐全、交易规范的全国性骨干农产品批发市场网络。改造提升农贸市场交易和配套设施,加强集贸市场管理,规范经营环境,降低经营成本。规范发展农产品期货市场,充分发挥引导生产、稳定市场、规避风险的作用。发展农产品现代流通方式,加强大型粮食物流节点、农产品冷链系统、鲜活农产品物流配送中心等农产品流通基础设施建设。开展"南菜北运"、"西果东运"现代流通综合试点。大力推进"农超对接",促进农产品电子商务健康有序发展,形成高效的农产品流通网络。培育和发展农村经纪人、农产品运销专业户、农产品流通企业等各类流通主体,提高农产品流通的组织化、产业化水平。

表2-3 中国"十二五"时期现代农业发展主要指标(2011—2015年)

类别	指标	2010年	2015年	年均增长(%)
农产品供给	粮食综合生产能力(亿吨)	>5.0	>5.4	
	粮食播种面积(亿亩)	16.48	>16.0	
	棉花总产量(万吨)	596	>700	>3.27
	油料总产量(万吨)	3230	3500	1.62
	糖料总产量(万吨)	12008	>14000	>3.12
	肉类总产量(万吨)	7926	8500	1.41
	禽蛋总产量(万吨)	2763	2900	0.97
	奶类总产量(万吨)	3748	5000	5.93
	水产品总产量(万吨)	5373	>6000	>2.23
	农产品质量安全例行监测总体合格率(%)	94.8	>96	>[1.2]
农业结构	畜牧业产值占农业总产值比重(%)	30	36	[6]
	渔业产值占农业总产值比重(%)	9.3	10	[0.7]
	农产品加工业产值与农业总产值比	1.7	2.2	[0.5]

续表

类别	指标	2010 年	2015 年	年均增长（%）
农业物质装备	新增农田有效灌溉面积(万亩) 农业灌溉用水有效利用系数 农机总动力(亿千瓦) 耕种收综合机械化水平(%)	 0.5 9.2 52	 0.53 10 60	[4000] [0.03] 1.68 [8]
农业科技	科技进步贡献率(%) 农村实用人才总量(万人)	52 820	>55 1300	>[3] 6.8
农业生产经营组织	农业产业化组织带动农户数量(亿户) 奶牛规模化养殖(年存栏 100 头以上)比重(%) 生猪规模化养殖(年出栏 500 头以上)比重(%)	1.07 28 35	1.3 >38 50	3.97 >[10] [15]
农业生态环境	适宜农户沼气普及率(%) 农作物秸秆综合利用率(%)	33 70.2	>50 >80	>[17] >[9.8]
农业产值与农民收入	农林牧渔业增加值年均增长率(%) 转移农业劳动力(万人) 农村居民人均纯收入(元)	 5919	 >8310	5 [4000] >7

注:1.[ ]内为五年累计数。

2. 820 万农村实用人才总量为 2008 年年底数。

3. 农村居民人均纯收入绝对数按 2010 年价格计算,增长速度按可比价格计算。

资料来源:《全国现代农业发展规划(2011—2015 年)》,2012 年 1 月 13 日由国务院印发。

▨ 思考题

1. 中国人口众多而土地、水资源稀缺,面对这样的国情,中国采用了哪些手段保障粮食安全?

2. 提高粮食生产能力的潜力在哪里?

3. 提高农业生产经营效益的途径和手段有哪些?

▨ 参考文献

1. 国家发展和改革委员会:《全国农村经济发展"十二五"规划》,2012 年 6 月。

2. 新华社:《中华人民共和国国民经济和社会发展第十二个五年规划纲要》,2011 年 3 月。

3.《中国统计年鉴2012》,北京:中国统计出版社,2012年。

4.[美]舒尔茨著,梁小民译:《改造传统农业》,北京:商务印书馆,2010年。

5.张培刚:《农业与工业化》,北京:中国人民大学出版社,2014年。

6.[日]速水佑次郎、[美]弗农拉坦著,吴伟东等译:《农业发展:国际前景》,北京:商务印书馆,2014年。

三、中国新农村建设如何进行

　　中国正经历有史以来规模最大的城镇化，预计 2030 年中国人口将达到峰值 15 亿，按照最乐观的估计，城镇化率可达到 70%，这意味着在短短 20 年中，将有 3 亿多人从农村进入城镇，难度之大，可想而知。即使如此，仍然有 4—5 亿农民生活在农村，因此，一方面必须积极稳妥推进城镇化，另一方面必须大力建设新农村，双轮驱动，并行不悖。

　　2005 年 10 月，中国共产党第十六届五中全会通过的《中共中央关于制定国民经济和社会发展第十一个五年规划的建议》（2006—2010）中指出："建设社会主义新农村是我国现代化进程中的重大历史任务。"要按照"生产发展、生活宽裕、乡风文明、村容整洁、管理民主"的要求，坚持从各地实际出发，尊重农民意愿，扎实稳步推进新农村建设。

　　那么，新农村建设如何开展？2004 年，中国共产党第十六届四中全会上提出"两个趋向"的重要论断:"纵观一些工业化国家发展的历程,在工业化初始阶段,农业支持工业、为工业提供积累是带有普遍性的趋向,但在工业化达到相当程度以后,工业反哺农业、城市支持农村,实现工业与农业、城市与农村协调发展,也是带有普遍性的趋向。"同年12月中央经济工作会议明确指出,中国现在总体上已到了"以工促农、以城带乡"的发展阶段。2012年11月,中国共产党第十八次全国代表大会提出,城乡发展一体化是解决农业、农村、农民问题的根本途径。要加大统筹城乡发展力度,增强农村发展活力,逐步缩小城乡差距,促进城乡共同繁荣。

从中国工业化的发展过程看,新中国成立后,为了迅速摆脱经济落后的局面,中国采取了重工业超前发展战略。当时,中国的社会经济发展水平相当低。1952年,全国人均国民生产总值仅50多美元,农业劳动力份额达83.5%,农业净产值的比重为70%。在这样的基础上搞工业化,农业必然成为筹集工业化资金的主渠道。据测算,1979年以前的29年,农业部门为国家工业化提供的资金约4500亿元。这种向工业倾斜的政策从全局和整体看是必要的、有效的,但问题是延续时间过长,使本来就落后的农业生产的物质技术条件得不到应有的改善。不仅如此,长期实行的城乡分割体制,还使城乡之间要素不能自由流动,大量的农村劳动力被束缚在土地上,农民实际上被排除在国家工业化进程之外。由于实行农村农业人口与城镇非农业人口两种户籍制度,造成农村居民与城镇居民权利和发展机会的不平等,加剧了城乡结构的失衡。虽然改革开放以来城乡关系得到逐步改善,但农业和农村在资源配置与国民收入分配中仍处于不利地位,农村居民和城镇居民在发展机会、社会地位等方面仍不平等,计划经济体制下形成的城乡分割的二元结构未从根本上改变,因而造成工农业发展失调和城乡发展失衡的局面没有扭转,城乡差距依然悬殊。

进入21世纪以来,从工业化发展阶段来看,中国人均GDP已超过1000美元,农业与非农产业的产值结构大约为15∶85,农业与非农产业的就业结构大约为 50：50,城镇化水平为 40%。这四项指标表明,中国已进入工业化中期阶段,国民经济的主导产业由农业转变为非农产业,经济增长的动力主要来自非农产业。根据国际经验,这时采取相应措施,以工业反哺农业,是带有普遍性的现象。例如,日本在战前处于以农养工阶段,20 世纪 50 年代末 60 年代初开始转向工业反哺农业阶段。韩国在 20 世纪 60 年代中期以前还从农业部门抽取工业化资本,自 60 年代末开始转向保护农业。

实行工业反哺农业,不仅与中国工业化所处的发展阶段有关,而且是由中国农业和农村发展所具有的特殊性、复杂性决定的。中国农业劳动生产率低,农业仍然是国民经济中承受风险最大的弱质产业。中国人口 60% 以上居住在农村,农民生活水平明显低于城镇居民,农村教育、科技、文化、卫生等事业的发展水平也明显落后于城市。在全面建设小康社会的进程中,农村面临的任务更为艰巨。从历史经验来看,农民安居乐业对于国家的稳定发展具有决定性的作用。只有加快农业和农村经济发展,增加农民收入,同时加强农村基层民主政治建设和精神文明建设,在广大农村形成和谐安定、健康向上的良好局面,保证广大农民安居乐业,农村社会稳定才有坚实的基础,国家长治久安也才有可靠的保障。

2006 年 2 月《中共中央国务院关于推进社会主义新农村建设的若干意见》的文件密集出台了破解社会主义新农村建设诸多深层问题的重大举措,新农村建设由此起步开局①。

新农村建设的关键是要树立统筹城乡发展的新观念,打破城乡分割的体制障碍,把农业发展放到整个国民经济的大格局中,把农村进步放到整个社会的进步中,把农民增收放到国民收入分配和再分配中,进而统筹规划政策、公共资源、基础设施及产业布局。

新农村建设将坚持"因地制宜、尊重民意、远近结合、体现特色、量力而行"的原则,在搞好县域村镇体系规划和村镇建设规划的同

---

① 参见本章附录:"十一五"规划:社会主义新农村建设重点工程(2006—2010 年)。

时,统筹安排农村基础设施建设和社会事业发展,建设农民幸福生活的美好家园。

(一) 加强农村基础设施建设

截至 2005 年年底,中国仍有近 5 万个村不通公路;一半的行政村没有通自来水;3 亿农村人口的饮水安全亟待解决;60%以上的农户还没有用上卫生厕所;2%的村庄还没有通电。因此,新农村建设中着力加强农民最急需的生产生活设施建设。

从 2006 年起,中央政府大幅度增加农村沼气建设投资规模。安排资金支持编制村庄规划和开展村庄治理试点。从各地实际出发制定村庄建设和人居环境治理的指导性目录,重点解决农民在饮水、行路、用电和燃料等方面的困难。引导和帮助农民切实解决住宅与畜禽圈舍混杂问题。加快实施农村饮水安全工程。加强农村公路建设,基本实现全国所有乡镇通柏油(水泥)路,东中部地区所有具备条件的建制村通柏油(水泥)路,西部地区具备条件的建制村通公路,健全农村公路管护体系。积极发展农村沼气、秸秆发电、小水电、太阳能、风能等可再生能源,完善农村电网。建立电信普遍服务基金,加强农村信息网络建设,发展农村邮政和电信,基本实现村村通电话、乡乡能上网。按照节约土地、设施配套、节能环保、突出特色的原则,做好乡村建设规划,引导农民合理建设住宅,保护有特色的农村建筑风貌。

到 2010 年年末,解决了 2.1 亿农村人口的安全饮水问题,大部分农村地区的电力基本实现了城乡一体化管理和服务,新建改建农村公路 186 万多公里,农村沼气用户达到 4000 万户,农村安居工程建设进展顺利。

根据"十二五"规划①,新农村建设将按照"饮水安全方便、能源清

---

① "十二五"规划全称是《中华人民共和国国民经济和社会发展第十二个五年规划纲要》。规划的起止时间为 2011—2015 年。"十二五"规划建议称,"十二五"规划期间是全面建设小康社会的关键时期,是深化改革开放、加快转变经济发展方式的攻坚时期。

洁便利、道路畅通便捷、住房安全舒适、环境整洁优美"的要求,加强农村基础设施建设,改善农村生产生活条件。

1. 加快农村饮水安全建设

坚持水量和水质安全并重,进一步加快建设进度,因地制宜地采取集中供水、分散供水和城镇供水管网向农村延伸等方式解决农村人口饮水安全问题,到2015年农村集中式供水受益人口比例提高到80%左右。强化工程运行管理,落实管护主体,加强水源保护和水质监测,确保工程长期发挥效益,让农民喝上洁净水、放心水。

2. 加强农村电力建设

实施新一轮农村电网改造升级工程,提高农村电力供电可靠性和供电能力,改善农村生产生活用电条件。加快城乡电力公共服务均等化进程,实现城乡用电同网同价。实施无电地区电力建设工程,全面解决无电人口基本用电问题,实现电力普遍服务。在保护生态和农民利益的前提下,科学规划、有序开发农村小水电,继续加强水电新农村电气化县建设,因地制宜实施小水电代燃料工程,搞好农村水电配套电网改造工程建设。

3. 加强以农村沼气为重点的清洁能源建设

继续推进农村户用沼气建设,切实加强建后管理和服务体系建设,提高户用沼气使用率。适应畜禽规模养殖快速发展实际,积极有序地开展大中小型沼气工程建设。加强沼气关键技术研发推广,促进沼气和沼渣沼液的高效利用。加快省柴节煤炉灶炕升级改造,推进大型秸秆能源化利用工程建设,引导适宜地区在农村新建和改造的住房中利用太阳能,推广使用太阳能热水器和太阳灶,加快构建清洁、经济、便利的农村能源体系。

4.加强农村公路建设

继续实施以通沥青(水泥)路为重点的通达、通畅工程,实现所有具备条件的东中部地区建制村、西部地区 80%以上的建制村通沥青(水泥)路。实施县乡道改造和连通工程,提高农村公路网络水平。统筹城乡交通一体化发展,基本实现乡镇通班车率达到 100%、建制村通班车率达到 92%。实施农村公路的桥涵建设、危桥改造以及客运场站等公交配套工程,加强农村公路安全设施建设,切实落实农村公路的养护和管理。

5.加强农村住房建设

鼓励有条件的地方通过多种形式支持农民依法依规建设自用住房。继续推进农村危房改造,合理确定补助对象和标准,强化工程质量安全管理,完善档案管理和产权登记,推动农村基本住房安全保障制度建设,改造农村危房 800 万户以上。加快国有林区(场)棚户区改造和垦区危房改造,基本解决国有垦区、林区、林场职工住房困难问题。继续实施游牧民定居工程,建设游牧民定居住房 24.6万户,实现全国游牧民定居目标。加快实施以船为家渔民上岸安居工程。

6.继续推进农村扶贫开发和水库移民后期扶持工作

贯彻落实《中国扶贫开发纲要(2011—2020 年)》,增加扶贫开发投入,将连片特困地区作为贫困攻坚主战场,加大对革命老区、民族地区、边疆地区扶持力度,坚持开发式扶贫方针,实行扶贫开发和农村最低生活保障制度的有效衔接,稳定解决扶贫对象温饱,尽快实现扶贫对象脱贫致富。全面落实水库移民后期扶持政策,加大资金整合和投入力度,加快库区和移民安置区基础设施建设和社会事业发展,不断改善水库移民生产生活条件。积极开展特困移民解困工作试点,集中攻坚,解决好特困移民的安全居住和生存发展问题。

四川省汶川县:新农村蜕变新生

汶川县位于四川省西北部、阿坝州东南部,是领略九寨、黄龙、四姑娘山、大草原风光的快速通道。全县幅员面积4084平方公里,距成都146公里,辖6镇7乡、118个行政村,震前全县总人口105436人(其中,农业人口67438人,羌族人口36705人)。汶川县是全国仅有的四个羌族聚居县之一,是阿坝州的工业基地,有"大禹故里、熊猫家园、羌绣之乡"的美誉。

2008年"5·12"汶川特大地震给汶川县带来了毁灭性的灾难,直接经济损失643亿元。面对突如其来的特大灾害,在党中央、国务院的亲切关怀下,在省州党委、政府的坚强领导下,在全国人民的无私援助下,全县各级干部群众大力发扬艰苦奋斗、不等不靠的精神,抗震救灾、灾后重建工作取得重大胜利。经济发展呈现逐步回升势头,社会大局保持稳定。

该县坚持以发展休闲农业和乡村旅游为主线,从特色效益种植业、现代畜牧业、特色林产业、农产品加工业等四个方面入手,重点打造"一村一特"、"一乡一主"的新村格局和农业产业模式,着力发展大产业、扶持大企业、培育大品牌。强力推进"两桃一花一牧"农业的规模化、标准化、产业化发展,大力发展甜樱桃、猕猴桃、花卉、现代畜牧业,带动性发展茶叶、中药材、特色水产业,倾力打造岷江河谷现代特色农业示范区,力争在未来5年内建成猕猴桃产业基地50000亩,年产量超过1000万公斤;建成大樱桃产业基地30000亩,年产量达1000万公斤;建成以鸡、鸭、猪、羊为主的现代畜牧业养殖基地,力争年出栏达到千万(头、只);建成岷江干旱河谷延伸地带现代花卉基地,力争年产花卉达1000万盆。

截至2011年6月,该县已发展甜樱桃基地20000亩、猕猴桃基地30000亩、花卉基地5000亩、茶叶基地5000亩、无公害蔬菜基地15000亩、推广杂交玉米良种40000亩;有4种食品获得绿色食品认证;新建畜禽圈舍23.25万平方米,发展规模户384户,户均年收入达1.6万元;

图 3-1   重建后的汶川（新华社发）

新建腊肉加工厂 2 个，规模养殖场 4 个，规模养殖小区 2 个；建成 70 条 400 公里农村公路，各乡镇、村组实施饮水工程 112 处，解决了农村 6.65 万人的饮水问题。

"十二五"规划：农村基础设施建设重点工程

农村饮水安全工程

采取集中供水、分散供水和城镇供水管网向农村延伸等方式，解决约 3 亿农村人口（含国有农林场）和农村学校师生的安全饮水问题。

农村供电工程

对未改造的农村电网进行全面改造，对电力需求快速增长而出现供电能力不足的农村电网实施升级改造。建成 1000 个太阳能示范村和 200 个绿色能源县。建设 300 个水电新农村电气化县和新增小水电装机容量 1000 万千瓦。

农村公路工程

新建和改造农村公路 100 万公里,实现所有具备条件的东中部地区行政村、西部地区 80% 以上的行政村通沥青(水泥)路。

农村沼气工程

建设户用沼气、小型沼气工程、大中型沼气工程和沼气服务体系,使 50% 以上的适宜农户用上沼气。

农村安居工程

完成农村困难家庭危房改造 800 万户。基本解决国有垦区、林区、林场职工住房困难问题。建设游牧民定居住房 24.6 万户,实现全国游牧民定居目标。

农村清洁工程

推进农村有机废弃物处理利用和无机废弃物收集转运,配套开展村庄硬化绿化。

资料来源:国家发展和改革委员会:《全国农村经济发展“十二五”规划》,2012 年 6 月。

(二)加快发展农村社会事业

“十一五”期间,国家重点加大政策扶持力度,着力普及和巩固农村九年制义务教育。对农村义务教育阶段学生免收学杂费,对其中的贫困家庭学生免费提供课本和补助寄宿生生活费。按照明确各级责任、中央地方共担、加大财政投入、提高保障水平、分步组织实施的原则,将农村义务教育全面纳入公共财政保障范围,构建农村义务教育经费保障机制。实施农村教师培训计划,使中西部地区 50% 的农村教师得到一次专业培训。鼓励城市各单位开展智力支农,加大城镇教师支援农村教育的力度。全面实施农村中小学远程教育。

加强以乡镇卫生院为重点的农村卫生基础设施建设,健全农村县乡村三级卫生服务和医疗救助体系。培训乡村卫生人员,开展城市医师支援农村活动。建设农村药品供应网和监督网。加强禽流感等人畜共患疾病防治。完善农村计划生育服务体系,实施农村计划生育家庭奖励扶助制度和"少生快富"工程。

加强县文化馆、图书馆和乡镇文化站、村文化室等公共文化设施建设,继续实施广播电视"村村通"和农村电影放映工程。到2010年,我国基本实现20户以上的已通电自然村全部通广播电视,全国农村将实现一村一月放映一场电影的目标。推动实施农民体育健身工程。农村影院、文化馆、图书馆等设施的普及,也把农民的传统日常生活概念大大拓展。进一步完善村务公开和民主议事制度,让农民群众真正享有知情权、参与权、管理权、监督权。

加强劳动力技能培训,培养造就有文化、懂技术、会经营的新型农民。支持新型农民科技培训,提高农民务农技能和科技素质。实施农村劳动力转移培训工程,增强农村劳动力的就业能力。实施农村实用人才培训工程,培养一大批生产能手、能工巧匠、经营能人和科技人员。

"十二五"期间(2011—2015年),新农村建设将按照"教育水平提高、卫生条件改善、文化生活丰富、就业公平体面"的要求,加快发展农村社会事业,提高农村人口素质,促进农村全面发展。

1. 办好农村教育事业

合理配置公共教育资源,重点向农村、边远、贫困、民族地区和革命老区倾斜。改善农村中小学办学条件,保留并办好必要的村小学和教学点,加强农村中小学寄宿制学校建设,加大农村中小学师资队伍建设力度,提高农村义务教育质量和县域内均衡发展水平。对于农村义务教育阶段学生,实施营养改善计划,政府免费提供教科书,免寄宿生住宿费,并为家庭困难寄宿生提供生活补助。加快普及农村高中阶段教育,落实好农村中等职业教育免学费政策。大力发展农村学前教育,加强农村幼儿园建设,努力提高农村学前教育普及程度,保证留守儿童入园。大规模开展农村实用人才培训,加快培养农村生产型、经营型、技能服务型实用人才,到2015年农村实用人才总量达到1300万人。

2. 加强农村医疗卫生体系建设

推进新增医疗卫生资源重点向农村倾斜。完善以县医院为龙头、乡镇卫生院和村卫生室为基础的农村三级医疗卫生服务网络。加快建设以县级疾病预防控制、卫生监督等为核心的农村公共卫生服务体系，扩大农村免费基本公共卫生服务范围，推行乡村卫生服务一体化管理。实施农村妇女住院分娩补助。积极预防农村重大传染病、慢性病、职业病、地方病和精神疾病，提高农村重大突发公共卫生事件处置能力，实施农村急救体系建设。

3. 繁荣发展农村文化体育事业

推进农村公共文化服务体系建设工程，改善农村文化基础设施，为农村居民免费提供文化信息资源共享、电影放映、送书送报送戏等公益性文化服务。加强农村基层广播电视和无线发射台站建设，全面解决20户以下已通电自然"盲村"广播电视覆盖，在有线网络未通达的农村地区开展直播卫星公共服务。继续加强农家书屋和农村阅览栏（屏）建设。积极开展农村特色文化活动。继续实施农民体育健身工程，改善农村公共体育设施条件。

4. 做好农村就业服务工作

完善城乡公共就业服务体系，加强农村劳动力就业综合服务平台建设，为农民转移就业免费提供就业咨询、职业指导、职业介绍、就业失业登记等服务。加快建立功能齐全、布局合理、方便可及的农村就业服务网络。

青海海东强化就业培训提升就业人员劳动技能

青海海东地区位于青海湖以东，辖6县，即平安县、乐都县、互助土族自治县、民和回族土族自治县、化隆回族自治县、循化撒拉族自治县。总面积1.32万平方公里，总人口162万人。2011年，海东地区生产总值达 219.37 亿元,全年农民人均纯收入 4599.83 元。

近年来,海东各级政府始终把就业再就业工作纳入重要议事日程,强化技能培训,将职业技能培训作为提升城乡劳动力创业就业能力的关键来抓,积极落实国家技能人才培养工程,大力实施"人才强区"战略,以职业技能培训为重点,依托农村劳动力转移培训"阳光工程"、"雨露计划"、进城务工人员培训和创业培训,共完成农村劳动力"阳光工程"技能培训 18.4 万人,进城务工人员培训 7.9 万人,下岗失业人员就业再就业培训 7.6 万人,创业培训 3068 人。

全区劳务输出实现了由数量型向质量型、由省(区)内向省外、由体力型向技能型、由短期工向长期稳定、由盲目无序向组织有序、由一般性劳务经济向创业经济的转变。达到了输出一批、发展一批、稳定一批、脱贫一批的目标,逐步形成了具有地方和民族特色的"化隆牛肉拉面"、"循化撒拉人家"等特色劳务经济和创业品牌。通过多年的努力,全区呈现出了劳务规模不断扩大,劳务收入不断增长,劳务水平不断提高,劳务品牌逐步显现,创业群体快速发展的良好局面。2012 年,海东着力将拉面经济、金秋拾棉、海西枸杞采摘作为劳务输出的重点,按照"政府引导、部门服务、劳务经纪人组织、群众自愿"的方式,有序组织输送农民工赴疆拾棉和赴海西等地从事枸杞采摘。2012 年,全区向新疆、甘肃等地引导组织输出季节性拾棉工61111 人,向海西组织输出枸杞采摘工 24758 人,实现劳务收入4.2 亿元。

预计到"十二五"末,全区城镇将新增就业人员 6 万人;农村劳动力转移就业累计达 300 万人(次),年均实现劳务收入 50 亿元;城镇登记失业率控制在 3.5%以内;完成各类人员就业培训 24 万人,其中下岗失业人员就业培训 4 万人,农村劳动力技能培训 16 万人,创业培训 1.5万人。

（三）提高农村社会保障水平

"十一五"期间（2006—2010年），中国探索建立与农村经济发展水平相适应、与其他保障措施相配套的农村养老保险制度。基本建立新型农村合作医疗制度。有条件的地方建立农村最低生活保障制度。完善农村"五保户"供养、特困户生活补助、灾民救助等社会救助体系。

到2010年年末，中国农村社会保障水平得到了明显改善。农村最低生活保障制度全面建立，96.3%的农村居民参加了新型农村合作医疗，新型农村社会养老保险试点覆盖面达到24%，5000多万农村居民得到最低生活保障。扶贫开发事业取得显著成就。

"十二五"期间（2011—2015年），中国将按照"保基本、广覆盖、多层次、有弹性、可持续"的要求，健全农村社会保障制度，提高农村社会保障水平，实现农村居民"老有所养、病有所医、困有所济"。

1. 实现新型农村社会养老保险制度全覆盖

建立健全新型农村社会养老保险制度，稳步提高新型农村社会养老保险基础养老金水平。完善被征地农民基本生活保障制度，实行先保后征。研究制定新农保与城镇居民社会养老保险制度、城镇企业职工基本养老保险制度间的衔接和保险关系转移接续办法，促进城乡养老保险一体化发展。

2. 完善新型农村合作医疗保障制度

逐步提高农村居民医疗保险人均筹资标准和财政补助水平，提高新农合最高支付限额和住院费支付比例。完善农村医疗救助制度，提高救助标准，扩大救助范围。加强城乡医疗保障制度衔接和资源整合，鼓励有条件地区建立城乡一体化的居民基本医疗保险制度。

3.加强农村社会救助体系建设

完善农村最低生活保障制度,将符合条件的农村老人全部纳入农村五保供养范围,实行分散供养和集中供养相结合。稳步提高低保标准,健全与物价挂钩的低保标准动态调整机制,力争农村低保标准年均提高10%以上。完善农村受灾群众临时救助制度,加大对农村残疾人生产扶助和生活救助力度,积极探索建立农民意外伤害保障机制和生育保障机制。

(四)推进农村环境综合整治

"十一五"时期,中国的生态建设和环境保护取得新进展。五年完成造林面积2527万公顷,森林覆盖率达到20.36%,新增治理水土流失面积23万平方公里,新增治理沙化土地面积1081万公顷,新增治理"三化"草地8017万公顷,退牧还草3240万公顷。全国已建立自然保护区2588处,50%的自然湿地得到有效保护,重点河湖生态修复成效明显,农业面源污染防治和农村环境综合整治积极推进。

"十二五"期间,国家将大力发展农业循环经济,推进农业清洁生产,开展农业废弃物资源化利用。加快测土配方施肥技术的推广应用,引导农民科学施肥,多施绿肥、有机肥,推广病虫草害生物防治,鼓励使用高效、低毒、低残留农药及生物农药,搞好农膜、农药包装物的回收再利用,推进秸秆综合利用,科学规划布局养殖场,加大畜禽、水产养殖污染防治力度,加强土壤污染监测,开展污染土壤(场地)治理修复,有效控制和治理农业面源污染。

支持有条件的农村地区开展垃圾集中处理,逐步建立户分类、村收集、乡(镇)中转、县(市)处理的垃圾收集清运与处理体系,引导条件暂不适宜农村地区实行源头分类、就地减量、资源化利用的垃圾处理模式。推进农村水污染综合治理,在规模较大的村庄和城市周边村镇推广污水集中处理。实施农村清洁工程,改善农村卫生条件和人居环境,到 2015 年完成 6 万个建制村的环境综合整治任务。强化农村工业企业污染排放监管,禁止工业和城市污染向农村扩散。

安吉建设生态文明美丽新农村

安吉县地处浙江省的西北部,距离上海 223 公里,省会杭州 65 公里。全县面积 1886 平方公里,常住人口 46 万,其中农业人口占 76%,辖 10 镇 5 乡 1 街道和 1 个省级经济开发区。安吉是著名的中国白茶之乡、中国椅业之乡、中国竹地板之都,被命名为全国首个"国家生态县"、全国首批"生态文明建设试点县"、国家可持续发展实验区、中国美丽乡村国家级标准化示范县、全国休闲农业与乡村旅游示范县、全国文明县城、国家卫生县城、国家园林县城、省级森林城市,荣获全国首个县域"中国人居环境奖"、"联合国人居奖",两度蝉联"长三角最具投资价值县市(特别奖)"。

从 2008 年起,安吉县全面开展"中国美丽乡村"建设行动,努力将安吉乡村建成"环境优美、生活富美、社会和美"的现代化新农村样板,美丽乡村覆盖面达到 85% 以上。

在美丽乡村建设中,安吉坚持四美原则。尊重自然美,充分彰显依山傍水、因势因地而建的生态环境特色。侧重现代美,坚持把生产发展放在首位,把生活富裕作为美丽乡村的前提和基础,融现代文明于自然生态中。注重个性美,因地制宜,因村而异,彰显一村一品、一村一景。构建整体美,强化全局战略思维,把全县当作一个大乡村来规划,把一个村当作一个景来设计,把一户人家当作一个小品来改造。各创建乡镇(开发区)、村对照行动纲要、实施意见和总体规划要求,从自身实际出发,将其他各类专项规划有机纳入美丽乡村建设整体规划,明确了发展目标和创建任务,合力推进美丽乡村建设。

2011 年,地区生产总值达到 222 亿元,财政总收入 29.1 亿元,其中地方财政收入达到 16.7 亿元,连续四年增幅居全省前列、全市第一。城镇居民人均可支配收入达到 2.8 万元,农民人均收入达到 1.4 万元,明显高于全省平均水平。与此同时,安吉的生态环境持续好转,"中国美丽乡村"建设成效逐渐凸显。围绕环境提升、产业提升、素质提升、服务提升等"四大工程"的实施,一批与群众生活密切相关的基础设施项目基本完成,农村特色主导产业、农民专业合作和现代家庭工业、农村休闲旅游等产业得到长足发展和提升,创建村的面貌焕然一新。美丽乡村已成为安吉继中国竹乡、国家生态县之后的第三个全国性品牌,成为全省新农村建设的示范工程、全县人民共建共享的民心工程。

图3-2 浙江省安吉县山川乡马家弄村的乡村景观吸引
不少游客前来参观(新华社记者鞠焕宗摄)

安吉县良朋镇迁迢村党支部书记康洪亮说,自从建设美丽乡村后,村里发生了大变化。村里的环境变得整洁美丽了,现在全村人都很重视保洁。过去很少有人到我们这个偏远山村来游玩,现在每到节假日,村里的每个"农家乐"几乎都是满满的,美丽乡村建设真是美了农村,鼓了我们农民的"钱袋子"。

（五）完善农村发展体制机制

"十一五"期间，中国农村改革实现新突破。包括全面取消农业税，"三农"投入大幅增加，农业补贴范围扩大、力度加大，主要农产品价格保护制度进一步健全，农业支持保护制度日益完善。集体林权制度改革全面推进，落实草原承包面积33亿亩，农村综合改革、农村金融制度改革不断深化。

同期，统筹城乡发展迈出新步伐。城乡二元体制障碍有所突破，农民工外出务工环境明显改善，全国农民工总数达到2.42亿人，其中外出农民工达到1.53亿人，成为推进城镇化的重要力量，城镇化快速发展。城乡规划、产业布局、基础设施、公共服务、劳动就业和社会管理一体化进程明显加快，城乡融合发展趋势明显。

但是，农村关键领域改革仍然滞后，城乡二元制度尚未根本消除，实现城乡资源要素合理配置仍面临体制性障碍。因此，"十二五"期间，中国将坚持不懈推进农村改革和制度创新，稳定和完善农村基本经营制度，充分发挥市场在资源配置中的基础性作用，完善国家对农业农村发展宏观调控，健全符合社会主义市场经济要求的农村经济体制机制，使农村经济发展充满活力。

1. 建立投入稳定增长机制

落实中央关于"三农"政策有关规定，确保各级财政对农业的投入增长幅度高于财政经常性收入增长幅度，预算内固定资产投资继续向农业农村建设项目倾斜，土地出让收益重点投向农业土地开发和农村基础设施建设。保证财政农业科技投入增幅明显高于财政经常性收入增幅，逐步提高农业研发投入占农业增加值的比重。2003—2012年的10年间，中央财政"三农"投入累计超过6万亿元，为赢得"三农"发展黄金期做出了重要贡献。在总量上，中央财政"三农"投入从2003年的2144亿元增加到2012年的1.228万亿元，翻了两番还要多；在速度

上,中央财政"三农"投入年均增长 21%,高于同期财政支出年均增长
4.5 个百分点;在比重上,中央财政"三农"投入占财政支出的比重从
13.7%提高到 19.2%,达到将近 1/5。

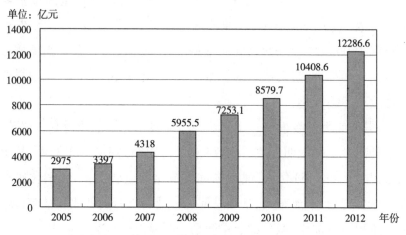

图 3-3　2005—2012 年中央财政"三农"的支出

资料来源:《人民日报》2013 年 1 月 22 日。

严格执行耕地占用税税率提高后新增收入全部用于农业的规定,
严格按照有关规定计提和使用用于农业土地开发、农田水利建设的土
地出让收益,严格执行新增建设用地土地有偿使用费全部用于耕地开
发和土地整理的规定。拓宽农业投入来源,鼓励和引导社会资本投入
农业农村,努力形成多元化投入新格局。

2.稳定和完善农村基本经营制度

坚持以家庭承包经营为基础、统分结合的双层经营体制,完善农村
土地承包法律法规和政策,全面推进集体林权制度改革,完善草原承包
经营制度,健全覆盖耕地、林地、草原等土地资源的家庭承包经营制度。
保持现有土地承包关系稳定并长久不变,全面落实农村土地承包地块、
面积、合同、证书"四到户",赋予农民更加充分而有保障的土地承包经
营权。完善土地承包经营权权能,依法保障农民对承包土地的占有、使
用、收益等权利。在依法自愿有偿和加强服务基础上完善土地承包经

营权流转市场,允许农民以转包、出租、互换、转让、股份合作等形式流转土地承包经营权,发展多种形式的适度规模经营,支持农民专业合作社和农业产业化龙头企业发展,加快健全农业社会化服务体系,提高农业经营组织化程度。

3. 有序推进农村土地管理制度改革

加快推进农村集体土地所有权、宅基地使用权、集体建设用地使用权的确权、登记、颁证工作。完善农村宅基地管理制度,严格宅基地管理,禁止违规多占宅基地,在尊重农民意愿、保障农民权益的原则下,依法盘活和利用好农村现有宅基地,探索开展农村闲置宅基地的退出和补偿机制。农村宅基地和村庄整理所节约的土地,首先要复垦为耕地,调剂为建设用地的必须符合土地利用总体规划,纳入年度建设用地计划,并优先满足集体建设用地。规范城乡建设用地增减挂钩改革试点,严格控制试点范围和试点规模,确保土地增值收益及时全部返还农村。

逐步建立城乡统一的建设用地市场。改革征地制度,严格界定公益性和经营性建设用地,逐步缩小征地范围,严格履行征地程序,完善征地补偿制度。提高农村土地征收补偿水平,依法征收农村集体土地,按照同地同价的原则及时足额给农村集体组织和农民合理补偿。在土地利用规划确定的城镇建设用地范围外,经批准占用农村集体土地建设非公益项目,允许农民依法通过多种方式参与开发经营并保障农民合法权益。将农村集体经营性建设用地使用权转让纳入现行的城市国有土地市场统一管理,对依法取得的农村经营性集体建设用地,必须通过统一有形的土地市场、以公开规范的方式转让土地使用权,在符合规划的前提下与国有土地享有平等权益。

4. 创新金融支农体制机制

加大对农村金融政策支持力度,拓宽农村融资渠道,加快建立商业性金融、合作性金融、政策性金融相结合,资本充足、功能健全、服务完善、运行安全的农村金融体系。引导农村储蓄存款主要用于农业农村,县域内银行业金融机构新吸收的存款,主要用于当地发放贷款。拓展农业发展银行支农领域,扩大邮政储蓄银行涉农业务范围。坚持农业银行为农服务的方向,稳定和发展农村服务网络。深化农村信用社改革,切实发挥其为农服务主力军作用。放宽农村金融准入政策,鼓励和规范发展多种形式的农村金融机构,加快培育村镇银行、贷款公司、农村资金互助社,鼓励有条件的地区以县为单位建立社区银行,有序发展农村小额贷款组织。加强农村信用体系建设,扩大农村有效担保物范围。发展农村保险事业,健全农业保险制度。支持符合条件的涉农企业上市。

5. 深化农村综合改革

推进集体林权和国有林区林权制度改革,完善草原承包经营制度。认真总结统筹城乡综合配套改革试点经验,积极探索解决农业、农村、农民问题的新途径。

6. 推进城镇化发展的制度创新

深化户籍制度改革,坚持因地制宜、分步推进,把有稳定劳动关系并在城镇居住一定年限的农民工及其家属逐步转为城镇居民。中小城市和小城镇要根据实际放宽落户条件,切实落实国家有关户籍制度改革的政策要求,逐步满足符合条件农村人口的落户需求。继续探索建立城乡统一的户口登记制度。大力改善对暂时不具备在城镇落户条件农民工的公共服务,逐步实现基本公共服务由户籍人口向常住人口覆盖。保证农民工随迁子女平等接受义务教育,并研究制定接受义务教育后在当地升学考试的办法。将与企业建立稳定劳动关系的农民工纳入城镇职工基本养老和医疗保险,以农民工、非公经济组织从业人员等为重点,扩大工伤、失业和生育保险覆盖面。多渠道多形式改善农民工居住条件,鼓励采取多种方式将符合条件的农民工纳入城镇住房保障体系。采取有针对性的措施,着力解决新生代农民工问题。扩大县域发展自主权,稳步推进扩权强县改革试点,逐步提高县级财政在省级财力分配中的比重,在有条件的地方探索省直接管理县(市)的体制。依法赋予经济发展快、人口吸纳能力强的小城镇在投资审批、工商管理、社会治安等方面的行政管理权限。

附录:"十一五"规划:社会主义新农村建设重点工程(2006—2010 年)

大型粮棉油生产基地和优质粮食产业工程 在粮食主产区集中连片建设高产稳产大型商品粮生产基地,继续建设优质棉基地、优质油料带。在 13 个粮食主产区的 484 个粮食主产县(场),建设万亩连片标准粮田,实施良种繁育、病虫害防控和农机装备推进等项目。

沃土工程 对增产潜力大的中低产田加大耕地质量建设力度,配套建设不同类型的土肥新技术集成转化示范基地,使项目实施区的中低产田耕地基础地力提高一个等级。

植保工程 完善县(市)级基层站点和省级分中心,建设一批生态和生物控灾示范基地、农药安全测试评价中心和生物技术测试区域中心。

大型灌区续建配套改造和中部四省大型排涝泵站改造 大型灌区续建配套和节水改造。更新改造湖南、湖北、江西、安徽四省已有大型排涝泵站。

种养业良种工程 建设农作物种质资源库、农作物改良中心、良种繁育基地,畜禽水产原良种场、水产遗传育种中心、种质资源场及检测中心等。

动物防疫体系 建设和完善动物疫病监测预警、预防控制、检疫监督、兽药质量监察及残留监控、防疫技术支撑、防疫物质保障六大系统。

农产品质量安全检验检测体系 建设国家级农产品质量标准与检测技术研究中心、农产品质检中心、区域性质检中心,省级综合性农产品质检中心和县级农产品检测站。

农村饮水安全 解决 1 亿农村居民饮用高氟水、高砷水、苦咸水、污染水和血吸虫病区、微生物超标等水质不达标及局部地区严重缺水问题。

农村公路 新建和改造农村公路 120 万公里,实现所有具备条件的乡镇和行政村通公路。

农村沼气 建设以沼气池、改圈、改厕、改厨为基本内容的农村户用沼气,以及部分规模化畜禽养殖场和养殖小区大中型沼气工程。

送电到村和绿色能源县工程 建成 50 个绿色能源示范县,利用电网延伸、风力发电、小水电、太阳能光伏发电等,解决 350 万户无电人口用电问题。

农村医疗卫生服务体系 以中西部地区乡镇卫生院为重点,同步建设县医院、妇幼保健机构、县中医院(民族医院)。

农村计划生育服务体系 以中西部地区县、乡计划生育技术服务站为重点,建设县级服务站、中心乡镇服务站、流动服务车等。

农村劳动力转移就业 加强农村劳动力技能培训、就业服务和维权服务能力建设,为外出务工农民免费提供法律政策咨询、就业信息、就业指导和职业介绍。

思考题

1. 如何理解城镇化发展和新农村建设的关系?

2. 中国的新农村建设主要从哪几个方面开展? 在完善农村发展体制机制上做了哪些探索?

3. 缩小城乡差距,您认为需要采取哪些政策工具?

参考文献

1. 国家发展和改革委员会:《全国农村经济发展"十二五"规划》,2012

年 6 月。

　　2. 新华社:《中华人民共和国国民经济和社会发展第十二个五年规划纲要》,2011 年 3 月。

　　3. 温铁军主编:《中国新农村建设报告》,福州:福建人民出版社,2010 年。

　　4. Song Hongyuan, Zhao Hai, and Xu Xuegao. "From Poverty to Overall Well-off: Reviewing China's Agricultural and Rural Development during the 20th Century", *China Economist*, 2012(5).

　　5. Han Jun. "Building a New Countryside: a Long-term Task in China's Modernization Drive", *China Economist*, 2007 (11). http://news. xinhuanet. com/ziliao/2011-03/28/c_121239866.htm.

　　6. http://english.gov.cn/special/rd_index.htm.

　　7. http://english.agri.gov.cn/.

改革开放以来,中国农民收入增长明显,特别是 2006—2010 年期间,接连跨越 4000 元、5000 元两个大关,2010 年达到 5919 元,扣除价格因素,年均实际增长 8.9%,是改革开放以来增长最快的时期之一。农民生活水平显著提高,耐用消费品成倍增长,消费结构进一步提升。农民衣食住行用全面改善,贫困人口生存和温饱问题基本解决。不过,这段时期中国城乡居民收入的差距并没有缩小。2009 年,城乡居民收入绝对差距扩大到 12000 多元,相对差距扩大到 3.33∶1。直到此后三年农民收入增速连续 3 年超过城镇居民,分别实际增长 10.9%、11.4% 和 10.7%,中西部地区增速普遍超过东部地区,中国城乡和区域收入差距缩小的态势才初步呈现。2012 年,全国农民人均纯收入达到 7917 元。

2012 年,中国共产党第十八次代表大会明确提出了国内生产总值和城乡居民人均收入2020年比2010年翻一番的目标。在实现城乡居民"收入倍增"中,重点和难点是农民增收。尽管近年来中国农民增收实现了连续九年快速增长,但仍低于同期国内生产总值和城镇居民收入增长速度;尽管近3年城乡居民收入差距有所缩小,但收入差距仍处于历史高位,而且城乡居民收入的统计口径还不相同,如按可支配收入同口径统计,城乡差别还要大。即使2020年实现了城乡居民"收入倍增",收入差距过大问题仍难以完全解决。因此今后一段时间,农民收入至少应与城镇居民收入同步增长,并力争超过,只有这样才能使城乡居民收入差距过大问题得到缓解。

为此,从政策层面需要从战略上研究采取综合措施,营造有利的环境条件。调整国民收入分配结构,在初次分配和再分配中向农民倾斜,促进农产品价格、农民工工资稳步提高,不断增加农业投入和对农民的补贴。充分挖掘农业增收潜力,着力扩大非农就业增收空间,壮大县域经济,继续促进农民外出务工经商,支持农民工返乡创业。努力增加农民财产性收入,推动农村产权制度改革,保障农民对集体资源和经营性资产收益的分配权。

(一)挖掘农业内部增收潜力

1. 通过农业产业化发展,引导农民优化种养结构,积极发展优质高效农业和特色农业,提高农业的经济效益

农业产业化是"小生产"对接"大市场"的一个现实途径。从国际经验来看,世界上很多国家的农民都有成熟的合作组织,可以提供产前、产中、产后的各种服务,日本90%以上的农户加入了农协组织,而中国农民的组织化程度还很低;发达国家的农产品加工程度一般都在90%以上,而中国只有30%;农业产业化龙头企业,总体上看数量偏少、规模偏小,产业化的各链条之间的利益连接机制还没有真正建立起来。

因此,依靠农业龙头企业、农民专业合作社等将农产品生产、加工、

销售一体化,将农业产前、产中、产后连成一个完整的产业体系。农户和企业之间或由固定合同联结,或由合作社负责收购、加工、销售,并给农户返还利润,使农民合理分享农产品加工、流通增值收益。

农民专业合作社破解"小生产大市场"困局

从 2007 年开始,陕西省大荔县农民周忠朝联合村里的蔬菜种植户,建立起以自己名字命名的"忠朝蔬菜专业合作社"。

"我们村里种洋葱、胡萝卜、大蒜、辣椒的很多,但是品种太多太杂,一家一户自己生产自己卖,不好销售。"周忠朝告诉记者,多年"单打独斗"的经历使大家逐渐意识到,只有联合起来才能有出路。几年来,加入合作社的蔬菜种植户统一品种、统一管理、统一销售,规模越做越大,目前已经有 800 多名社员。

"组织合作社前,一斤辣椒只能卖 10 元,现在统一品种、统一管理,质量和口碑都上去了,一斤能卖到 20 元。"周忠朝说,目前加入合作社的社员种植蔬菜,每亩能赚 7000 元至 8000 元。

过去,千家万户小农生产造成土地集约化程度不高,产量和质量均难以保障。农民专业合作社把分散的农户组织起来,根据市场信息统一组织种植,促进了规模化、标准化经营。同时,合作社通过统一提供农资、对成员进行内部监督管理等手段,为农产品质量安全提供了重要保障,信誉的建立反过来促进了销售的提升。

业内专家表示,农民专业合作社提高了农民市场谈判地位,延伸了产业链条。合作社在生产环节能更多地依靠市场行情组织"订单生产"避免盲目投资,在流通环节组织"农超对接"、"农校对接"等平台降低物流费用,能有效促进农民增收。

《中国农民专业合作社发展报告(2006—2010)》提供的数据显示,目前"全国入社农户的收入普遍比非成员同业农户高出 20%以上"。

资料来源:《农民专业合作社能否破解农产品"小生产大市场"困局(节选)》,新华网,2011年 10 月 30 日,http://news. xinhuanet. com/fortune/2011 - 10/30/c_111133437_3.htm。

2. 拓展农业功能,利用农村田园风光、山水景观、乡风民俗等资源,发展"农家乐"、休闲农业、旅游农业和手工制品经营等

成都发展休闲农业,打造"五朵金花"

四川省成都市锦江区在城乡结合部的红砂、幸福、万福、驸马、江家堰、大安桥6个行政村,建设成了占地12平方公里的以"花香农居"、"幸福梅林"、"江家菜地"、"东篱菊园"、"荷塘月色"命名的"五朵金花"为品牌的观光休闲农业区,已成为国内外享用盛名的休闲旅游娱乐度假区,被评定为国家4星级风景旅游区。

"五朵金花"的快速发展,主要得益于规模化经营,破解农民单家独户闯市场的风险,走出了一条专业化、产业化、规模化的发展之路。五个景区实现一区一景一业错位发展的格局。"花香农居"以建设中国花卉基地为重点,全方位深度开发符合观光产业的现代化农业,主办各种花卉艺术节,促进人流集聚。"荷塘月色"以现有1074亩水面为基础,大力发展水岸经济,建设融人、水、莲、蛙为一体的自然景观。"东篱菊园"依托丘陵地貌,构建菊文化村,引导游客养菊、赏菊、品菊,陶冶道德精神情操。"幸福梅林"用3000亩坡地培育20万株梅花,建设以梅花博物馆为主要景点的梅林风景。"江家菜地"把500余亩土地平整成0.1亩为一小块的菜地,以每块每年800元租给城市市民种植,丰富市民和儿童对发展绿色产业的兴趣。

"五朵金花"观光休闲农业不仅整合了成都市城郊区域之间的农村旅游资源,而且将农村旅游与农业观光休闲、古镇旅游、节庆活动有机地结合起来,形成了以农家乐、乡村酒店、国家农业旅游示范区、旅游古镇等为主体的农村旅游发展业态,在不断提升成都市旅游总体实力的同时,还丰富了农村旅游的内涵,促进了农村观光休闲农业的可持续协调发展。不仅改善了农村的人居环境,改变了农民的生活习惯,也改变了传统的单家独户的农业生产方式,引导农业生产经营规模化、产业

化经营,土地产出效益大幅增加。由每亩种粮食年收入200—300元,蔬菜或种花年收入2000—5000元提高到上万元。

图4-1　四川省成都市锦江区三圣乡红砂村新貌(新华社记者王晔彪摄)

通过景区建设,在区内从事多种开发经营的3000多户农民(11500多人),全部就地转为市民,解决了9790个农民的就业安置,加快了城乡一体化的步伐;带动了商贸业、服务业等相关产业和县域经济发展;"五朵金花"旅游景区每年对地方财政收入贡献达近千万元。

3. 结合农业结构调整,发挥各地比较优势,支持发展"一村一品",培育一批特色鲜明、类型多样的专业村、专业镇

陕西省:"一村一品"帮助农民增收

2002年4月,陕西省委主要领导与时任日本大分县知事平松守彦正式签署了开展经济合作与交流协议,正式引进"一村一品"模式(OVOP)。在前期大量调研的基础上, 2007年陕西省政府以1号文件

下发了《陕西省实施一村一品千村示范万村推进工程规划》,一村一品工作在陕西开始全面实施。通过几年的努力,陕西一村一品工作取得了一定成效。

一是产业基础初具规模。截至 2010 年年底,全省一村一品示范村已达 3823 个,一乡一业示范乡镇 186 个,省级休闲农家明星村 20 个;主导产业从业农户 180 万户,从业人员 500 多万人;主导产业涉及粮、果、畜、菜、手工艺、农产品加工以及休闲农业等 12 个领域;创建农民专业合作社 6250 个;与龙头企业有效对接的示范村 551 个,有专业批发市场的示范村 165 个。

二是区域板块加速形成。依托区域资源优势,科学布局,加大投资,先后建立了洛川(苹果)、镇坪(生猪)、泾阳(蔬菜)、石泉(蚕桑)、武功(手工艺品)等 11 个一县一业建设县区,积极推进包括 18 个县区在内猕猴桃、设施瓜菜、茶叶、魔芋、花椒 5 个优势产业区(带)建设,加速了优势产业区域板块的形成。一村一品发展整体呈现集中连片、整体推进、板块联动的发展格局,正在由一村一品向多村一品、一乡一业和一县一业加快转型。

三是知名品牌不断涌现。在一村一品示范村中,获得省(市)以上名牌产品的示范村 288 个,获得地理标志产品保护的 148 个,有注册商标的 239 个,分别占示范村总数的 7.5%、3.9% 和 6.3%。主导产品获得无公害农产品、绿色食品、有机农产品认证的示范村达到 471 个,占示范村总数的 13.3%。洛川苹果、周至猕猴桃、韩城花椒、清涧红枣、陕南绿茶、秦川肉牛、凤翔泥塑等农特产品闻名中外,已成为当地经济发展的特色产业和农民增收的主要来源。

四是典型样板脱颖而出。按照一村一品发展模式,全省已经涌现出了以周至县裕盛村为代表的龙头企业带动型生产模式,以眉县第二坡村为代表的服务组织带动型生产模式,以泾阳县花马村为代表的专业市场带动型生产模式,以大荔县黄营村为代表的农村能人带动型生产模式,以平利县龙头村为代表的特色资源依托型生产模式,以礼泉县袁家村为代表的民俗文化开发型生产模式等一批发展一村一品先进典型,有效带动了当地农民增收致富和农村经济快速发展。

五是农民增收成效显著。2010年,全省一村一品示范村农民人均纯收入达到5800元,较全省农民人均纯收入4105元高出41.3%;较2006年示范村农民人均纯收入2940元增加2860元,增长97.3%,年递增18.5%;来自主导产业(产品)的收入占总收入的70%以上。

资料来源:《陕西:一村一品舞"农"头》,http://gb.cri.cn/27824/2011/10/27/4985s3416208.htm(2013年2月15日检索)。

(二)积极发展农村第二、第三产业

2003年,中国农村4.9亿劳动力中转移到乡镇企业就业的有1.35亿。然而,在可以预见的将来,即使有越来越多的农民进城,农村劳动力供大于求、就业不充分的问题仍将长期存在。因此,扩大农村劳动力就业,必须多形式、多层次、多领域全面展开。通过挖掘农业内部的就业容量,进一步拓展农村第二、第三产业的就业空间。

1. 大力发展农产品加工业

加快发展农产品产地初加工,改善产地初加工设施设备,降低产后损失,提升入市品级。以资源为基础,以市场为导向,提升农产品精深加工水平,发展粮油、糖料、果蔬、肉类、水产、乳制品和农业特色资源加工业,生产优质、安全、卫生、方便、营养、附加值高的农产品加工制品。优化农产品加工业布局,引导农产品加工企业向农产品优势产区集聚、向园区集中。支持农产品加工企业加快技术改造,改善装备条件,改进工艺技术,提升产品质量,培育市场占有率高的名牌产品。

2. 提升乡镇企业发展水平

引导乡镇企业加快转型升级,加大科技创新力度,调整优化产业结构,完善经营管理机制,提高从业人员素质,提升企业核心竞争力。推进乡镇企业节能减排,开展清洁生产,发展循环经济。鼓励有条件的乡镇企业通过跨地区、跨行业的联合、兼并、重组、收购、控股等方式,组建大型企业集团。科学规划,促进乡镇企业向县城、小城镇及园区集中,提高聚集效应。落实和完善财政、税收等优惠政策,加强对乡镇企业担保、贷款、上市融资等方面的金融支持,为乡镇企业发展创造良好环境。支持乡镇企业广泛参与现代农业发展、农业农村基础设施和公共服务建设。

3.加快发展农村第三产业

适应农村经济发展需要,大力发展农村金融、信息、科技等生产性服务业。支持商贸企业及供销合作社、农民专业合作社等合作组织发展农资连锁经营,推行农资信用销售。深入实施"万村千乡"市场工程,引导城市大型商贸流通企业等向农村延伸服务,推进农村电子商务体系建设,发展高效的农村物流配送体系,提高农村物流效率。面向农村居民生活需要,积极发展通信、文化、餐饮、旅游、娱乐等生活性服务业,丰富服务产品类型,扩大服务供给,提高服务质量,满足和方便农民多样化的生活需求。适应农村人口老龄化和居住方式变化,积极发展农村养老服务和社区服务业。

依托电子商务实现农民就地创业的新路径
——江苏省睢宁县沙集镇农民电子商务发展情况调查

电子商务作为信息化时代的标志性营销手段,以其低廉的交易成本、简化的贸易流程、无限拓展的市场空间、不受地域限制的贸易条件,为新时期农民就地创业带来了前所未有的便利。江苏省睢宁县沙集镇农民依托电子商务把生意做到全国乃至新加坡等国家和地区,探索出了一条以信息化带动工业化、农村产业化的农民就地创业的新路径。该镇东风村被第十三届中国国际电子商务大会评为"中国电子商务农村创业优秀奖",沙集镇被 2010 年网商大会组委会评为"最佳网商沃土"奖。

一、主要做法

1. **典型引路、内生发展。**农民注重现实的特点,决定了电子商务这一新的交易方式和生产方式在农村推广需要靠能人带动、典型示范。2006 年,被称为沙集镇网商"三剑客"的东风村青年孙寒、夏凯和陈雷开始利用网络进行创业。选择的产品从销售一些小的挂件和家具饰品开始,逐步发展到销售简易拼装的板式家具。为提高利润率,2007 年年底由孙寒率先投资 10 万元建起家具生产作坊,一改单纯的销售为生产销售相结合,"三剑客"的网销创业之路越走越好,极大地激发了农民依托电子商务开展就地创业的内生动力。在家的老人、妇女、残障人员,在外打工的农民,甚至在大型企业的中层管理人员也回乡加入了依托电子商务创业的行列。胡翠英作为家庭主妇,其丈夫、儿子常年在外打工,看到网销能赚钱,把丈夫、儿子都叫回家,买了电脑,开通网络,儿子设计、儿媳负责网络销售,开起了家庭作坊。徐州大地集团的中层管理人员刘兴利与爱人一道回到故乡东风村开起了现代化的"三实"家具公司。"三剑客"的电子商务不仅迅速扩展到整个东风村,而且扩展到整个沙集镇,现在已辐射到周边的凌城镇、高作镇,甚至宿迁市的耿车镇和安徽泗县山头镇。

2. **规模聚集、产业升级。**电子商务的开展催生了沙集镇家具生产产业及配套产业的规模扩张和产业链拓展,板材加工、家具配件、物流快递等相关配套产业不断发展壮大,产业链不断拉长。沙集镇家具生产厂已发展到 200 余家,网店专业服务商 1 家,家具配件门市 2 家,板材加工厂 6 家,物流快递企业 16 家。随着产业规模的扩大,产业升级也提上日程。目前,沙集镇家具行业从最初以家庭成员为主的作坊式生产向现代化公司运作发展,从简单低档家具向复杂高档家具发展,从千篇一律向个性定制发展,从一味模仿向自主创新发展,从冒牌贴牌向自主品牌发展。比如,沙集镇 2010 年申请注册商标 50 多个,购买外地商标使用权 100 多个。

3. 行业自律、规范发展。为规范行业行为,避免行业恶性竞争,确保持续健康发展,同时发挥整体优势,在原材物料采购、电信网络价格、物流成本等方面增加话语权,沙集镇成立了电子商务协会,通过经验分享、联合采购、开展业务培训等措施,吸引同行会员加入,制定同行共同遵守的制度,规范农民网商的经营行为。协会会长孙寒说:"现在参加协会的会员有200多名,经过大家协商,各项规章制度基本建立,我们正在制订'沙集家具质量技术标准'和'网销客服服务规范',以更好地规范行业生产和服务。"

4. 跟进服务、后置管理。一个新兴产业的兴起和发展离不开党委政府的服务和管理。睢宁县和沙集镇党委政府充分尊重和积极保护农民依托电子商务就地创业的热情,在金融、电信、道路、治安、消防、培训、法律等方面提供优质服务,努力为农民创业营造良好的外部环境和有利条件。比如,为鼓励农民开设网店,实施宽带入户工程;为方便物流车辆通行,县财政出资拓宽村内道路;为方便夜晚发货,对村庄进行了亮化;为消除火灾隐患、以防万一,成立了消防队;为加强对农村妇女网络知识的培训,县妇联成立了网络培训中心。沙集镇的电子商务源于农民的自发行为,为充分保护农民创业的内生动力,最大限度地提供创业空间,县委县政府实施后置管理,即除为农民创业提供服务之外,政府部门一律不得主动介入实施管理。用县委书记王天琦的话讲,"除非他们亲自提出要求,否则政府不得介入。"

二、取得的成效

1. 繁荣了农村经济

依托电子商务创业在沙集已成燎原之势,沙集镇的农民网商已有1000多户,开办网店近2000家,2010年的销售额超过3亿元。胡翠英家过去是全村有名的贫困户,通过开网店,去年纯收入10万多元。长期在安徽捡破烂的王从章通过开家具厂网络销售,去年纯收入达到20多万元。当地农民形象地说,"网店开在家里头,幸福生活有奔头"。

2. 加快了产业转型

沙集镇农民人均土地不足一亩,且多为盐碱地,原来村里的人除了外出打工,就是回收废旧塑料、烧制砖瓦、加工粉条和面粉。沙集镇党委书记黄浩形象地称作"路北漏粉丝,路南磨粉面,沿河烧砖瓦,全乡收破烂。"这些产业虽然增加了农民的收入,但都带来了不同程度的环境污染、资源浪费等问题。农民电子商务的开展,带动了其他产业元素的大力跟进,促进了产业链条的延伸拓展,加快了经济结构的转型升级。从 2009 年开始,东风村家具网销产业已超过了原有的废旧塑料回收加工等产业,越来越多从事"老四样"的经营户实现了转型。

3. 增强了农村活力

工业化和城镇化浪潮将农村的青壮年劳动力特别是乡村精英吸引到城市,农村多为老弱妇孺,新农村建设主体严重缺失,农村缺乏生气,这已经成为制约新农村建设,缩小城乡差距,打破城乡二元结构的最大障碍。以沙集镇东风村为例,该村有 4000 余人,过去在外打工的有 1000 多人,最多时高达 2000 多人。现在,东风村农民电子商务的成功实践,像一块超强磁铁吸引在外打工的农民返乡创业,目前 90% 以上的外出打工人员选择在本村依靠电子商务创业,昔日荒凉的乡村,变成了热火朝天、欣欣向荣的创业创新的热土,重新焕发出勃勃生机。

4. 促进了社会和谐

过去由于农民外出打工,农村"空巢"家庭居多,老人得不到很好赡养,儿童缺乏父母的关爱,夫妻长期分居感情疏离,一些无所事事者游手好闲,这都带来一系列社会问题,影响到社会的和谐稳定。现在,外出打工者回家创业,"空巢"问题基本解决,人们安居乐业,正如沙集镇党委书记黄浩所言,"家家户户无闲人、人人手中有猴牵",无事生非的少了,社会治安好了,当地刑事案件和民事纠纷都明显下降。

资料来源:王友明编写,中国浦东干部学院,2014 年。

全国示范村:常熟蒋巷村的发展

  蒋巷村位于江苏省常熟市、昆山市、太仓市三市交界的阳澄水网地区的沙家浜水乡。全村 186 户,800 多人,村辖面积 3 平方公里。村里湖面波光粼粼,岸边垂柳依依,园中错落有致,小道曲径通幽。它常令初到这里的外来客感到惊奇。40 年前这里还是荒滩恶水,百姓住着茅草棚,患着血吸虫病,是整个常熟县(今常熟市前身)最穷的地方。可40 年后的今天,蒋巷村成了全国文明村、全国农村现代化建设示范村、中国小康建设十佳红旗单位。

  蒋巷村的发展之路成为人们关注的焦点。

  20 世纪 60 年代后期,蒋巷村在村党委书记常德盛的带领下开始向贫穷落后宣战。蒋巷村村民用两只肩膀一双手、两只箩筐一根扁担,前后历时 20 年,把 1700 亩低洼地、贫瘠地平均填高了 1 米多,同时,清理河塘,用淤泥肥田,提高肥力。20 世纪 70 年代后期,昔日的荒滩野地成了肥沃松软的"海绵田",蒋巷村的稻、麦单产独占常熟鳌头。蒋巷村在发展农业的同时,还把眼光瞄向了工业。20 世纪 80 年代中期起,苏南乡镇企业异军突起,呈现出以工业化带动农业现代化、农村城镇化的新趋势。蒋巷人办起了生产新型建材彩钢复合板的轻质建材厂,如今,从轻质建材厂起步的江苏常盛集团有限公司已经发展成为华东地区最大的轻重钢结构及轻质建材企业,成为国家级企业集团,产品被认定为江苏省该行业唯一的名牌产品。10 多年来,该集团不仅上交国家税收 2 亿多元,而且累计投入新农村建设资金上亿元,为蒋巷村率先实现小康奠定了雄厚的物质基础。"发展服务业,创办农业生态观光游"成为蒋巷村的一个大动作。仅 2003 年,蒋巷村就接待海内外宾客 5 万多人。国家旅游局已将蒋巷村定为全国农业旅游示范点。凭借科学、自然、人文交集的环境特点,产业、休闲、居住相宜的生活空间,生产、生活、生态结合的现代化新农村,蒋巷村建设成周边各大城市的又一个后花园和度假胜地,旅游业成为蒋巷村新的经济增长点。

  目前,蒋巷村又结合农业、种植业结构调整,合理配置土地和河塘资源,建起了集农业经济、自然环境、生态效益于一体的"生态种植园",实现了经济效益、社会效益、生态效益的和谐统一,标志着蒋巷村进入了农业主体循环、科学种田的新天地。

图4-2　蒋巷村的农民别墅(新华社记者陈琪摄)

2010年全村经济总产值12亿元,主体工业产值销售超过10亿元,旅游收入突破1200万元,村民人均收入超过2.5万元(不包括集体福利和别墅房补贴)。人均社区股份制分红6000元。从1995年开始,蒋巷村率先启动农民集中居住区建设,由村统一代建,按造价减半供给农户。蒋巷村还专门为老年人建造了100套老年公寓,每套住房平均50多平方米,按三星级宾馆标准配备用具,老年人可自由选择居住。不过,村里鼓励老人与子女住别墅,每年发给2000—3000元奖金;如果老年人选择入住公寓,则不发奖励也不收房租。从2001年起,蒋巷村全村实现养老保险、医疗保险等五大保险的全覆盖,做到了"基本生活包、老残有依靠、就业促勤劳、小康步步高",彻底解决了农民的后顾之忧。

中国农业与农村发展

（三）发展壮大县域经济

县域经济是城乡经济的结合部、汇合点，加快县域经济发展步伐，对于活跃农村经济、推进农村富余劳动力向非农产业和城镇转移、加快城乡一体化进程、推动城乡经济协调发展具有战略意义。

1. 加快培育县域主导产业

发挥比较优势，改善发展环境，依托重点骨干企业，加快培育县域主导产业，带动配套产业、关联产业发展，促进产业集群发展。统筹规划县域产业园区建设，推进园区整合发展，完善园区基础设施，加强园区管理创新，提升园区服务水平，增强园区承载和聚集功能，引导企业向园区集中、资源向园区整合、资金向园区流动、人才向园区汇集，促进产业园区特色化、规范化、集约化发展。鼓励中西部地区依托园区承接东部地区产业转移。

小商品、大市场：中国小商品城——浙江义乌

义乌为中国浙江省金华市下辖县级市，金华—义乌（浙中）和杭州（浙北）、宁波（浙东）、温州（浙南）并列浙江四大区域中心城市。义乌位于浙江省中部，地处金衢盆地东部，市境东、南、北三面群山环抱，义乌南北长 58.15 公里，东西宽 44.41 公里，面积 1,105 平方公里。义乌建县于公元前 222 年，1988 年撤县建市，截至 2012 年年底，义乌户籍人口为 753312 人，登记流动人口数为 159.5 万，实际在册人数 137.7 万，主要来自江西、河南、安徽、贵州、浙江等省份。

义乌手工业历史悠久。1978 年党的十一届三中全会以后，全民、集体和乡镇工业迅速发展。1984 年全面贯彻工业体制改革，扩大企业自主权，乡镇企业普遍实行经济承包责任制，全民和县属集体所有制企业。"十一五"期间（2006—2010 年）义乌市工业生产总值由 2005 年

的 593 亿元上升到 2009 年的 972 亿元,年均增长 13.1%,基本形成了"小商品、大市场,小企业、快集群"的制造业发展格局,小商品制造占全市工业产值的 70% 以上。

义乌是中国最富裕的地区之一,在福布斯发布 2013 年中国最富有 10 个县级市排名第一。义乌是全球最大的小商品集散中心,中国小商品城就坐落于浙江中部义乌市,创建于 1982 年,是中国最早创办的专业市场之一。现拥有营业面积 470 余万平方米,商位 7 万个,从业人员 21 万多,日客流量 21 万余次,经营 16 个大类、4202 个种类、33217 个细类、170 万个单品。是国际性的小商品流通、信息、展示中心。被联合国、世界银行与摩根士丹利等权威机构称为"全球最大的小商品批发市场"。2013 年中国小商品城市场成交额 683.0235 亿元,连续 23 年登上全国专业市场榜首。

中国小商品城由中国义乌国际商贸城、篁园市场、宾王市场三个市场簇群组成,几乎囊括了工艺品、饰品、小五金、日用百货、雨具、电子电器、玩具、化妆品、文体、袜业、副食品、钟表、线带、针棉、纺织品、领带、服装等所有日用工业品。其中,饰品、袜子、玩具产销量占全国市场 1/3 强。物美价廉,应有尽有的特色鲜明,在国际上具有极强的竞争力。

中国小商品城是我国最大的小商品出口基地之一,商品已出口到 219 个国家和地区,年出口 57 万多个标准集装箱,外贸出口占 65%,外国企业常驻代表机构数达 3059 家居全国县域首位,常驻外商达超 1.3 万名,联合国难民署、外交部等机构在义乌建立采购信息中心,有 83 个国家和地区在市场设立进口商品馆,"买全球货、卖全球货"的格局初步形成。

2006 年以来,国家商务部先后发布了义乌中国小商品城指数和《小商品分类与代码》行业标准,从而使义乌市场这个"世界超市"取得了全球小商品贸易定价、定标话语权,实现了由输出商品到输出标准和规则的飞跃。

2012 年,义乌市实现地区生产总值 803 亿元,比上年增长 10.2%,

图4-3　义乌国际商贸城一期饰品专区大通道一派繁忙(新华社发)

人均生产总值达到 107009 元(按 2012 年平均汇率折算为 16952 美元),增长 9.6%。三次产业比例优化为 2.6∶41.6∶55.8。

2. 积极发展小城镇

以县城和中心镇为重点,培育发展一批规模较大、辐射带动能力强的小城镇。强化土地利用总体规划的整体管控作用,加强小城镇规划工作,合理确定小城镇开发边界,强化规划约束力,走集约式城镇化道路,努力实现城镇面积扩张与人口产业集聚的合理匹配。加强小城镇基础设施建设,提高小城镇综合经济实力,增强小城镇公共服务和居住功能,吸纳农村富余劳动力就近就地转移就业、返乡创业和落户定居。

(四) 促进农民转移就业

1. 拓宽农民就业渠道

加大对农民转移就业培训的支持力度,为农民工提供职业技能培训和技能鉴定补贴,根据市场需求开展订单培训、定向培训,切实提高农民转移就业能力。结合农村基础设施项目建设,扩大农民就地转移就业规模。农村第二、第三产业和县域经济要更加重视发展劳动密集型产业,带动农民就近转移就业。加强农民外出就业信息引导,组织开展劳务输出对接,促进农民外出转移就业持续增长。落实好农民工创业扶持政策,为有创业需求的农民工免费提供创业咨询指导、创业培训、创业项目推介等服务,提供创业小额担保贷款贴息,引导农民工返乡创业,以创业带动就业。

2. 加强农民工劳动权益保护

建立统一规范灵活的人力资源市场,促进城乡劳动者平等就业。全面推行劳动合同制度,着力提高农民工合同签订率,规范劳务派遣用工和企业裁员行为。建立健全农民工工资决定和正常增长机制,健全工资支付保障机制,完善最低工资和工资指导线制度,逐步提高最低工资标准,努力实现农民工和城镇就业人员同工同酬。改善农民工劳动条件,保障安全生产,加强职业病防治和农民工健康服务。健全协调劳动关系三方机制,发挥政府、工会和企业作用。加大劳动保障监察立法和执法力度,加强劳动人事争议调解仲裁服务体系建设,为农民工免费提供劳动关系协调、劳动人事争议调解仲裁和劳动保障监察执法维权等服务。

江苏省昆山市五项措施打造农民工法律援助直通车

江苏省昆山市地处江苏省东南部,位于上海与苏州市区之间,总面积 927.68 平方公里,其中水域面积占 23.1%。昆山是"百戏之祖"昆曲的发源地,中国大陆经济实力最强县级市,连续多年被评为全国百强县之首。2010 年 9 月,昆山与维也纳、新加坡等 5 城市获该年度联合国人居奖。

近年来,大量外来务工人员不断涌入昆山,目前已有 130 多万新昆山人在昆工作生活,数量远远超过本地户籍人口,同时,各种与农民工有关的矛盾纠纷也不断出现,使得农民工法律援助案件也不断增多。为更好地维护好广大农民工群众的合法权益,促进社会和谐、稳定,2011 年,昆山市法律援助中心力推五项措施,着力打造农民工法律援助直通车。

一是加强农民工法律援助工作队伍建设。调整充实农民工法律援助骨干律师队伍;加强相关业务培训;强化工作考评,奖优罚劣,筑牢农民工法律援助工作的人才基础。

二是加强农民工法律援助知识宣传。积极开展"新市民法律讲堂"系列法制培训班,在农民工数量集中乡镇和企业开展短期培训班,讲解法律知识,扩大法律援助知晓面。

三是畅通受理环节,提高办案速度。在受理环节中,及时、快速地完成指派和材料交接,在办案过程中,探索和推行调解优先原则,促进问题迅速解决,降低成本,提高效率。

四是整合资源,强化农民工法律援助网络。加强与工、青、妇、劳动保障、法院等部门的横向联系,全面掌握农民工维权动态,积极协调、畅通农民工维权过程中的相关环节,便于律师取证、调档、立案等工作的开展,缩短农民工维权时间。

五是进一步规范农民工劳动法律援助站的工作。努力发挥南京大学法学院的人才和学术优势,通过调研,积极开展更具针对性的、更贴近农民工实际需求的法律服务工作,把农民工法律援助站打造成昆山法律援助的新亮点。

资料来源:江苏法律援助网,http://www.chinalegalaid.gov.cn/China_legalaid/content/2011-02/15/content_2473224.htm? node=24963(发布时间 2011 年 2 月 15 日,检索时间 2013 年 2 月 15 日)。

(五)努力增加农民转移性收入

1. 全面取消农业税

从 2006 年 1 月 1 日起,中国全面取消除烟叶以外的"农业四税"

（农业税、屠宰税、牧业税、农业特产税），结束了 2600 多年农民按地亩
缴税的历史。2006 年全面取消农业税后，与农村税费改革前的 1999
年相比，中国农民每年减负总额超过 1000 亿元，人均减负 120 元左右。
这是中国农业发展与世界惯例接轨的标志性事件。从国际上看，当一
个国家经济发展到一定程度，无一例外地要对农业实行零税制，并给予
相当的财政补贴。在经济全球化的宏观背景下，中国取消农业税，采取
"少取、多予、放活"的政策，无疑顺应了时代的要求。

2. 对农业实施补贴

中国从 2002 年开始搞种粮补贴试点，到 2004 年全面推开，现在实
行"农业四补贴"（包括种粮农民直接补贴、农用生产资料综合补贴、良
种补贴和农机具购置补贴），但即使每年补贴 1000 多亿，平均到每个农
民个体也只有 200 多元人民币，占农民人均纯收入的 4% 不到。因此，
随着国家财力的提升，需要完善农业补贴政策，逐步加大补贴力度。按
照增加总量、优化存量、用好增量、加强监管的要求，不断强化农业补贴
政策，完善主产区利益补偿、耕地保护补偿、生态补偿办法，加快让农业
获得合理利润、让主产区财力逐步达到全国或全省平均水平。继续增
加农业补贴资金规模，新增补贴向主产区和优势产区集中，向专业大
户、家庭农场、农民合作社等新型生产经营主体倾斜。落实好对种粮农
民直接补贴、良种补贴政策，扩大农机具购置补贴规模，推进农机以旧
换新试点。完善农资综合补贴动态调整机制，逐步扩大种粮大户补贴
试点范围。

3. 其他支持政策

此外，继续实施农业防灾减灾稳产增产关键技术补助和土壤有机
质提升补助，支持开展农作物病虫害专业化统防统治，启动低毒低残留
农药和高效缓释肥料使用补助试点。完善畜牧业生产扶持政策，支持
发展肉牛肉羊，落实远洋渔业补贴及税收减免政策。增加产粮（油）大
县奖励资金，实施生猪调出大县奖励政策，研究制定粮食作物制种大县

奖励政策。增加农业综合开发财政资金投入。现代农业生产发展资金重点支持粮食及地方优势特色产业加快发展。积极增加农业保险保费补贴品种并扩大覆盖范围,开展并逐步扩大设施农业保费补贴试点。

4. 不断提高基本公共服务水平

增加新型农村社会养老保险基础养老金,逐步提高新型农村合作医疗人均筹资标准、财政补助水平和报销水平,农村最低生活保障标准年均增长10%以上。

5. 继续加大扶贫投入力度

中国是世界上人口最多的发展中国家,发展基础差、底子薄,不平衡现象突出。特别是农村贫困人口多,解决贫困问题的难度很大。中国的减贫,在很大程度上就是解决农村的贫困问题。

20世纪80年代中期以来,中国政府开始有组织、有计划、大规模地开展农村扶贫开发,先后制定实施《国家八七扶贫攻坚计划(1994—2000年)》、《中国农村扶贫开发纲要(2001—2010年)》、《中国农村扶贫开发纲要(2011—2020年)》等减贫规划,使扶贫减贫成为全社会的共识和行动。中国的农村扶贫开发,促进了社会和谐稳定和公平正义,推动了中国人权事业的发展和进步。

2001年,中国政府发布了《中国的农村扶贫开发》白皮书。10多年来,中国国民经济平稳较快增长,综合国力不断增强。在这一进程中,国家把扶贫开发纳入国民经济和社会发展总体规划,制定和实施有利于农村贫困地区发展的政策措施,把扶贫投入作为公共财政预算安排的优先领域,把贫困地区作为公共财政支持的重点区域,不断加大对贫困地区的扶持力度,切实提高扶贫政策的执行力。

(1)农村政策。中国是一个传统的农业大国,农村人口多,贫困现象突出。实行有利于减贫的农村政策,对于消除农村贫困问题十分重要。10多年来,国家实行统筹城乡经济社会发展的方略和工业反哺农业、城市支持农村与"多予少取放活"的方针,全面促进农村经济社会的发展,使贫困地区和农村贫困人口普遍受益。具体举措包括免除农业税,直接补贴,逐步建立和完善农村社会保障体系,推进农村饮水、电力、道路、沼气等基础设施建设和农村危房改造等。推行集体林权制度改革,使农民真正拥有林地承包经营权和林木所有权,落实各项优惠政策,发展林下经济和森林旅游,增加农民收入。不断加大强农惠农富农和扶贫开发的投入力度,中央财政用于"三农"的支出从 2003 年的 2144.2 亿元人民币增加到 2010 年的 8579.7 亿元人民币,年均增长 21.9%,公共财政覆盖农村步伐明显加快。国家的一些强农惠农富农政策率先在贫困地区实行。其中,免征农业税试点、农村义务教育"两免一补"政策(对农村义务教育阶段贫困家庭学生免书本费、免杂费、补助寄宿生生活费)、对国家新安排的公益性基本建设项目减少或取消县及县以下配套,率先在国家扶贫开发工作重点县实行。一些强农惠农富农政策向贫困地区和贫困人口倾斜。中央财政在农村最低生活保障、新型农村合作医疗和新型农村社会养老保险的制度安排上,对中西部地区给予较大支持。2010 年,民政部门资助参加新型农村合作医疗 4615.4 万人次,资助资金 14 亿元人民币,人均资助 30.3 元人民币。

(2)区域政策。20 世纪末,中国政府开始实施西部大开发战略。中国的西部地区,自然条件相对恶劣,基础设施建设相对滞后,贫困人口比较集中。10 多年来,西部大开发安排的水利、退耕还林、资源开发等项目,在同等条件下优先在贫困地区布局;公路建设加快向贫困地区延伸,把贫困地区的县城与国道、省道干线连接起来;基础设施建设项目尽量使用贫困地区的劳动力,增加贫困人口的现金收入。国家相继出台一系列区域发展政策,促进西藏和四川、云南、甘肃、青海四省藏区以及新疆、广西、重庆、宁夏、甘肃、内蒙古、云南等地经济社会发展,并把农村扶贫开发作为政策重点加以推进。

(3)农村社会保障制度。为贫困人口提供基本的社会保障,是稳定解决贫困人口温饱问题的最基础手段。2007 年,国家决定在全国农村全面建立最低生活保障制度,将家庭年人均纯收入低于规定标准的所有农村居民纳入保障范围,稳定、持久、有效地解决农村贫困人口温饱问题。农村最低生活保障标准,由县级以上地方政府按照能够维持当地农村居民全年基本生活所必需的吃饭、穿衣、用水、用电等费用确定。截至 2010 年年底,全国农村低保覆盖 2528.7 万户、5214 万人;2010 年全年共发放农村低保资金 445 亿元人民币,其中中央补助资金 269 亿元人民币;全国农村低保平均标准为 117 元人民币/人、月,月人均补助水平为 74 元人民币。国家对农村丧失劳动能力和生活没有依靠的老、弱、孤、寡、残农民实行五保供养,即在吃、穿、住、医、葬等方面给予生活照顾和物质帮助。10 年间,五保供养逐步实现了由集体福利事业转型为现代社会保障制度,所需资金由农民分摊转由国家财政负担。到 2010 年年底,全国农村得到五保供养的人数为 534 万户、556.3 万人,基本实现"应保尽保",全国各级财政共发放农村五保供养资金 96.4 亿元人民币。2009 年,国家开展新型农村社会养老保险试点工作,到 2011 年 7 月已覆盖全国 60%的农村地区,共有 493 个国家扶贫开发工作重点县纳入试点,覆盖率达到 83%。新型农村社会养老保险实行个人缴费、集体补助、政府补贴相结合的筹资方式,基础养老金和个人账户养老金相结合的待遇支付方式,中央财政对中西部地区按中央确定的基础养老金给予全额补助,对东部地区给予 50%的补助。2010 年,中央财政对新型农村社会养老保险基础养老金补贴 111 亿元人民币,地方财政补助资金 116 亿元人民币。2004 年,国家出台了规范的最低工资制度,对保障以农民工为主体的劳动者的劳动报酬权益发挥了积极作用。

(4)提高扶贫政策执行力。政策实施成功与否,关键在于执行。中国政府把建立工作责任制、加强干部队伍和机构建设作为保障扶贫政策执行力的关键,采取有效措施保证扶贫政策的落实。按照"省负总责、县抓落实、工作到村、扶贫到户"的要求,实行扶贫开发工作责任到省、任务到省、资金到省、权力到省。把扶贫开发作为国家扶贫开发工作重点县政府的中心任务,由县负责把扶贫开发的政策措施落实到贫困村和贫困户。实行扶贫工作党政"一把手"负责制,把扶贫开发的效果作为考核这些地方政府主要负责人政绩的重要依据。加强贫困地区干部队伍建设,将贫困地区县级领导干部和县以上扶贫部门干部的培训纳入各级党政干部培训规划,采取挂职锻炼、干部交流等方式充实和加强贫困地区干部队伍。加强扶贫开发统计监测,为科学决策提供依据。加强贫困地区基层组织建设,改进基层干部思想作风和工作作风,推进社会治安综合治理,维护贫困地区社会稳定。充实和加强各级扶贫开发的工作机构,稳定人员,改善条件,提高素质,增强扶贫开发的组织领导和协调管理能力。国务院有关部门把扶贫开发作为一项重要工作,结合各自职能,认真贯彻落实扶贫政策。

2012年,中国扶贫开发投入力度进一步加大,中央财政综合扶贫投入2996亿元,比上年增长31.9%。28个省区市财政预算安排专项扶贫资金147.8亿元,中央定点扶贫直接投入帮扶资金(含物资折款)18.98亿元,帮助引进各类资金90.34亿元。

截至2012年年底,国务院已全部批复了11个集中连片特殊困难地区区域发展和扶贫攻坚规划,全国片区扶贫攻坚规划全面启动,部分民生工程和基础设施项目率先实施,310个单位参与定点扶贫,首次实现对国家扶贫开发工作重点县的全覆盖。全国扶贫对象总规模下降到9899万人,占农村户籍人口的比例下降到10.2%。

"中国式扶贫"政策呈现三特征

中国国务院新闻办公室2011年11月16日发布的《中国农村扶贫开发的新进展》白皮书表示,中国提前实现了联合国千年发展目标中贫困人口减半目标,为全球减贫事业做出重大贡献。中国的扶贫开发政策有三个特征。

——坚持开发式扶贫和社会保障相结合。引导贫困地区和贫困群众以市场为导向,提高自我积累、自我发展能力。2001—2010年,中国592个国家扶贫开发工作重点县人均地区生产总值年均增长17%,农民人均纯收入年均增长11%,两者的增幅均高于全国平均水平。到2010年年底,农村低保覆盖2528.7万户,5214万人,新型农村社会养老保险等覆盖范围不断扩大。

　　——坚持专项扶贫和行业扶贫、社会扶贫相结合。编制以财政专项扶贫资金为主要资源的专项扶贫开发规划,分年实施。水利、交通等部门将贫困地区作为各自发展重点,党政机关和企事业单位进行定点扶贫,东西扶贫协作,军队和武警部队支援,社会各界参与,形成有中国特色的社会扶贫方式,推动贫困地区发展,增加贫困农民收入。

　　——坚持外部支持与自力更生相结合。通过专项扶贫资金、财政转移支付、部门项目建设、社会各界捐助、引进利用外资等途径,不断加大对贫困地区的资金投入。贫困地区自强不息,投工投劳,依靠自身力量改变贫困落后面貌。据不完全统计,截至 2010 年,中国扶贫领域共利用各类外资 14 亿美元,加上国内配套资金,直接投资总额近 200 亿元人民币,近 2000 万贫困人口受益。

资料来源:《中国农村扶贫开发的新进展》白皮书,2011 年。参见中国新闻网,http://www.chinanews.com/cj/2011/11-16/3464376.shtml(发布时间 2011 年 11 月 16 日,检索时间 2013 年 2 月 15 日)。

思考题

　　1. 除了帮助农业转移人口进入城镇,实现非农就业外,您认为中国农民通过就地工业化、城镇化、农业现代化等增加收入的措施手段,是否有效? 您认为政府、市场、社会可以从哪些方面帮助农民增加收入?

　　2. 中国采取了哪些措施,帮助大量贫困人口实现脱贫?

　　3. 您所在国和中国农业、农村情况有哪些相似和差异之处? 您认为今后可以在哪些领域开展交流与合作?

参考文献

　　1. 李克强:《农村公共产品供给与农民发展》,北京:中国社会科学出版社,2013 年。

　　2. 韩长赋:《中国农民工的发展与终结》,北京:中国人民大学出版社,2007 年。

3. 谢春涛主编:《中国城镇化:亿万农民进城的故事》,北京:新世界出版社,2014 年。

4. 秦晖:《农民中国:历史反思与现实选择》,郑州:河南人民出版社,2003 年。

5. 朱玲:《减贫与包容:发展经济学研究》,北京:中国社会科学出版社,2013 年。

6. 新华社:《中华人民共和国国民经济和社会发展第十二个五年规划纲要》,2011 年 3 月。

7. http://english.agri.gov.cn/.

Preface

What is the state system of China? How has the Communist Party of China (CPC) managed to exercize long-term governance and to lead the Chinese people from one victory to another? What are the 'secrets' of the CPC's governance? What is China's development road? What significant strategies have been adopted in China? What is the next step in China's development? Why has China been able to achieve such rapid economic development? These are just some of the many questions frequently asked by the international community, especially foreign political parties and statesmen on their visits to China. For the purpose of providing answers to these questions and enabling readers to be informed about the real China and the CPC, we arranged for the *Understanding Modern China* Series (hereinafter referred to as the Series) to be written, to serve as elementary documents introducing the CPC, as well as China's development road, development theories and development experience.

The Series is inspired by the new philosophies, new ideas and new strategies for the country's governance put forward by General Secretary Xi Jinping since the 18th National Congress of the CPC, aimed at the following aspects: strenuously reflecting the development vision of 'the Chinese Dream' and the development prospects of the 'Two Centenary' goals; strenuously reflecting the coordinated promotion of the overall situation of a 'five-pronged approach to building socialism with Chinese characteristics to build up socialist economy, socialist democracy, socialist advanced culture, socialist harmonious society and socialist ecological civilisation; and the strategic arrangements for the 'Four-Pronged Comprehensive Strategy' comprehensively completing the building of a moderately prosperous society in all respects, comprehensively deepening reform in all respects, comprehensively advancing the rule of law, and comprehensively exercising strict discipline for the party; strenuously reflecting the 'new normal' facilitating and leading China's economic development and the implementation of the 'five major development concepts' to promote innovative, coordinated, green, open and shared development; strenuously reflecting the three major economic development strategies of the 'Belt and Road', the coordinated development of Beijing, Tianjin and Hebei province, and the Yangtze river economic belt. On the basis of a great number of fresh cases and experiences, the Series tells China's story, transmits China's voice, analyzes China's problems, and offers China solutions.

The Series has been written on the basis of telling China's story and transmitting China's voice, oriented around the following four aspects: the first is to illustrate the new measures taken to deepen reform since the 18th National Congress of the CPC, the new ideas on economic development and the new philosophy on foreign affairs, on the basis of an all-round introduction to the achievements since the reform and opening up; the second is to analyze the reason for the achievements, the underlying operating law, and the process of evolution, while presenting the development achievements of China's economy and society; the third is to keep to problem orientation and demand orientation, rather than attempt to be all-embracing and systematic, so as to clear up targeted doubts and confusion on the basis of the demands of foreign readers; the fourth is to introduce China not only in terms of 'where it is coming from', but also in terms of 'where it is going', for the purpose of enabling readers to know about China's historical development process on the one hand, and on the other hand, exemplifying and clarifying how China assures the organic unification of its past, present and future, the organic combination of legacy and innovation, and how China is planning its future development.

Under the guidance of the International Department of the CPC Central Committee, the writing of the Series has been organized by China Executive Leadership Academy Pudong (CELAP).

The International Department of the CPC Central Committee is the functional department of the CPC in charge of foreign affairs. So far, the CPC has established connections of various types with more than 600 political parties and organizations in over 160 countries and regions, which include left-wing and right-wing parties; both ruling parties and opposition parties. Foreign affairs work is of paramount importance to the CPC, and an indispensable component of national diplomacy as a whole, whose target is to promote state-to-state and people-to-people communication and understanding.

CELAP is a national leadership institution in China, and as a platform on which international cooperative training and exchange are carried out, CELAP has held fast to its characteristics of internationality and openness since March 2005 when it was founded. CELAP spares no effort in implementing international cooperative training, with target participants being foreign political parties and statesmen, high-ranking business executives and senior professionals. By the end of 2015, CELAP had offered training programs to more than 6,000 participants from over 130 countries, and thus has won wide recognition and received a favorable reception from the countries, regions and participants that are involved.

To cater for the needs of foreign participants, CELAP initiated the writing of the Series at the beginning of 2012, and after four years of modifications and improvements, the finalized manuscripts were completed at the end of 2015. The first batch of 10 books to be published in this Series are: *China's New Strategies for Governing the Country; The Communist Party of China: the Past, Present and Future of Party Building; China's Reform, Opening Up and Construction of Development Zones; The Framework of the Chinese Government and Public Services; A New Analysis of Urbanization in China; China's Agriculture and Rural Development in the Post-Reform Era; The Evolution of China's Diplomacy in the Modern Era; Leadership Selection and Appointment in China; Leadership Education and Training in China;* and *Shanghai – the 'Pacesetter' of China's Reform and Opening Up.*

The authors of the Series are mainly professionals in CELAP, and functionaries and specialists in the Development Research Center of the Shanghai Municipal People's Government, Shanghai Institute for International Studies and Hangzhou Research Center for Urban Studies.

The Series is published in Chinese and English, with the English translation done mainly by senior professors at Shanghai International Studies University, to whom thanks are due. Gratitude also goes to the People's Publishing House for its great support and positive suggestions in the process of writing and translating.

Writing such a series of textbooks for mature foreign students is a first in China. Constructive criticism is welcome, for the Series as a new endeavor can hardly be free from mistakes.

Editorial Committee of the *Understanding Modern China* Series
January 2016

Alain Charles Asia (ACA) Publishing Ltd is delighted to be associated with the People's Publishing House to bring this series of 10 *Understanding Modern China* books to an English-speaking readership.

ACA, formerly known as ACP (Alain Charles Publishing) Ltd Beijing, was founded in October 1989 and was the first foreign-owned publishing company to be allowed to open an office in China.

In 2007, ACP Beijing was renamed ACA Publishing Ltd to better reflect its focus on China and the Asia-Pacific region. The company specialises in publishing books about China for international readers and has offices in Beijing and London.

ACA Publishing Ltd,

April 2016

Contents

Introduction

I. Objectives

In the late 1970s, China kicked off a series of reforms in its rural areas. Since then, world-shaking changes have taken place and agriculture production has increased. China has ranked first in the world by output of grain, oil, vegetables, fruit, eggs and aquatic products for many consecutive years, creating a miracle of feeding nearly 20% of the world's population with 9% of its arable land. Rural economic development has been achieved through a balanced and all-round development of farming, forestry, animal husbandry and fishery. Based on quality production, optimal regional arrangements, industrialization and standardized management, modern agriculture has basically taken shape. The fast development of secondary and tertiary industries in rural areas has changed the employment structure and promoted development in small towns. The great improvements in farmers' living standards and their increased income have turned China from a country lacking basic necessities into a moderately affluent society, and China has become the first country to achieve the United Nations (UN) Millennium Development Goal of halving the number of its people living in poverty. Rural public services including education, healthcare and social security have greatly improved.

China's successful rural reforms have accumulated a rich store of experience for transforming its economic systems and attracted worldwide attention. China is willing to exchange ideas and share its best practices, address resource and environmental challenges together with other countries, and make life better for all, which is part of our globalization initiatives. According to *The State of World Food Insecurity 2012* released by the UN Food and Agriculture Organization (UNFAO), among the 868 million

(868m) people who are chronically malnourished and even more who suffer from hunger, 850m are living in the rural areas of developing countries. It is of great importance for nations to communicate, share and make common efforts, and this book is published to make a contribution in this regard. It introduces the basic systems in rural China and elaborates how China promotes modern agriculture based on specific local conditions, builds a new countryside and helps farmers become rich despite having a large population and limited arable land and resources. Case studies are provided for better understanding.

We sincerely hope to give our readers, especially those who are foreign officials, experts and researchers who may come for communication and research to the China Executive Leadership Academy Pudong (CELAP), a sound understanding of China's agriculture and rural development through this book and also answers to the questions which they may be interested in such as how China safeguards food security, alleviates poverty and helps farmers get rich. It will be a great honor for us if the book inspires agriculture and rural development in other developing countries.

II. Scope

This book is divided into four chapters. Chapter One provides a brief introduction to China's agriculture, rural areas, farmers and rural systems, which will help readers gain an overall understanding about the development of China's agriculture and rural areas since the initiation of the reform and opening-up program and the current situation. The second, third and fourth chapters respectively focus on agricultural development, rural construction and farmers' income growth.

Chapter One introduces the basic conditions of China's agriculture, rural areas and farmers, the development of economic and organizational systems, including the household contract responsibility system, the rural land ownership system, the rural enterprise development system and the rural governance system. Section one of this Chapter gives a brief account of the basic conditions of China's agriculture, rural areas and farmers. Section two provides the background and an overview of the course of China's rural reform which mainly covers three important stages: 1) the combination of centralized and decentralized management on the basis of household contractual management in the late 1970s; 2) the agricultural products circulation system reform and the market-oriented reform of the rural economy starting in the

1980s; and 3) the coordination of urban and rural development since the early 21st century. Section three digs deeper into the rural land tenure system and the two-tier management system that combines centralized and decentralized management on the basis of household contractual management. Section four recounts how the expansion of township enterprises has promoted secondary and tertiary industries and forecasts their future development. Section five describes the rural governance structure which is composed of township-level local government administration and village-level self-governance.

Chapter Two focuses on how China promotes agricultural modernization. After a brief review of the progress made in China's agriculture, a detailed account is given in five dimensions. Section one introduces the measures adopted by the Chinese government to stabilize grain production. The stabilization of grain production is a perennially important strategy as it is critical for safeguarding food security. Section two describes the direction of the strategic structural adjustment of China's agriculture. The adjustment aims to enable the agricultural sector to create more economic benefits. Section three discusses how to promote technological innovation and applications in agriculture. Sections four and five are about agricultural modernization policies and measures: the improvement of agricultural facilities and equipment, and systemization and institutionalization of agricultural production and operation.

Chapter Three focuses on the construction of the new countryside since 2005. After an introduction to the background, it gives a detailed account of the progress and implementation measures. Section one is about improving rural infrastructure, including drinking water, power supply, clean energy, rural roads, housing, poverty relief, development and the follow-up support for migrants from reservoir construction sites. Section two talks about speeding up rural social services, including education, healthcare, culture, sports and employment services. Section three introduces the efforts made by the Chinese government to improve social security and address farmers' concerns by building a sound pension, healthcare and social assistance system under the principles of providing basic benefits, achieving full coverage, covering multiple levels, and ensuring flexibility and sustainability. Section four is about how the rural environment and living conditions are improved through developing circular agriculture and improving rural production. Section five discusses how to improve the rural economic system by promoting rural reform and institutional innovation.

Chapter Four explores how to narrow the rural-urban income gap and increase farmers' incomes. Farmers' incomes mainly come from business operation, salary and fiscal transfers. Section one is about creating added value through agricultural industrialization, developing 'leisure agriculture' and tapping the grain production potential by helping villages specialize in a certain field based on local conditions. Section two is about increasing famers' incomes through the development of secondary and tertiary industries in rural areas, by promoting agricultural product processing, the growth of township enterprises, producer services and consumer services. Section three is about developing the county-level economy by transferring rural labor to non-agricultural industries and urban areas. Section four focuses on helping farmers find jobs in cities through providing vocational training and employment information, supporting farmers to start up their own businesses and protecting their labor rights. Section five is about increasing farmers' transfer income and introduces China's development support and poverty alleviation policies in terms of tax breaks, subsidies and social security.

III. Key Points

This book aims to introduce the institutional concepts and practical policies adopted by the Chinese government to promote China's agricultural and rural development over the past three decades, thereby giving foreign readers a basic understanding of how China's rural reform fits into China's overall reform and opening-up program. A knowledge of China's national conditions and political and economic systems is essential to develop a good understanding.

IV. Reading Suggestions

In order to gain a good understanding, we suggest: first, reading through Chapter One to understand China's agricultural and rural situation and the economic and social systems in the rural areas, which will help you understand the rural reform policies in the following chapters; second, trying to answer the questions at the end of each chapter which will help you find out more; and third, evaluating the references listed at the end of each chapter which will be a good tool for further study.

Since the book attempts to make a succinct and systematic analysis and summary of China's agriculture, rural areas and farmers, it is nearly impossible to detail everything. So if you have the opportunity to make field trips, you will get a better understanding of China's agricultural and rural development and the efforts made by Chinese farmers to pursue a happy life.

Chapter 1

Main Systems of China's Agriculture, Rural Areas and Farmers

I. The Current Situation of China's Agriculture, Rural Areas and Farmers

China is a large developing country with a population of 1.347bn in 2011, with nearly half living in rural areas. In some sense, China is sustaining a large population with relatively limited arable land. Improving agricultural production, ensuring food security and increasing famers' incomes have always been the primary goals of China's economic development. The Communist Party of China (CPC) and the State Council have made agriculture a top priority of the national economic development agenda and agriculture, the rural areas and farmers are also the top priorities of the government's work. In November 2012, the 18th National Congress of the CPC made it clear that by the year 2020, the modernization of agriculture and the construction of the new countryside must produce obvious effects as they are the prerequisites for a moderately affluent society. After years of hard work, China has freed itself from a long-term shortage of agriculture products and achieved a basic balance in supply and demand. Farmers are no longer suffering from shortages of food and clothing, and have become reasonably affluent. China has succeeded in feeding nearly 20% of the world's population with 9% of its arable land. This is not only a basis for China's further reform and opening up but also a great contribution to the development of mankind.

The decade since 2003 has witnessed the fastest development of China's agriculture and rural areas, from which Chinese farmers have benefited to an amazing extent. Grain production has gone up year after year. In 2012, the annual production increased to 589.57m tonnes from 430.7m tonnes in 2003, representing an annual average increase of 17.5m tonnes. Scientific and technological progress accounts for 54.5% of grain output growth; the total

1

power of agricultural machinery reached one 1,000GW; integrated farming mechanization reached 57%; the penetration of improved grain varieties reached 96% and for the first time the grain yield per *mu* (about 0.0667 hectares) reached 350kg, which is responsible for 80.5% of the increase of total grain production. At the same time, the secondary and tertiary industries in the rural areas have developed with a strong momentum. The gross output of township enterprises exceeded Rmb6 trillion (US$897bn); the output value of agricultural product processing exceeded Rmb15 trillion (US$224bn); the total output value of agricultural reclamation surpassed Rmb500bn (US$74.7bn), and the total value of of agricultural product imports and exports surpassed US$170bn, in which exports amounted to US$65bn, reaching an all-time high.

The per capita net income of Chinese farmers has grown fast in recent years, rising from Rmb2,622 in 2003 to Rmb7,917 in 2012, with an annual increase of over Rmb540. It is gratifying that the growth in per capita net income of farmers has been higher than the growth of per capita disposable income of urban residents, promising to reduce the income gap between urban and rural residents. At the same time, the Chinese government has expedited the lifting of all constraints on farmers who want to find a job, to do business or to settle down in the cities. By the end of 2011, the total number of migrant workers in China exceeded 250m, of which over 30m have migrated with their families. Migrant farmers, also called migrant workers, have become the main source of labor in many industries in China. Such a massive flow of agricultural labor has fueled the commercial and industrial development in urban areas and contributed a lot to the socio-economic integration of urban and rural areas, creating new spaces for developing modern agriculture and promoting the income growth of farmers. Compared with 2002, the number of people employed in agriculture has dropped by over 70m in China, and the agricultural population in the rural areas has dropped by over 12%, giving each farmer another 20% or more of land for cultivation. In 2011, farmers' per capita income from salary was Rmb2,963.4 (compared with Rmb702.3 in 2000), accounting for 42.5% (31.2% in 2000) of the total per capita net income of farmers; farmers' per capita income from household business has increased by Rmb1,794.7 and its share of farmers' per capita net income has dropped by 17.2% over the same period. Farmers' income from salary has become a key driver in increasing their income in the 21st century.

Over the last decade, China has made great achievements in promoting agricultural and rural development and increasing farmers' incomes, primarily through implementing a series of policies aimed at strengthening agriculture, benefiting farmers and raising rural living standards. These incentives include: abolishing agricultural tax; deepening the reform of township institutions; providing direct subsidies for grain producers; setting minimum grain purchase prices; shifting the focus of infrastructure construction and social undertaking development to rural areas; ensuring rural compulsory education funds; running the new rural cooperative medical system; granting subsistence allowances in rural areas; running a new type of rural endowment insurance system; conducting collective forest tenure reform; making a clear commitment to keep existing land contract relationships stable and unchanged for a long time; raising subsidies for people living below the poverty line in rural areas by a big margin and giving classified guidance to the reform of the urban household registration system. The implementation of these policies which meet the real needs of Chinese farmers has greatly stimulated development momentum, creating a golden age for agricultural and rural development in China.

II. The Course of Structural Reform in Rural Areas

1. Background of reform

After the founding of the People's Republic of China (PRC) in October 1949, the Chinese government was faced with the problem of how to build socialism in a country with weak economic foundations. From 1949 to 1978, China learned from the Soviet Union and established a highly centralized planned economic system. It took 10 years to establish an independent and relatively complete industrial system and national economic system. However, as time passed, the highly centralized planned economic system could no longer meet the needs of the rapid development of China's economy and the country's fast-growing productivity. People's enthusiasm, initiative and originality were limited by this system, resulting in the loss of vitality and resilience in the socialist economy. The conflict between the national economic system and high productivity mainly manifested itself in China's rural areas, especially in the agricultural sector. The prevailing egalitarianism during the period of the people's communes (1958-1978) greatly dampened farmers' enthusiasm for production. Therefore, China's rural institutions had to be reformed to solve these problems at the roots and liberate the productive forces.

The 11th Central Committee of the CPC held its third plenary session in 1978, which lasted from December 18 to 22. Taking scientific stock of China's internal situation and prevailing global trends, and drawing on the experience and lessons of China and other countries in socialist construction, the CPC Central Committee decided to shift the focus of party and government work to socialist modernization. The strategy of 'reform and opening up' was adopted, which set China on a new course toward socialism. Reforms then started in the rural areas, including restoring and expanding the autonomy of rural communes and production brigades; allowing private plots, household sideline production, collective sideline production and rural trading; implementing the agricultural production responsibility system paying remuneration according to output; increasing the purchasing prices of grain and some other agricultural products; and adopting policy support for the development of a diversified economy. All these reforms have brought about remarkable changes in agriculture.

2. Progress of reform

After 30 years of continuous exploration and development, China's rural reform has proceeded through a series of trials and experiments featuring the gradual decentralization of agricultural policies, including local pilot programs and across-the-board implementation. Overall, China's rural reform has gone through three phases.

The initial phase of China's rural reform was the shift from the rural production and operational system to the household contract responsibility system, which started at the end of the 1970s. A basic rural economic system was established to safeguard farmers' autonomy in agricultural production, paving the way for later development of a market economy in China's rural areas. The second phase of China's rural reform was the market-oriented reform beginning in the mid-1980s, including the reform of the circulation system for agricultural products (to lift controls on the pricing and operation system of agricultural products) and ownership reform. Township enterprises could then be owned by individuals and joint households, not just people's communes and production brigades, and later the private economy grew on the basis of private ownership, which drove the development of diversifed economic sectors. Market-oriented reform in China's rural areas contributed a lot to the development of agriculture and the rural economy. The third phase of China's rural reform started in the early 21st century, aimed at formulating fundamental strategies to integrate economic and social development in urban and rural areas. The first reform was the change in the rural taxation system carried out step by step since 2000. Based on the regulation and integration of rural taxes and administrative charges, the central government first reduced agricultural tax rates, and then abolished all the four taxes on agriculture, namely agricultural tax, livestock slaughter tax, animal husbandry tax and tax on agricultural and forestry specialty products in 2006. Later state-owned farms were included in the rural tax system. As a result, the total tax burden on farmers was reduced by Rmb133.5bn. The central government also provided direct subsidies for grain producers, including direct grain subsidies, subsidies for purchasing superior crop varieties, subsidies for purchasing agricultural machinery and tools, and subsidies for purchasing general agricultural supplies. These subsidies totaled Rmb140.6bn by 2011. The grant of subsidies to farmers put an end to the regime of agricultural taxation in China that lasted 2,600 years and marked a new era of government subsidies for agricultural development. The reform of rural taxation was followed by the reform of agricultural product imports and exports. After China's accession to the World Trade Organization (WTO) in late 2001, China's agricultural sector was opened up to international investors, and China's agricultural products began to reach international markets. Third, the central government boosted general reforms targeting township institutions, compulsory education in rural areas and fiscal management systems at county and township levels. Fourth, the government also pushed forward the construction of a new socialist countryside and a new model of urbanization in accordance with the principle of coordinating urban and rural development.

Under the impetus of rural institutional reform, the dynamics and mechanisms of agricultural and rural development were also changed. There was a shift from a planned economy to a market economy where market mechanisms played an increasingly important role in agricultural and rural development. The methods and circumstances of agricultural and rural development were revolutionized, so a new type of farmer and modern technology were needed to develop a modern agriculture sector which would be able to participate in international competition. China's agricultural and rural development entered a new stage and the overarching goal is to comprehensively build a new socialist countryside and an affluent society.

Table 1-1: China's rural reform policy measures

Period	Key Policy Measures	Effects
1978-1984	Household contract responsibility system	Extraordinary development of agriculture
	Higher prices for agricultural products	Record-high grain output
	15-year term of land contracting	Rapid growth of farmers' incomes
1985-1999	Abolition of unified and fixed state purchase of agricultural products	Slowing down of agricultural growth
	Developing agricultural products market	Enlarged scope of agricultural market
	Adjusting rural economic structure	Diversified agricultural production
	Developing township enterprises	Diversified rural economic structure
	Instituting macroeconomic control	Slowing down of farmers' income growth
	Raising grain prices and intensifying reform of the circulation system	Accelerated agricultural production growth
	Establishing an agricultural market system	Changed supply and demand pattern for agricultural products
	30-year land contract system	Substantial rise in proportion of non-agricultural industries
	Rapid rise of township enterprises	Sharp rise of non-agricultural employment
	Liberalization of the household registration system and the emergence of 'migrant workers'	Rapid growth of farmers' incomes
2000 to date	Overall reform of rural taxation system	Abolition of agricultural tax
	Reform of agricultural products circulation system	China's agricultural sector open to international players
	Accession to the WTO	Restoration of growth of farmers' incomes
	Coordinating urban and rural development	All-round socio-economic development in China's rural areas
	Overall rural reforms and the construction of a new socialist countryside	Coordinated urban and rural economic development

Source: *30 Years of Rural Reform in China*, p2, Song Hongyuan, China Agriculture Press, March 2008.

III. Rural Land System and Basic Operational System

1. Rural land system

Article 2, Clause 1 of *The Land Management Law* of the PRC stipulates that China adopts and implements a socialist public land ownership system, namely, ownership by the whole people and collective ownership by the working people. According to this provision, land in China falls into two categories: land owned by the state on behalf of the whole people, and land collectively owned by farmers. According to Article 8 of the same law, land in urban districts is owned by the state, while land in rural and suburban areas (except when otherwise stated by law), including land reserved for house construction, and farmland and hills allocated to individual farmers for agricultural production, is collectively owned by farmers.

The land system plays a fundamental role in rural areas, underlying almost all other systems and institutions. It has a great influence on rural stability and social justice as it affects the allocation of land resources and land use efficiency. Since the reform and opening-up program started in the late 1970s, China has made great progress in defining and protecting farmers' land rights by increasing the market's role in allocating land resources, strengthening the protection of cultivated land, enhancing the state's control over land use, and improving the legal framework for land ownership. Yet despite the achievements, the land ownership system in rural areas is far from perfect. It still needs further reform to achieve better rural-urban integration, thus realizing the goals of scientific development. Guidelines for further reform are provided by the *Decision of the CPC Central Committee on Major Important Issues in Advancing Rural Reform and Development* (hereafter refered to as the Decision) issued at the third plenary session of the 17th CPC Central Committee in 2008. According to the Decision, further reform will carry on under the principles of clear ownership, land use control, economical and intensive use of land, and strict management.

(1) Establish systems to protect arable land and economical land use

Uphold strict protection of arable land. China is one of the countries with the biggest scarcity of land in relation to population in the world. To tackle the serious arable land shortage, the Chinese government has developed a series of strong protective policies regarding arable land in recent years to curb the trend of using cropland for urban construction, industrial park construction and other non-agricultural projects. Although these policies have had some effect, they have not substantially slowed down the conversion of agricultural land to non-agricultural purposes, mainly because of the massive demand for land for construction in both urban and rural areas, the lack of long-term compensation incentives for conserving arable land, and the illegal occupation of land. To safeguard the bottom line of preserving 1.8bn *mu* (120m hectares) of arable land, we must tighten control over land use and implement a stricter arable land protection policy. First, governments at every level must take responsibility for conserving arable land and basic farmland in their administrative districts. Second, the principles governing use of arable land for non-agricultural purposes are: compensation first followed by occupation;, maintenance of a general balance between occupation and compensation by not crossing provincial, district or municipal boundaries; preventing the tendencies of occupation without compensation, occupation before compensation or occupying more and compensating less and occupying superior land but compensating poorly. Third, basic farmland will be zoned nationwide to make sure that the total area of basic farmland does not shrink, basic farmland is not used for non-agricultural purposes, and the quality improves. For primary crop production areas which are given higher goals for arable land and basic farmland conservation, the state will put in place compensation mechanisms including economic incentives to mobilize local governments and farmers to protect cultivated land.

Basic farmland definition:

Basic farmland is arable land that is not allowed to be converted to non-agricultural use for a very long period, and basic farmland conservation is a legally authorized administrative act to conserve basic farmland to meet the long-term demand for agricultural products due to population growth and the development of the national economy for a given period. Basic farmland to be conserved includes the following categories: arable land used for grain, cotton and oil-bearing crop production bases approved by the land administration department of the State Council or the local people's governments at and above the county level; high and stable yielding farmland; arable land with good water conservancy and water and soil conservation facilities, and medium and low-yield land where the execution of an improvement plan is in progress or medium and low-yield land that is transformable; vegetable production bases for large and medium-sized cities; experimental plots for research and teaching; and other arable land designated as basic farmland protection areas as stipulated by the State Council.

Provisions on basic farmland protection are formulated in the 'PRC Land Management Law', the 'Regulations on the Protection of Basic Farmland', and other regulations issued by the PRC's Ministry of Land and Resources and the key regulations are as follows:

1. *Basic farmland protection planning system: People's governments at all levels will, in the process of compiling the overall planning for land utilization, list basic farmland protection as one of the contents of the planning, expressly defining the arrangements for the layout, quantitative targets and qualitative requirements of basic farmland protection.*

2. *Basic farmland protection zoning system: Zoning and demarcation of basic farmland protection zones should be carried out with the village (township) as the unit, organization for the implementation of which should be conducted by the relevant land administration department of the people's government at the county level in conjunction with the relevant department of agriculture administration at the same level.*

3. *Licensing system for occupation and use of basic farmland: No unit or individual can change or occupy basic farmland in a protection zone that has been demarcated in accordance with the law. In the event of inability to move away from basic farmland protection zones in site selection for such major construction projects as state energy, communications, water conservancy and military installations that require occupation of basic farmland involving diversion to other use of agricultural land or land requisition, it must be subject to the approval of the State Council. It is prohibited to occupy basic farmland by changing land use planning at any level of government.*

4. *Basic farmland occupation and compensation balancing system.*

5. *System to prohibit destruction or waste of basic farmland, or leaving it idle: Kiln building, house construction, tomb building, sand digging, quarrying, mining, earth gathering, piling up of solid wastes or other activities that destroy basic farmland by any unit or individual within basic farmland protection zones is prohibited. Occupation of basic farmland by any unit or individual for the development of forestry industry, fruit industry and digging of ponds for fish farming is prohibited. Leaving basic farmland idle or barren by any unit or individual is prohibited.*

6. *Basic farmland protection accountability system: This will be an important metric when evaluating the performance of government officials.*

7. *Basic farmland supervision and monitoring system: Local people's governments above the county level will establish a system of supervision and inspection to protect basic farmland, organize at regular intervals the relevant departments of land administration, agriculture administration as well as other departments concerned to conduct inspections for the protection of basic farmland and submit a report in writing of any problem discovered to the people's government at the next higher level.*

8. *Basic farmland local construction and environment conservation system: Relevant government departments of agriculture administration at all levels and contractors of basic farmland should take measures to fertilize the soil and protect farmland from being polluted.*

On 11 October 2012, the Ministry of Land and Resources held a video conference to promote the development of pilot counties to build high-standard basic farmland, requiring 500 pilot counties to accelerate the construction of high-standard basic farmland. During the 12th Five-Year Plan period (2011-2015), no less than 200m mu (13.3m hectares) of high-standard basic farmland (concentrated parcels of basic farmland with stable high yield which is resistant to natural disasters and meets the requirements of modern agriculture) is to be constructed, to ensure that the total area of high-standard basic farmland nationwide amounts to 400m mu (26.7m hectares).

The toughest policy will be enforced to promote economical land use. At present, uneconomical use or even waste of land is still a prominent problem in both urban and rural areas. As research results show, China's per capita land use for urban construction amounts to more than 130 square meters (sqm), higher than the average of 82.2sqm in developed countries and 83.3sqm in developing countries; the economic output of industrial land is far lower than the average of developed countries; and the use of land for construction in rural areas is very inefficient. To solve the conflict between conserving arable land and meeting the need for construction plots, we must make economical, intensive and efficient use of the existing land for construction rather than blindly expanding construction on green land. First, we must control the increase of land used for new construction projects. Second, we must make more efficient use of the existing construction land by integrating scattered construction land plots in urban areas, encouraging increased capacity and more intensive development of inefficiently used construction land, reforming non-urbanized areas in towns and cities, fast-tracking the transformation of urban ghettos, to increase land use efficiency and promote land-saving technologies and methods of construction. Third, we must explore new spaces for construction. On condition that the environment is not to be damaged, we must encourage development of uncultivated land and waste land, and promote use of vertical development and underground spaces.

(2) Protect farmers' rights to the contractual use of land, and improve the market for transfer of contractual operating rights

Farmers must be empowered to use land on the basis of contractual operation. The introduction of the household contractual responsibility system separated land use rights from collective land ownership. It is clearly stated in the Decision that the current land contract relationships should remain stable and unchanged in the long term, which is the basis of China's land system in the rural areas. Farmers have a strong desire for stable land rights. We must protect farmers' rights to occupy, use and benefit from contractual use of land. Reducing uncertainties in land contractual relationships is helpful to satisfy farmers' expectations in the long term.

The regulation of the transfer of contractual land use rights. The market for circulation of contractual land use rights has developed a lot since the late 1970s when China launched the reform program in rural areas which liberalized such transfers. After years of trials, a system of policies, laws and regulations has been developed, including the principle of legal, voluntary and compensatory transfer, and different policy requirements for contractual land use right transfers in different periods. In line with previous policies, the *Decision* provides that farmers may transfer contractual land use rights in the form of subcontracts, leases, exchanges, assignments or joint-stock cooperation under the principle of legal, voluntary and compensatory transfers; areas where conditions are mature may develop various forms of moderately large-scale operation in forms such as big specialized household operations, family farms and farmers' professional cooperatives. The *Decision* also proposes 'three must nots' with regard to transfer of land operation rights: must not change the nature of collective ownership; must not change the land use; and must not harm farmers' land contractual rights and interests. To be more specific, collective farmers' ownership must not be changed into state ownership through transfer of contractual management rights or when a rural villager turns into a city dweller, and where the change of land ownership is necessary, it should go through certain legal processes. Farmland must be used for agricultural purposes only, and no individual or collective contractee may transfer or lease any agricultural land for any non-agricultural purposes. No individual or organization can seize or withhold the proceeds from the transfer of contractual land use rights which belong to farmers. No administrative means may be used to coerce contractual land use rights transfers; land circulation agencies should be tasked to better manage and facilitate the circulation of contractual land use rights.

In November 2014, a joint circular was issued by the General Office of the CPC Central Committee and the General Office of the State Council: *Opinions on Guiding the Systematic Transfer of Rural Land Operation Rights to Develop Appropriately Large-Scale Operations in Agriculture.* It points out that in the process of China's industrialization, informatization, urbanization and agricultural modernization, the development of appropriately large-scale operations in agriculture has become a general trend and the transfer of contractual land use rights is speeding up. Promoting the transfer of contractual land use rights and developing appropriately large-scale operations in agriculture have proved to be essential for building modern agriculture, as both can optimize the allocation of land resources, improve productivity, ensure food security and supply of the main agricultural products, promote new agricultural technologies, improve performance of agricultural operation and increase farmers' incomes. Yet the transfer of contractual land use rights and development of appropriately large-scale operations will be advanced in a prudent and smooth way, considering the large population and varied conditions across the vast rural areas of China.

To promote the transfer of contractual land use rights and development of appropriately large-scale operations, the following guidelines must be observed: First of all, a comprehensive modern agricultural operation system will be built on the basis of household operations, cooperation among households, enterprises and governments, and utilization of social intermediary services, and a modern agriculture system will feature modern Chinese characteristics including the application of advanced technologies, appropriately large-scale operations, strong competitiveness in the market, and friendliness to the environment. The system aims to achieve food security, increase agricultural output and promote the growth of farmers' incomes. The ownership rights, contractual land use rights and land operation rights will be separated. Household operations will be the fundamental form, while new operators will be cultivated and diverse forms of appropriately large-scale operations in agriculture will be developed. The development of appropriately large-scale operations will be aligned with the process of urbanization and labor migration from rural areas to urban areas, with the advancement of agricultural technologies and production means, and with the development of social intermediary services for agricultural operations. As a result, farmers must participate in and benefit from the transfer of contractual land use rights and the development of appropriately large-scale operations in agriculture.

The specific measures are as follows: First, the system of land contract operation rights in rural areas and contract relationships will be stabilized by improving the registration and certification of land contracts. Second, the transfer of land contract operation rights will be subject to better regulation through encouraging innovation in the method of transfer, and better supporting services for and control over the transfer of contractual rights will give effective support to large-scale grain production. Third, new forms of collective operation will be explored based on household operation through encouraging cooperation among households, and modern farming entities will be encouraged which can be run as enterprises, and therefore new business entities in agriculture will be cultivated through improved regulation and risk prevention. Lastly, diverse social intermediary services and up-to-date professional training for farmers will be provided and trading cooperatives will be utilized to establish a social service system.

(3) Promote land requisition system reform

In recent years, compensation for requisitioned land and requisition procedures have become more regulated thanks to local governments' land requisition reforms. Yet rather than creating benefits for farmers thus bridging the urban-rural gap in the process of urbanization and industrialization, land requisition has caused problems for farmers and enlarged the gap. The number of landless farmers is increasing due to large-scale land requisition. Social security and employment of landless farmers have become a tricky issue because of low requisition compensation. Therefore the *Decision* provides a solution to the problems by intensifying land requisition reform as follows:

Strictly defining the land for public good from that for commercial construction. It is provided in the constitution that the state may requisition land for public good with compensation in accordance with laws and regulations. Yet there is no clear definition on public good in laws and regulations such as *the Land Management Law*. Massive land requisitions in the name of public good have been used for commercial construction. According to the *Decision*, the scope of land subject to requisition will gradually be narrowed down by clearly defining the public good in land requisition. Farmers will be allowed to participate in and protect their legal rights and interests through various means in the process of the development and management of those non-public welfare projects with approval to use collective land in rural areas beyond the scope of land used for urban construction determined in the land use plan.

Establishing reasonable compensation rates and mechanisms. According to the *Land Management Law*, compensation for land requisition and labor resettlement are based on the average annual output value of the requisitioned land in the three years before requisition rather than on the location, socio-economic development and supply-demand relations in the requisitioned area, and the use and market value of the land after requisition, which leads to low compensation for farmers on requisitioned land. To improve the land requisition compensation mechanism, the *Decision* proposes to requisition collective land in rural areas according to law, make timely compensation for collective organizations and farmers in accordance with a unified standard, protect their information, participation, supervision and appeal rights, and develop a coordination and arbitration mechanism to provide legal assistance for land requisitioned from farmers in dealing with disputes over land requisition compensation problems.

Taking good care of the employment, housing and social security issues of farmers whose land has been requisitioned. Promote employment of farmers through various means such as providing professional training and produce favorable policies on loans, tax and sites for farmers whose land has been requisitioned seeking self-employment. Include the social security expenses of farmers whose land has been requisitioned into the compensation. Where the compensation cannot cover the expense, local governments should set aside money from their revenue on lending state-owned land use rights to fund it. Where social security issues affecting farmers whose land has been requisitioned haven't been solved, local governments should not approve the requisition. Where land requisition has surpassed a certain level, farmers may get some land for residential building and independent operation, on which they may develop projects to earn stable, long-term income.

(4) The system of residential building sites in rural areas

Residential building sites refer to plots of land used by farmers for the construction of their residences, including housing, accessories and courtyards. The land used for residential building sites in rural areas covers a very wide and large area, and is still increasing fast. Therefore the *Decision* provides for improvements in the residential building site system in rural areas by:

Regulating the management of residential building sites. The measures include: sticking to the policy of one residential building site per rural household; reorganizing the messy residential arrangements in rural areas to make it more orderly and concentrated, thus making economical use of land to facilitate infrastructure construction; encouraging farmers to build residences in a relatively concentrated way of their own accord on condition that their rights and interests are observed; renewing the decaying inner villages to make more efficient use of present residential building sites. The land saved from the reorganization and reform of present residential building sites will be reclaimed in the first place, and those earmarked for construction in compliance with land use plans will be put into the annual land use schedule of that year and prioritized to meet the needs of land for collective construction projects.

Protecting famers' usufructuary rights over residential building sites. A clearer definition of rights over residential building sites can better protect farmers' interests and fundamental habitat rights, which is also what farmers are expecting. Farmers' right to acquire, use and benefit from the land as residential building sites will be well protected through compensating farmers whose land for residential building gets requisitioned and prohibiting land requisitions against farmer's wills for non-agricultural purposes.

(5) The system of rural collective construction land

Rural collective construction land refers to the land used for building farmers' residences as well as manufacturing and service projects in rural areas, including construction land for the development of township enterprises, public facilities as well as for housing. At present, such land cannot circulate in the market because the land market in China is not sound or mature enough, and there is an obvious imbalance between urban and rural development. The *Decision* proposes to reform the system of rural collective construction land to create a unified construction land market in both urban and rural areas, which offers a very important policy direction for the reform of the system for collective construction land in rural areas. Such land entering the market on par with state-owned construction land may help develop a collective construction land price mechanism in rural areas which ensures equal rights and benefits for rural and urban areas, thus forming land prices that really reflect supply-demand relations in the market, and optimizing the allocation of land resources.

A unified construction land market is necessary for better regulation of the land market. Rural collective construction land blindly entering the market can be very disruptive, causing violations of rules, affecting land use planning, and resulting in ineffective control over total land supply. Therefore, regulating the trading of land will be a priority in the management of land resources in rural areas in the future. The *Decision* points out that the land acquired through legal transfer on the open unified land market will enjoy the same rights and benefits as state-owned construction land, as long as it doesn't violate government land use plans. The property value of rural collective construction land is becoming increasingly evident as China urbanizes and industrializes. Well regulated transfer of the utilization rights over rural collective construction land can help develop a unified construction land market accommodating orderly competition in both urban and rural areas, thus preventing political power from interfering with land prices and tapping the enormous economic potential of rural collective construction land.

2. Basic operation system for rural areas

(1) The establishment and development of a two-tier operation system

A two-tier operation system for the rural areas was established in the late 1970s during the agricultural reform based on household contract operations and the combination of centralization and decentralization. The two-tier operation system in agriculture is one of the most significant breakthroughs achieved in China's reform and opening up. In 1982, the basic principles of the household contract responsibility system were confirmed by the Central Government in its Document No. 1. In 1983, the household contract responsibility system was further defined as a two-tier operation system that combined unified collective operation and decentralized household operation in the Central Government's Document No. 1: *Several Problems in Current Rural Economic Policies*. In 1993, the household contract responsibility system and the two-tier operation system were added into the *Constitution* at the second session of the eighth NPC. In June of the same year, they were added into the Agriculture Law as amendments. In 2002, the household contract responsibility system was enhanced following the issue of the *Rural Land Contract Law of the PRC*. In 2007, the property attributes of the contractual operation rights of land were defined in the *Property Law*, which clearly defines farmers' contractual land operation rights. Over the past 30 years, the operation system in rural areas has become more and more enhanced and consolidated.

China's two-tier operation system in rural areas can be construed as follows. First, main production materials such as rural land are public or collectively owned. Land in rural and suburban areas, except where it is state-owned, is collectively owned by farmers, including residential building sites, private plots and private hill land. The rights of possession, use, usufruct and disposal over such land belongs to all farmers as a collective or, in some cases, in the form of rural collective organizations. Second, household contract operation is fundamental. It has been clearly provided for in the *Rural Land Contract Law* that China resorts to a system of contract operation of land in rural areas. Land in rural areas may be contracted to households in a collective, while land unsuitable for households to contract, such as land on barren mountains, valleys, hills and wasteland, may be leased out through bidding, auctions and public discussion. Third, China adheres to a two-tier operation system in rural areas. Unified collective operation and decentralized household operation are combined through contracts prescribing rights and responsibilities of all parties.

(2) Improvement of the basic operation system

During the past 30 years since the reform and opening-up program was launched in 1978, the basic operation system for rural areas has been maintained and greatly improved by the following means: First, industrialized operation of agriculture. The concept of industrialized operation of agriculture was put forward in the mid-1990s, aiming to transform the growth pattern of agriculture, create a channel connecting rural households to the market, and adapt agriculture to the market economy. By the end of September 2012, organizations of various kinds focusing on the industrialization of agriculture totaled 280,000, and more than 110m households were involved in the industrialized operation of agriculture, and their average annual income increased by Rmb2,400 (US$386). Second, professional cooperatives of farmers. Professional cooperatives are organizations established by farmers to hedge against risks as part of the market economy which started to take shape and went into operation in the 1980s. In 2007, *The Law of the PRC on Farmers' Professional Cooperatives* was enacted, which paved the way for and gave more potential to the development of farmers' professional cooperatives. There were more than 150,000 professional cooperatives at the end of 2008 involving more than 38.7m rural member households, accounting for 13.8% of all rural households in China and 55.12m non-member rural households were also involved as non-members. Usually one cooperative can comprise 100 to 200 households on average and the member households' average annual income can increase by about 20%, twice as high as the growth rate of common non-member households. Third, a social intermediary service system for agriculture. Such a system has an obvious advantage in solving problems which individual households cannot handle in the market. Currently, the system has been decentralized from government domination to involve multiple players including related government departments, agricultural enterprises and farmers' professional cooperatives. It covers various areas such as public welfare, mutual assistance and profit-seeking agricultural operation, and offers services before, during and after agriculture production. Fourth, innovation in forms of agricultural operation. Besides traditional household operation, new diversified forms of operation such as moderately large-scale operation, commissioned farmland operation and joint-stock (or equity-based) cooperative operation have also appeared as rural labor continues to transfer and the social service system for agriculture improves.

On the whole, the household contract system has proved to possess strong vitality through nationwide practice, and achieved enormous success in the following four dimensions:

Second, it has also helped optimize the rural employment structure. The two-tier operation system has given farmers who had been tied to the collective communes strong autonomy in making decisions concerning agricultural production. Along with the growth of township enterprises and the advancement of the secondary and tertiary sectors, a great amount of rural surplus labor has transferred to non-agriculture sectors and migrated into cities and towns, resulting in a tremendous change in the rural employment structure. In addition, it was so commonplace to have a part-time job that the workforce dedicated to agricultural production has been decreasing as a percentage of the total workforce and in terms of the absolute number of farmers as well. In 2012, the total number of rural migrant workers was 3.9% more than the previous year and rose to 262.61m, of which 163.36m migrant workers had migrated between provinces, and the remaining 99.25m had moved locally or within provinces, representing increases of 3.0% and 5.4% respectively.

Third, it has remarkably improved farmers' living conditions. The household contract responsibility system gave farmers the rights of autonomous operation and production on their farm land, which boosted their enthusiasm for production and helped increase their income substantially. Since the reform and opening up in the late 1970s, a continuous and rapid increase in farmers' incomes has drastically improved their living conditions. The per capita net income of farmers jumped from Rmb134 (US$21.50) in 1978 to Rmb7,917 (US$1,275.40) in 2012, and their per capita income rose at an average annual rate of 8% from 2004. China fulfilled the UN Millennium Development Goals objective of reducing the population living in extreme poverty by half ahead of the schedule (MDG 1), thus making an essential contribution to the global poverty reduction effort. China's rural population has made a historic leap from having no adequate food and clothing to leading a generally affluent life, and are now aiming at comprehensive affluence.

Fourth, it has advanced and improved a range of reform and opening-up policies. China's reform and opening up started in the rural areas, and agricultural reform started with household operation. On the basis of household contractual operations fully integrated with the establishment of the two-tier operation system, the highly centralized people's communes were brought to an end, releasing the potential of rural productive forces and boosting China's rural socio-economic development to a great extent, which was the basis of China's national development and prosperity in the following decades. Moreover, its implementation started China's march towards comprehensive reform and paved the way for China's economic system reform. It has led directly to the formation of a socialist market economy.

IV. Development of Township and Village Enterprises (TVEs)

1. The emergence of TVEs

Township and village enterprises (TVEs), then called 'commune and brigade enterprises', emerged in China in the mid-1950s. As a byproduct of the strategy of heavy industry priority in the 1950s, China played down the commune and brigade enterprises and strictly curbed their development, only allowing them to run local plants with local natural resources and materials, and to sell the products within the local area. In addition, the circulation of goods and transportation were prohibited, and no private businesses were allowed. The commune and brigade enterprises had hardly grown at all before China's reform and opening up in late 1978. There were

1.52m commune and brigade-run TVEs in China in 1978, averaging one TVE per 1,924 people in the rural areas. TVEs employed 28.27m farmers, accounting for 9.2% of the total rural workforce; and their gross output reached Rmb49.1bn (US$7.9bn), 7.17% of the national GDP and 24.1% of the output of the rural areas.

The fourth plenary session of the 11th Central Committee of the CPC, held in September 1979, adopted the *Decisions on Some problems in Speeding up the Development of Agriculture* in which the CPC and the government recognized the significant role TVEs could play in supporting rural economic development. Nevertheless, the development of TVEs was still impeded by the planned economy system. At that time, only collective enterprises were allowed and the distribution and pricing of TVEs' products were under strict government control. TVEs had no right to make managerial decisions, recruit employees and distribute profits. Some areas even went so far as to close down or suspend TVEs, and the number of TVEs decreased to 1,346,400 in 1983, lower than in 1978.

TVEs emerged as a new force to be reckoned with after 1984, however. With the nationwide adoption and implementation of the household co-production contractual responsibility system in China in 1983, agricultural productivity substantially improved and surplus labor in rural areas increased. The price of grain and sideline products shot up several times after 1978, which boosted farmers' incomes to an extent which allowed them to invest in their individual businesses. Meanwhile, farmers were becoming enthusiastic about setting up enterprises to further increase their income. They ran them either as part of collective enterprises or as independent enterprises, but both propelled the development of the rural economy. Under such circumstances, TVEs embraced rapid development. The number of TVEs surged to 6,065,200 by the end of 1984, 4,718,800 more than in the previous year, including 516,600 new village-run enterprises, and individual and private businesses started to boom. TVEs maintained a sound development momentum in 1985. There were 12,225,000 TVEs in China by the end of 1985, including 10,123,000 individual businesses run by farmers.

2. The development of TVEs

Along with the abolition of people's communes and production brigades in 1983, commune and brigade-run enterprises were renamed as TVEs, and cooperative, private and individual enterprises in which farmers had a stake were expanded according to a document issued by the Central Committee of the CPC and the State Council in March 1984. More importantly, this official document made it legally possible for farmers to own private businesses in individual names or groups.

From 1984 to 1988 was the most glorious period in the history of TVEs which increased dramatically in terms of their number, although the growth rate slowed down a bit. TVEs broke away from the restrictions in terms of ownership, businesses and industries. The original owners changed from communes and brigades to towns and villages and even individuals, and the portfolio of rural businesses expanded from production and trading of grain and relevant agricultural byproducts to a wide range including secondary and tertiary sectors such as manufacturing, commerce, transportation and construction. By 1988, the gross output of TVEs was equivalent to 24% of China's GDP and 58% of China's total rural output; and the employees working for TVEs accounted for 23.8% of the total rural labor force. TVEs paved the way for farmers to get rich and accounted for half of the rural economy.

However, the rapid development of TVEs gave rise to a collection of problems. What made things worse was that China suffered from severe inflation in 1989, which disrupted the national economy. The loans TVEs borrowed from the Agricultural Bank of China and rural credit cooperatives totaled Rmb84.786bn (US$13.6bn), which was five time higher than 1984 and strained those banks. Since TVEs lagged behind in technology, their rapid growth had been natural resources and energy intensive. The Chinese government started to adjust the economic system to restore economic order in 1989, which in turn led many TVEs to close down or transfer, and lots of employees lost their jobs and returned to the farmland. In a word, TVEs experienced hardly any growth between 1989 and 1991. Their development suffered a great setback.

TVEs recovered in 1992 and have boomed since then with the advances in economic system reform and the improvement of the macroeconomic environment. A series of reforms were conducted to redefine ownership and introduce new operational mechanisms for TVEs. TVEs also managed to improve their product quality, reduce their costs and increase their efficiency via technological development and talent acquisition and development. In an effort to bridge the development gap among TVEs in different regions, the Chinese government gave the less developed central and western regions special incentives to promote TVEs' development. In addition, the government strove to develop industry clusters in industrial parks or satellite towns. Scattered TVEs were integrated into clusters.

Therefore, China's TVEs experienced a second boom from 1992 to 1996. There were 23.36m TVEs employing a total of 135m workers in 1996, which was 1.2 times and 1.4 times higher than 1991 respectively. Farmers working for TVEs comprised 29.8% of the total rural workforce, which was 7.8% higher than 1991; and the gross output of TVEs was Rmb1.7659 trillion (US$284.4bn), 5.9 times more than in 1991. TVEs had become a major component of China's rural economy.

The *Law of the PRC on TVEs* was enacted on January 1, 1997 with the aim of facilitating the sound and sustained development of TVEs. The enactment of this law meant that the TVEs' rights and interests would be duly protected and also that they would operate under legal regulation. In the meantime, the TVE environment changed. China was plagued by commodity shortages for a relatively long period before 1998, whereas China's economy turned from a shortage (seller's) economy into a buyer's market with sufficient supply of commodities after 1998. There were also a wide range of other problems, like the lack of competitiveness on the part of smaller TVEs, the lack of managerial competence on the part of managers, and environmental pollution and depletion of resources caused by TVEs. In this context, rural enterprises were forced to accelerate their restructuring and systemic innovation starting from 1998 and focused on the following three aspects: their growth model shifted from extensive (externally driven) growth to intensive (internally driven) growth; the rapid increase in individual and private businesses diversified the ownership mix; and TVEs became a component of China's modern industrial system.

TVEs have profoundly altered China's rural economy landscape, which used to be mainly agriculture and grain production. The gross output of the former commune and brigade enterprises accounted for only 37% of the total agricultural output in 1978. After a decade's fast and sound development, the total output of TVEs in the secondary and tertiary sectors amounted to Rmb485.4bn (US$78.2bn) by the end of 1987, which exceeded the total output value of agriculture for the first time, accounting for104% of the total agricultural output. It was a milestone, indicating a bright prospect for China's rural development. The gross value of TVEs was 68.68% of the rural economy, which made TVEs a powerhouse in the rural economy of China.

The emergence and development of TVEs has revolutionized the development of China's rural economy and provided an immediate channel for deploying surplus rural labor. TVEs absorbed 2.416m of the surplus workforce in 2011, contributing to the optimization of the rural labor structure, alleviation of China's employment pressure and increase of productivity via scaled agricultural operation. Like the household contract responsibility system, TVEs were also key to the realization of affluence in rural China. In 2011, the wages TVEs paid their employees totaled Rmb59bn (US$9.5bn) and workers in TVEs earned annual incomes of Rmb24,420 (US$3,933), which boosted the farmers' goal of leading a better life.

However, there were also several bottlenecks restricting TVEs' development: disadvantaged geographical location in the rural areas; limited reform of ownership; backward technical equipment; shortage of managerial talent and technicians; limited access to financing due to small-scale operation; and underdevelopment in China's central and western regions. To make TVEs a cornerstone of the rural economy under such circumstances, the following measures will apply: further enhancing the reform of ownership to define property rights; attracting and retaining various competent professionals to quicken the technical transformation and innovation; optimizing the management mechanisms; bringing the scattered TVEs to key or central towns to form clusters or company groups with scale operation; and paying special attention to environmental conservation in the countryside.

V. The Governance Structure of Towns and Villages

1. 'Town government and village administration' since the start of reforms

With the start of economic reform in 1978, specifically the adoption of the household contract responsibility system in the rural areas, the collectivized land system dissolved and farmers regained their autonomy in production and distribution of goods. The people's commune system gradually dissolved, too, and lost its power, leading to dramatic changes in rural governance at town and village level.

The so-called 'town government and village administration' consists of two levels: 'town government' and 'village administration'. 'Town government'is the lowest level of government in China governing the rural areas on behalf of the state, while 'village administration' is an autonomous body governed by a villagers' committee which practices democratic elections, democratic decision-making, democratic management and democratic supervision. Town government embodies state power whereas village administration is the embodiment of social rights and power. The former is the predominant power while the latter is the foundation for the exercise of power. In particular, the above-mentioned two local organizations are different in four aspects: the nature of power, the structure of power, the execution of power and the hierarchy of power.

First, in terms of the nature of power, given that the Chinese constitution stipulates that all power in the PRC belongs to the people, the state power exercised by town government offices and the autonomous power belonging to village administration all rest with the people. Evidently, they share the same source of power but are quite different in nature. Town government represents the extension of state power into the rural areas, whereas village administration represents the vigorous growth of social power. The relationship between town government and village administration is the relationship between state government power and grassroots social power. This is also an important difference between the structure of town government and village administration, and that of the people's commune system.

Second, in terms of the structure of power, the town is the lowest level of government in the countryside, its organ of power is the town people's congress, the town government is the executive organ of its power, and the town party committee exercises unified leadership of the town people's congress and the town government. On the other hand, village administration provides autonomy for the grassroots masses of farmers, the decision-making organ of its power is the village council or village representative council, the executive organ of its power is the village committee, and the village party branch is the core of grassroots leadership and gives prominence to the party's unified leadership.

Third, in terms of the exercise and operation of power, a town, as the representative of state power, exercises state power over the rural areas pursuant to the constitution, and is obliged to carry out the administrative orders and regulations of the central government within its local jurisdiction. Thus, it becomes a local implementer of state policy. Meanwhile, as an autonomous body, a village committee is formed through democratic election, adopts democratic decision-making processes, implements democratic management, and is subject to democratic supervision. Along with two vice chairmen and other members of the village committee, the chairman of the village committee is elected by the villagers; and villagers also take the initiative in discussing and handling the management of the village and formulating the village regulations. The autonomous village committee is indeed an embodiment of the power of the villagers.

Fourth, in terms of the purpose of the exercise of power, a town, at the lowest level of the state government hierarchy, assumes the responsibility of enforcing government policies to fulfill the tasks and goals imposed by its higher authorities. It is basically responsible to the higher authorities. However, a village committee is beyond the realm of state governance. A village committee is responsible to the individual villagers. It is organized via direct democratic election by the villagers by which they manage their own affairs, educate themselves and serve their own needs.

Local governance consisting of 'town government and village administration' is a unique administrative model for China's rural areas, conceived by the upper levels in China to serve the development of the socialist market economy with its distinct feature of socialism with Chinese characteristics. A town government is a centralized administrative body exercising state power; a village committee is an autonomous mass organization based on common regulations and equal rights of villagers in decision-making concerning the management of village affairs. So when one talks of village administration with respect to town government, village administration is the cornerstone., 'Town government and village administration' is a defining characteristic of China's rural politics.

2. Exploring new mechanisms of local governance

In the new historical period, China's rural governance has entered a new phase of development. To facilitate the construction of harmonious rural communities, the grassroots organizations must play a more positive role and optimize their potential by exploring new local governance mechanisms and redefining the relations between, including the rights, duties and limitations of, various governance bodies. The following measures need to be enforced to create synergy among all related sectors:

First, the relationships between town and village governments and village committees must be redefined by law, to enhance the relevant legal system. Enacted in 1998, *The Village Committee Organization Law* established that a village committee is the primary autonomous mass organization, and should operate under the guidance of the town and assist the town government in its work. On this basis, the pertinent regulations must be developed and specified so as to further define the limits of power between the town government and the village committee, and also to clarify the means and the extent to which a town should guide the work of a village committee and a village committee should assist the work of a town.

Second, further improvements should be made to the mechanisms governing the autonomy of village committees to enhance their autonomous capabilities. A village committee plays a significant role in rural autonomy. As a mass autonomous organization, the village committee is a governance body organized by the villagers themselves in which the villagers manage their own affairs, educate themselves, and serve their own needs, which stimulates the villagers' enthusiasm to deal with their own affairs. The key to improving the autonomy of village committees is to clearly define the responsibilities and work procedures of the CPC branch in the village and the village committee, which means seeking a coordinated and sound relationship between CPC leadership and villagers' autonomy.

Third, it is imperative to advance town government reform and to improve local governance to suit the rapid development and changes in rural areas. As China seeks new mechanisms of rural governance in the construction of a new countryside, it is important to transform a town government from a management-model into a service model of government; a town should be mainly responsible for facilitating the advancement of social undertakings and the construction of a harmonious society. Its focus should rest on enhancing public services and social administration. A town should transfer its operative, community and social services to non-government agencies. For instance, a town could adopt market-oriented methods such as bidding and tendering, contracting, renting, and charging to encourage private organizations to perform public services and social administration.

Fourth, support and incentives should be given to boost the development of rural social service organizations. Rural social service organizations in China have remained underdeveloped, since the vast majority of villagers are not well organized and therefore lack the institutional access to participate in village autonomy. Except for those villagers who are elected as delegates to the people's congresses or party congresses, or members of the village committee, villagers have limited opportunities to voice their opinion on certain public affairs concerning their own village. In the less developed areas, village enterprises are too small to support the rural economy, which in turn creates an illusion that the town is mainly responsible for the local economic growth. With the industrialization of agriculture and development of the market economy, farmers increasingly need to set up and join organizations to secure their interests and hedge against market risks. The ultimate goal is for villagers to realize self-management, self-education, and self-service, and to make them the key players in rural governance.

Over 98% of 589,000 Village Committees in China's Rural Areas Practice Direct Elections

On March 13, 2013, a press conference was held at the Media Center by the Press Center of the First Session of the 12th National People's Congress.

In answer to a question on China's democracy at the village level, Jiang Li, Vice Minister of Civil Affairs, noted that "democratic election of village committees is the most common practice in the socialist politics with Chinese characteristics among Chinese villagers. By the end of 2012, some 589,000 village committees had been established throughout the country, and most of the provinces, autonomous regions and municipalities directly under the central government had elected their eighth or ninth committees. What's more important is that 98% of the village committees have been directly elected and the average participation rate of villagers in such elections is above 95%. The latest round of direct elections for village committees started in 2011, and will conclude by the end of this year. In terms of voters, it will become the most widely participated-in election anywhere in the world: there will be 600m participants. The process involves secret ballots and open vote-counting, with secret ballot booths being very common, villagers are now able to elect their village committees in accordance with their own will. Democratic elections have become an important part of community-level democracy in rural China while, of course, village self-government also includes democratic decision-making, democratic management, and democratic supervision. Grassroots political democracy will become a reality when the above four practices are fully implemented in rural areas.

Chapter 2

How to Promote the Modernization of China's Agriculture

As a developing country with the biggest population in the world, China's per capita share of natural resources, especially agricultural resources, is inadequate. In China, the per capita arable land is 1.38 *mu* (0.092 hectare), per capita fresh water is 2,134 cubic meters (in 2007), and per capita forest is 10.2sqm (2012), which represents respectively 40%, 33% and 11% of the world average; and per capita grassland is 33% of the world average.

Thanks to the advancement of comprehensive rural reform, including the nationwide adoption and implementation of the household contract responsibility system since 1978, the establishment and improvement of the socialist market economy. and the deepening of reform and opening up, China has improved the efficiency of its agricultural resource allocation and optimized the structure of crop cultivation, and therefore the overall productivity of agriculture has risen notably and grain output has been drastically increased to 400m tonnes, then to 500m tonnes, which boosted China's domestic food availability from being in short supply to being in balanced supply, making China self-sufficient in grain supply for its people. China has seen an unprecedented level of growth and improvement in the agricultural sector since the beginning of the 21st century, mainly in the development of modern agriculture and radical changes in the mode of production in agriculture. Over the last decade, agricultural machinery has been widely applied, quality seed and good agricultural practices have been promoted, and the management of grain production has steadily improved in China. Quality seed coverage for major grain crop varieties exceeds 96%, and the increase in per unit area yield has contributed over 80% to overall growth in the total grain output. Technology has become a strong boost for agricultural development, and the contribution of technology to agricultural growth reached 54.5% in 2012, which was 6.5 percentage points higher than in 2006. China's agricultural machinery has also been promoted in most grain producing areas, and its agricultural mechanization rose to 57%, which was 19 percentage points up from 2006. China has seen a great change in agricultural production from dependence on human power and animal power to mechanization.

Table 2-1: China's Major Agricultural Product Output (unit: million tonnes)

Year	Grain (Cereals, beans, potatoes)	Oil-bearing products	Cotton	Fruit	Meat	Dairy products	Aquatic products
2001	452.637	28.649	5.324	66.580	60.139	11.229	37.959
2002	457.058	28.972	4.916	69.520	61.058	14.004	39.549
2003	430.695	2.811	4.860	145.174	64.433	18.486	40.770
2004	469.470	30.659	6.324	153.409	66.087	23.684	42.466
2005	484.022	30.771	5.714	161.201	69.389	28.648	44.199
2006	498.039	30.594	6.746	172.399	70.890	33.025	45.836
2007	501.600	24.610	7.600	181.363	68.657	36.334	47.475
2008	528.710	29.528	7.492	192.202	72.787	37.815	48.956
2009	530.820	31.543	6.377	203.955	76.499	36.777	51.164
2010	546.477	32.301	5.961	214.014	79.258	37.480	53.730
2011	571.208	33.068	6.589	227.682	79.578	38.107	56.032

Source: China Statistical Yearbook 2012, China Statistics Press

Table 2-2: China's world ranking by major agricultural products

Agricultural products	1978	1980	1990	2000	2007	2008	2009	2010
Cereals	2	1	1	1	1	1	1	1
Meat①	3	2	1	1	1	1	1	1
Cotton	3	3	1	1	1	1	1	1
Soybeans	3	3	3	4	4	4	4	4
Peanuts	2	2	2	1	1	1	1	1
Rapeseed	2	2	1	1	1	2	1	1
Sugar cane	7	9	4	3	3	3	3	3
Tea	2	2	2	2	1	1	1	1
Fruit②	9	10	4	1	1	1	1	1

Source: FAO statistics
Notes:
① Before 1990, the ranking was measured by the output of Pork, Beef, and Mutton.
② Excluding melon plants.

China sees 11th consecutive bumper harvest (2003-2014)

[Xinhua, Beijing, December 4, 2014] Data from the National Bureau of Statistics (NBS) show that China witnessed an 11th consecutive year of growth in its grain harvest in 2014. With an increase of 5.16m tonnes, up 0.9% from the previous year, China's grain output totaled 607.099m tonnes.

According to the NBS, with a growth of 4.577m tonnes, up 0.8% from the previous year, the main crop yield reached 557.269m tonnes in 2014, including maize, grain, wheat, barley, Chinese sorghum, buck wheat and oats.

According to the sample survey among farmers and investigation of agricultural producing organizations by the NBS throughout China's provinces, municipalities and autonomous regions, the total area for grain cultivation was 112.7383m hectares (1.691074bn mu), 0.7% up from the previous year; and the average grain output was 5,385tonnes/hectare (t/ha), 0.2% higher than 2013.

Source: *Farmer's Daily*, December 10, 2014

http://www.farmer.com.cn/newzt/sylz/gz/201412/t20141210_1000395.htm

Due to the ever increasing market demand and the constraints of natural resources and the environment on agricultural production, it is essential for China to transform its agricultural development model and promote sustainable modernized agriculture in the coming years. According to the 12th Five-Year Plan (2011-2015), China will promote industrialization, urbanization, and agricultural modernization simultaneously. The development of modern agriculture is a key step to transform the model of economic development and build an affluent society; it is also an inevitable step in building a new socialist countryside in China through increasing overall agricultural productivity and farmers' incomes.

I. Safeguarding National Food Security

At the Central Conference on Rural Work in December 2013, Chinese President Xi Jinping stressed the strategic importance and pointed out the direction of deepening rural reform to sustain long-term sound and steady economic growth and social development. The meeting also put forward the specific objectives of China's rural reform and stressed that to build a moderately prosperous society, the key is to improve the living standards of farmers, which is based on the fact that agricultural modernization has lagged behind in China's Four Modernizations and become a hurdle in China's progress towards a better-off society. Furthermore, the meeting noted that "a strong agricultural sector is the prerequisite for a strong China, a beautiful countryside is the prerequisite for a beautiful China and better-off farmers are the prerequisite for a prosperous China". By sticking to the long-term principle of industry supporting agriculture and the urban areas supporting the rural areas, and by means of a series of supportive policies and measures to boost rural development, China will continue to put agriculture, farmers and rural areas on the top of its agenda and prioritize the advancement of agriculture, farmers and rural areas.

The meeting communique also noted that food security for the country's enormous population is the first and foremost challenge facing China. The bowls of the Chinese, in any situation, must rest soundly in our own hands, so to speak. Our bowls should be filled mainly with Chinese grain. When a country is basically self-sufficient in food supply, it can grasp the overall situation for socio-economic growth. Hence, it is vital to stick to a national food security strategy based on domestic supply, which relies on increased production capacity and advanced science and technology, and moderate imports. And the following measures, which are the focal points in ensuring self-sufficient food supply and adequate food storage, are essential and should be implemented: stabilize the grain producing areas, and maintain the existing arable land area at not less than 1.8bn *mu* (120m hectares) to safeguard the existing arable land area against any decrease; stimulate and protect the 'two enthusiasms' of farmers to produce food, and motivate the main food production areas to increase grain output at the same time; maintain a reasonable level of food storage and guarantee proper food distribution in case of emergency, for which the central government will assume the main food security responsibility, and work together with provincial and town-level governments to provide financial aid for grain production; make better use of domestic and foreign markets and resources, keep imports stable and accelerate the pace of agricultural globalization; and advocate economical consumption of food, increase public awareness of the need to conserve food and make it a common practice nationwide.

The central government has made it clear that China will keep cereals basically self-sufficient and staple foods absolutely secured. Given the availability of natural resources, China will focus on maintaining self-sufficiency in the main grain products; and it is important to note that it is impossible to rely on the international market to feed China's huge population. Largely because international grain prices are lower than the domestic market, however, China has increased its grain imports in recent years to meet the diversified demand of its population for food products. Imports of three main grains - rice, wheat and corn - account for a meager 2.4% of the total domestic grain output. China will continue to import several food varieties that are in short supply domestically in the future. On the other hand, insisting on China's self-sufficient food security strategy and taking into consideration farmers' employment so as to increase their income, China will not sharply increase its import of grain products.

China will take the following measures to significantly increase domestic grain production:

1. Stabilize the land area sown to grain. We must protect arable land, especially basic farmland, control the use of agricultural land for non-agricultural purposes, and expand arable land through land reconsolidation and reclamation to ensure that the total arable land is no less than 1.8bn *mu* (120m hectares) and the soil resilience has been regenerated. In order to maintain the cultivated land at no less than 1.56bn *mu* (104m hectares), including 475m *mu* (31.7m hectares) of rice fields, China has been working to demarcate basic farmland conservation areas throughout the country. China is also working hard to select a number of arable and productive grain production bases for permanent conservation. In addition, it is important to raise the potential multiple cropping index to safeguard a steady arable land area of over 1.6bn *mu* (106.7m hectares), including a stable grain land area of 1.26bn *mu* (84m hectares).

2. Optimize the mix of grain varieties. China will optimize grain production according to local geological and climate conditions in different regions of China: by promoting double-cropping rice production in southern China; by expanding the growing area of quality Japonica rice in northeastern China; by gradually replacing Indica rice with Japonica rice in the area between the Yangtze River and the Huai River; and by encouraging the cultivation of quality wheat for specific end-use. At the same time, we will expand the corn planting acreage to cultivate quality corn for specific end-use; encourage farmers to produce more high-oil and high-protein soybeans to ensure China's self-sufficiency in soybeans; increase the production of coarse grains and promote the cultivation of quality varieties of potatoes.

3. Increase the per unit area yield of grain. China will select quality new grain varieties and speed up their propagation and cultivation so as to improve the cultivation ratio of quality seed for grain production. We will transform traditional agricultural practices and employ new methods to develop China's agricultural mechanization in a professional and systematic manner, including the application of industrialized seedling nurturing and greenhouse seedling nurturing. The practice of deep ploughing to loosen and turn over the soil on arable land will be promoted which is helpful for alleviating soil compaction and improving crop yields. High-yield cultivation technologies, such as the use of sowing seeds without ploughing and formula fertilization after soil testing, will also be promoted. And local land and climate conditions in different regions will be taken into account to ensure large-scale sustainable food increases.

With the rapid advancement of industrialization and urbanization, China's natural resources have been strained and farmland contamination has been aggravated. Taking all these circumstances into consideration, the central government, especially the authority responsible for agriculture, is adopting decisive measures to protect and improve the quality of arable land. The overall goal is to develop high-quality farmland through improving rural agricultural facilities; to raise the soil fertility of cultivated land to a new level - 0.5% higher - by 2020, and to increase the content of organic matter in the soil by 0.5% as well; and to upgrade the quality of cultivated land to effectively avert any further increase in acid land, saline-alkali land and farmland contaminated by heavy metals via: enriching soil fertility to enhance water and nutrient conservation; curbing the overuse of chemical fertilizers and pesticides; and reducing organic matter accumulation in heavy metal-contaminated farmland soil. Under huge pressure to fix its worsening farming environment, China will formulate guidelines to improve the quality of arable land in different regions with specific solutions; setting national standards for upgrading the quality of arable land; protecting the existing arable land properly in accordance with *The Regulations on the Protection of Basic Farmland*; and demarcating basic farmland preservation areas all over the country.

A tiny rice seed changes the world

The UN's World Food Program (WFP) executive director James Morris told reporters while he was in Beijing for a two-day visit that the UNWFP would end food aid to China by the end of 2005. The UNWFP said its 26-year program of food aid to China would officially stop from 2006 onwards, and called on Beijing to play a bigger role as a global donor. Since the hybrid rice developed by Yuan Longping was planted all over China, China has been able to feed its population, which is 20% or more of the world's total, with less than 10% of the world's total arable land.

In 1973, together with his teammates, Yuan Longping successfully cultivated a type of hybrid rice species which had great advantages. The new hybrid rice type has been grown on half of the country's rice fields since then, ensuring a sufficient food supply for over one billion Chinese and forcefully answering the question of 'who will feed China'.

At a national conference on hybrid rice held in October, Yuan Longping circulated a paper entitled Utilization of 'Wild-Abortive-type (WA)' Seed Selection 'Three-Line System' of Development and unveiled the first successfully bred 'three-line system' of Indica hybrid rice species.

In 1976 China started large-scale planting of hybrid rice, with the total area sown to three-line hybrid rice reaching 2.08m mu (138,666.7 hectares), with an increase in output of over 20%. For this huge contribution, Yuan Longping was granted new China's first National Top-Grade Invention Award in 1981.

In 1982, at an academic conference of the International Rice Research Institute, renowned Chinese scientist Yuan Longping, was for the first time publicly acknowledged as the world's 'father of hybrid rice'.

In 1986, he further proposed a strategy for breeding hybrid rice with a step-by-step method to gradually develop three-line, two-line and super hybrid rice. His method was accepted as part of China's National 863 Program, and he was appointed head of a research team comprising 16 partners from all over China. Two-line hybrid rice was planted nationwide in 1995, contributing to an average annual increase of 5% to 10% over the three-line system.

Soon afterwards, Yuan pointed out that it was necessary to carry out the heroic task of developing super hybrid rice in phases, and advocated a new technology which could effectively improve the photosynthesis effect by combining selected quality seed with hybridization.

In 2000, the objective of producing 10.5t/ha (700kg/mu) for Phase I super rice was attained, and the Phase II objective of 12t/ha (800kg/mu) was accomplished in 2004. A Phase III super rice breed developed under Yuan's guidance yielded 13.5t/ha (900kg/mu) in a small-scale pilot field in 2005.

The introduction and development of hybrid rice ended the food shortage in China, and also provided an essential solution for reducing worldwide starvation. From Asia to America and even as far afield as Africa and Europe, this super-yield hybrid rice was nicknamed 'oriental magic rice', 'giant rice', 'waterfall rice', and is even ranked alongside ancient China's four major inventions (papermaking, printing, the compass and gunpowder).

Yuan has received a list of awards for his innovative contributions in developing hybrid rice, such as the Wolf Prize for Agriculture and the World Food Prize in 2004. He was also elected as a foreign associate of the US National Academy of Sciences in 2006.

Source: Xinhua Net, 25 August 2009

http://news.sina.com.cn/c/2009-08-25/175918508894.shtml

China's father of hybrid rice: Yuan Longping

Yuan Longping, born on September 7, 1930 in Beijing, now lives in Changsha (capital city of Hunan Province). He is an expert in hybrid rice breeding. He is highly acclaimed as the father of hybrid rice for his enormous contributions to the development of hybrid rice. He is also a member of the Chinese Engineering

Academy. He was elected as a foreign associate of the US National Academy of Sciences in 2006, received an honorary doctoral degree from Macau University of Science and Technology in 2010, and won Malaysia's Mahathir Science Award in 2011.

Currently, he is a member of the Standing Committee of the 12th National Committee of the Chinese People's Political Consultative Conference (CPPCC), and also vice chairman of the CPPCC Hunan Provincial Committee and of the Hunan Provincial Association for Science and Technology. He is the director general of the China National Hybrid Rice Research & Development Center and Hunan Hybrid Rice Research Center. He is also the honorary dean of several colleges in China, including the College of Agronomy and Biotechnology of China's Southwest University in Chongqing, Huaihua Vocational and Technical Collage and Hunan Biological and Electromechanical Polytechnic. He is a professor at Hunan Agricultural University and a visiting professor at China Agricultural University. He also acts as chief consultant for the UN's FAO. In addition, he is an honorary president of the 1st World Chinese Association of Healthy Eating.

4. Enhance the development of major grain producing regions. Major grain producing provinces, cities and counties are the vital elements in ensuring China's food security. China's 13 major grain producing provinces account for 75% of the national total in terms of output, 80% in terms of grain circulation in the market, and 90% in terms of transport to other areas. More than 400 major grain producing counties claim a grain output of more than 1bn *jin* (500,000 tonnes) which accounts for 54% of the total national output, and 33 major cities (prefecture-level cities) produce a grain output of over 10bn *jin* (5m tonnes), and their combined output accounts for 43% of the national total. The major agricultural regions constitute an essential 'safety net' for China's food security.

A total of 800 major grain-producing counties have been identified as the key areas in planning to build more than 100bn *jin* (50m tonnes) of grain production capacity. We will increase investment, speed up the development of new production capacity and build core grain-producing areas and major grain-production counties in non-core areas into stable high-yield commercial grain-production bases. On the premise of protecting the ecological environment, we will develop food production reserves when appropriate depending on the overall grain supply and demand situation.

Yushu Municipality, Jilin Province: planned construction as a major grain-producing area

Yushu Minicpality in Jilin Province is one of the important commodity grain-producing bases in China and is described as "the greatest bread-basket in China". In 2010, Yushu Municipality was listed as one of the first 50 modern agricultural demonstration zones.

In 2011, the city's agricultural area reached 379,000 hectares, of which 347,000 hectares was sown to grain. In 2011, the city's grain output reached 6.2bn jin (3,100m tonnes), hitting an all-time high and winning for Yushu the title of "the national grain production pacesetter county (city)" for eight consecutive years. The municipal government has implemented scientific planning of its demonstration zone construction, including developing one-million-mu high-standard farmland, overall mechanization, developing a vegetable production base, facilitating an animal husbandry industry production base and agricultural industrialization.

1. *Yushu Municpality has vigorously promoted land scale management, on the condition that the land ownership remains unchanged. In 2011 the city's land circulation area reached 870,000 mu (58,000 hectares), and it fostered 500 large-scale grain production households, incubated 436 farmer entrepreneurs and set up 330 farmers' cooperation organizations.*

2. *Yushu Municipality has promoted mechanization of farming and introduced a large amount of advanced equipment. The city had 28,510 vehicles, of which 13,493 were large tractors. And the city's agricultural mechanization level stood ahead of other parts of China.*

3. *Yushu Municipality has developed irrigation works and added water-conservation irrigation facilities to 100,000 mu (6,667 hectares) of farmland in order to increase grain yield. The municipality has realized high-density corn planting, which could raise the yield by 30%.*

4. *Relying on agricultural science and technology, Yushu Municipality has collectively put agricultural funds into the construction of high-standard farmland, investing Rmb45m (some US$7,22m) into the construction of 410,000 mu (27,333 hectares) of high-yield demonstration farmland. The municipality has promoted synthetic technical measures to increase yields including: formula fertilization after soil testing; adopting conservation-oriented ploughing technology; planting maize in wide and narrow rows*

allowing some land to lie fallow;.destroying farmland rodents; and achieving widespread coverage of Trichogramma wasps to control crop damage by Asian corn borer insects.

5. *Continue to expand construction of northern China's winter vegetable production base. In all, 26 new vegetable parks have been built and 1,440 solar greenhouses as well as 1,560 normal greenhouses, bringing the total number to 44,000, and total vegetable production was worth Rmb1.8bn (US$290m). The municipality aims to basically raise the average greenhouse ownership to one per household within 10 years, turning Yushu Municipality into a 'northern Shouguang' (Shouguang Municipality is a renowned vegetable production base in Shandong Province).*

5. To improve the incentive mechanisms for encouraging food production. We will establish and perfect a compensation mechanism for the major grain-producing areas, including encouraging policies and measures to support major grain-producing areas. We will also strengthen the incentive measures for major grain-producing counties, linking fiscal support to grain-growing areas, grain yield, grain circulation in the market and the amount of grain transported to other areas. The funding for county-level agricultural infrastructure construction will be phased out for major grain-producing counties. Instead, a grain subsidy system will be established, and concrete measures of granting direct subsidies according to the grain growing area, grain yield and the amount of grain sold to the state will be explored, to fully and most effectively stimulate grain production and ensure farmers' benefits.

In order to encourage the use of rural land for grain production, the *Opinions on Guiding the Transfer of Rural Land Operation Rights and Encouraging Moderate-Scale Agricultural Management* was issued by the State Council in November 2014. This provides that first, new subsidies will be granted to scale grain production operators; second, land operators will be encouraged to participate in food production by means of a sectoral planning for the major grain-producing areas, functional grain-producing areas and creative high-yield project areas and relative supporting policies; third, we will keep the land-transfer price at a reasonable level, thus reducing the food production costs and stabilizing the grain area planted to grain.

II. Promote Strategic Restructuring of Agriculture

1. Optimizing the arrangement of agricultural regions. At the planning level, China will tailor measures to suit local conditions and give full play to the advantages of each area. We will encourage and support advantageous areas to focus on planting grain, cotton, oilseed, sugar crops and other staple agricultural products. We will strengthen the construction of bases for vegetables, fruit, tea, flowers, silkworm cocoons and other horticultural products, and develop livestock and aquatic production zones with distinctive features of their own. We will accelerate the establishment of a strategic arrangement of agriculture comprising 'seven zones and 23 belts', with the Northeast Plain, North China Plain (also known as the Yellow River, Huai He and Hai He River Basin), Yangtze River Basin, Fen River-Wei River Plain, Hetao Irrigation Area, South China, Gansu and Xinjiang as the main agricultural production zones, with other agricultural areas as important components.

> *China maps out strategic arrangements for agriculture comprising 'seven zones and 23 belts'*
>
> *According to The National Master Plan for Functional Zoning issued by the State Council in late 2010, China will establish strategic arrangements for agriculture comprising 'seven zones and 23 belts'.*
>
> *'Seven zones and 23 belts' refers to the seven main agricultural production zones and 23 agricultural products including wheat, maize and cotton. The seven zones are: the Northeast Plain, North China Plain, Yangtze River Basin, Fen River–Wei River Plain, Hetao Irrigation Area, South China, Gansu and Xinjiang, in which basic farmland is the basis, and the other agricultural areas are important components.*

The Northeast Plain will build high-quality rice, special corn, soybean and livestock belts.

The North China Plain will build high-quality special wheat, high-quality cotton, special corn, soybean and livestock belts.

The Yangtze River Basin will build high-quality rice, high-quality special wheat, high-quality cotton, oilseed rape, livestock products and aquatic belts.

The Fen River-Wei River Plain will build high-quality special wheat and special corn industry belts.

The Hetao Irrigation Area will build a high-quality special wheat belt.

South China will build high-quality rice, sugar cane and aquatic belts.

Gansu and Xinjiang will build high-quality special wheat and high-quality cotton belts.

In addition, we will also actively support the development of other agricultural zones and other characteristic agricultural products with advantages, which need the necessary policy guidance and support from the state according to their specialty. These agricultural products and belts include: the Southwest and Northeast China wheat belt, the Southwest/Southeast China corn belt, South China's high-protein soybean and vegetable soybean belt, North China's oilseed rape belt, Northeast, North, Northwest, Southwest and South China's potato belts, Guangxi, Yunnan, Guangdong and Hainan Provinces' sugarcane belts, Hainan, Yunnan and Guangdong Provinces' natural rubber belts, Hainan's tropical agricultural product belts, coastal regions' pig belt, Northwest China's beef and mutton belts, Beijing, Tianjin, Shanghai and Northwest China's dairy belts, and the Yellow Sea and the Bohai Sea's aquatic belts.

2. Vigorously developing the animal farming industry. We will strengthen and expand animal husbandry, enhancing breed improvement and animal disease prevention and control, and promoting scale, standardized, intensive and modernized livestock and poultry farming. We will promote the healthy and stable development of pig farming and actively support the construction of standardized scale pig feed production bases (farms). We will improve pig farms' rearing conditions, epidemic prevention and manure treatment, and strengthen the construction of the public live pig disease prevention and control system. We will enhance the subsidy system for pig farming and the quality-breed promotion policy, and further strengthen the support for pig production via credit loans and insurance. We will continue to implement the incentive policy for top pig-producing counties (farms). We will accelerate the restructuring of the dairy industry and ensure the quality and safety of dairy products, thus promoting the lasting and sound development of the industry. We will step up promotion of beef and mutton production, stabilize the development of poultry and egg production and encourage the development of special livestock breeding. We will promote the healthy development of the aquatic products industry, expand ecological aquacultural farming, and assist and grow ocean fishing.

3. Accelerating the development of resource-efficient agriculture. We will promote the application of channel seepage prevention, pipeline transport of water, spray irrigation, drip irrigation and other water-conservation agricultural technologies. Efforts will be made to promote high-efficiency water-saving irrigation and to raise the area of farmland covered by water-saving irrigation facilities by 50m *mu* (3.3m hectares). Efforts will also be made to develop rain-fed agriculture. We will speed up the construction of rain-fed agriculture demonstration bases, adopt plastic mulching, rainwater collection for supplemental irrigation, conservation ploughing and other techniques. We will advocate intensive farming, develop intercropping techniques and promote stereoscopic planting, thereby raising land use efficiency. We will raise the efficiency of agricultural inputs by promoting the application of agricultural technologies that economise on the use of seeds, fertilizer, pesticide and energy.

Developing rain-fed agriculture in arid regions

Gansu Province, located in northwest China, has 36m mu (2.4m hectares) of dry land, accounting for 70% of all its arable land. Gansu receives average annual rainfall of 300mm, most of which occurs between July and September. The harsh climate is not favorable for agriculture. In recent years, however, Gansu has produced bumper harvests with record highs.

The high output results from the development of science and technology. Whole-film double-furrow sowing, or two furrows (one wide and one narrow) both covered with plastic mulch, have increased the efficiency of re-using rainwater by retaining it in the soil to water crops. The mulch reduces evaporation; the furrows transform the spring rainfall into available water resources by collecting it in seeding furrows through rainwater harvesting surface to make it possible for seeds to fully absorb the rainfall. By using this method, the efficient use of rainfall

41

has doubled. It is estimated that the normal annual corn yield increases by 35% more than half-film planted corn, and the potato yield grows by 30% more than open field potatoes.

A steady high output relies on planting crops that are suited to the climate. As whole-film double-furrow sowing is becoming popular, Gansu is restructuring its agriculture, increasing the high-yield autumn crops such as corn and potatoes while reducing winter wheat in the arid areas. Statistics show that in 2010 there were about 12.74m mu (850,000 hectares) of corn land, compared with 6.97m mu (465,000 hectares) in 2000; the potato land expanded to almost 10m mu (670,000 hectares) from about 6.26m mu (417,000 hectares); the ratio of summer crops to autumn crops changed to 38:62 from 51:49. Nowadays, corn and potatoes have become a crucial support for Gansu's stable and increasing agricultural output.

"Last year, I harvested 13 tonnes of corn and earned a lot of money. I used cornstalks to feed my cattle, and used their manure to fertilize the land. They've benefited from each other," said Ma Shaoyuan, a 70-year-old farmer in Zhoujiazi Village, Qijia Town, Guanghe County, Gansu Province. Over 10m mu (670,000 hectares) of land has been planted with corn, increasing the total grain output and providing fodder for livestock grazing. Guanghe County, together with several other counties in Gansu, is exploring a circular agriculture model: dry farming – cornstalks – cattle and sheep breeding – biogas-organic fertilizer – grain output increase. In 2010, the proportion of livestock grazing in Gansu increased to 45%, 7% higher than in 2000.

Gansu: the 'hope project' showcasing film technology application on arid plateau

4. Actively develop urban agriculture. Capitalizing on the science and technology, human resources and market space in urban areas, we will strive to deepen and strengthen the development of functional agriculture, including technology-intensive agriculture, facility agriculture, ecological agriculture, quality agriculture and agritourism. To secure 'vegetable baskets' in the suburbs of large and medium-sized cities, China is supporting the construction of farming bases for the production of vegetables and other fresh produce.

Shanghai: A leader of modern urban agriculture

Shanghai is 'far removed' from agriculture due to its limited agricultural resources and low agricultural output as a percentage of its GDP. However, the city has become an agricultural powerhouse for its urban agriculture development model and high average yield.

Although there is not much arable land available here, Shanghai enjoys advanced science and technology, human, finance, information and market resources, which make it a front-runner in modern urban agriculture. Shanghai's agriculture, which is only 0.6% of its GDP, has delivered a stable supply of agricultural products for years, and especially 90% self-sufficiency in leafy greens. Among 50 major cities in China, Shanghai ranks behind 30 cities in the vegetable price index. With a small population working in agriculture, Shanghai boasts the most modern agricultural parks, amazing high-tech agricultural services and agricultural innovation. It has also enhanced agriculture by integrating it with the secondary and tertiary sectors. The average profit per mu (0.0667) is nearly Rmb5,000, much higher than China's average. Over 1.6m mu (over 100,000 hectares) of arable land serves as a natural and seasonal wetland, a green ecological belt around Shanghai. Agritourism here is now thriving and offers recreation and education, which are becoming a more popular choice for weekend plans among people in downtown Shanghai.

In the past 20 years, Shanghai has witnessed different stages of agricultural development, including the rise of modern urban agriculture. It took the earliest step among all large cities in China toward this new type of agriculture.

In the mid-1980s, Shanghai transformed its rural agriculture into suburban agriculture, a fragile and self-reliant industry that could only provide fresh food and primary agricultural products to the urban areas. At the beginning of the 1990s, as the demand for agricultural products in urban areas increased,

Shanghai set higher aims for agricultural development. In Shanghai's Ninth Five-Year Plan, the government claimed that the goal of developing urban agriculture was to boost ecological balance, tourism, high-tech agriculture demonstration and exports for foreign exchange. Shanghai's urban agriculture then started. In the late 1990s, Shanghai moved toward modern urban agriculture. As the urban and suburban areas were quickly integrated, the counties and rural districts became an important part of Shanghai. The agricultural support system consisting of finance, science and technology has been improved. Modern facilities and technologies such as greenhouses, sprinklers and drip irrigation have been widely applied for agriculture which has attracted many tourists and students.

In 2007, at the Ninth Shanghai Municipal Party Congress, Xi Jinping, then Secretary of the CPC Shanghai Municipal Committee, stated that Shanghai as an international modern metropolis would give priority to efficient ecological agriculture and promote its influence in economy, ecology and services.

In Shanghai's 12th Five-Year Plan for Modern Agriculture, the government declared the goals of developing efficient ecological urban agriculture, promoting its influence in the economy, ecology and services, and ensuring efficient supply and quality of agricultural products. The government's focus was on a multi-functional modern agriculture.

Shanghai is now transforming the traditional production-oriented agriculture into a modern urban agriculture aiming at the same time at the economy, ecology, high-tech demonstration and services. Agriculture as a percentage of Shanghai's GDP will keep decreasing in the future while it is increasingly integrated and efficient.

Source: *Farmers' Daily*, April 23, 2012.

http://www.farmer.com.cn/jjpd/hyyw/201204/t20120423_713100.htm

5. Developing forestry products. Efforts are being made to enhance: the cultivation of high-quality seedlings and precious tree species; the construction of strategic timber reserves for industrial and commercial purposes; the promotion of forest tourism, bamboo industry, flower seedlings and plants, wildlife breeding and utilization industry, and sand industry; the development of woody crops and oil-bearing plants such as tea-oil trees, walnuts and other specialized forest products; and the development of the underwood economy.

6. Ensuring the quality and safety of agricultural products. People who produce and sell agricultural products need to be educated about the importance and their responsibility for quality and safety. To achieve agricultural standardization, we will improve the system of agricultural product quality and safety standards, especially concerning the safety of agricultural inputs, residues of pesticides and veterinary drugs, and the regulation of cultivation practices. A quality tracking system must be established to protect registered trademarks and enforce the geographical indication (GI) protection system. China should promote green, pollution-free, organic food and GI agricultural products. The quality safety inspection system for agricultural products must be strengthened to improve routine monitoring and supervision of the quality and safety of agricultural products. Supervision over the production, acquisition, storage, processing, and sales of agricultural products must also be regulated. Illicit drugs, illegal chemicals and other agricultural inputs that are potentially harmful to human health are prohibited. We will carry out a risk assessment of the quality and safety of agricultural products to improve our risk control capabilities.

III. Accelerate Agricultural Scientific and Technological Innovation and the Widespread Application of Technology

1. Enhancing agricultural technological innovation capability. Based on China's basic national conditions, China should try to establish an agricultural technological innovation system that meets the needs of modern agriculture. To create a better atmosphere for agricultural innovation, we should try to increase the proportion of agricultural projects in the national science and technology program, to set up more innovation funds for agricultural technological development, and to support the construction of national agricultural hi-tech demonstration zones and national agricultural technology parks. Reforms should be carried out for agricultural research institutes, including improving the operation and evaluation mechanisms of scientific research projects, building a business-oriented strategic alliance for agricultural technological innovation, and supporting high-tech enterprises to engage in the research and development of agricultural technologies and in national-level high-tech projects, which would help to establish an advanced mechanism for agricultural innovation. Agricultural education and technology training should also be strengthened to speed up the development of human resources for agricultural technological innovation.

2. Making breakthroughs in critical basic theory and key technologies.
China will promote basic research in agriculture, especially in agricultural, biological gene regulation and molecular breeding; in resistance mechanisms for crops, forests, animals and plants; in efficient use of agricultural resources; in ecological rehabilitation of crops and forests; in pest control; and in biosafety and agricultural products safety. Meanwhile, we will speed up the development of cutting-edge technologies and aim to achieve innovative results in agricultural biotechnology, new materials, advanced manufacturing and precision agriculture. Efforts will be made in the innovation, integration and promotion of cost-effective and energy-saving agriculture, water-efficient irrigation, agricultural equipment, new types of fertilizers, animal disease control, processing and storage, circular agriculture, offshore agriculture and rural livelihood. To create an information-based agriculture, we will work on data collection and management, resource research, weather and natural disaster forecasting and early warning systems.

3. Strengthening and consolidating the seed industry. Besides the conventional breeding research, China will increase the investment in basic and public research to enhance the collection, conservation and identification of germplasm resources; to develop innovative breeding theories and technologies; to improve breeding materials; and to generate new genetically modified organisms and high-yield seed varieties. We will modernize the whole seed industry based on production, education and research to acquire the functions of seed cultivation, breeding and marketing. Large competitive seed enterprises will be established through integrating industry resources, optimizing resource allocation, raising market access standards and promoting mergers and acquisitions among seed enterprises. Innovation will be emphasized in biological breeding as well as in improving animal and plant varieties. We will also attach great importance to the construction of high-performance seed breeding bases and new seed variety demonstration zones in counties and towns that play an important role in the production of crops, cotton and oil-bearing plants. Seed market supervision will also be strengthened by improving and completing the validation, protection and withdrawal policies, and upgrading the administrative licensing of seed production and operation.

Li Denghai: father of China's compact hybrid maize

Li Denghai, born in Laizhou City, Shandong Province in September 1949, is known as the 'father of China's compact hybrid maize' and is as renowned as Yuan Longping, the 'father of hybrid rice'.

In the past 30 years, Li has achieved seven record highs in the yield of summer maize and set a record of 1,402.86kg per mu (21.043t/ha) in 2005 which still stands to this day, allowing each mu to feed 4.5 people, whereas in the past that used to feed only one person. He was the first to develop the compact hybrid maize that includes 52 national and local-level approved varieties. The maize varieties that Li cultivated have been introduced onto nearly 1bn mu (67,000 hectares) of land, achieving a profit of Rmb100bn.

After graduating from middle school in 1972, Li joined the agricultural technology team of his village as the team leader. He was impressed when he discovered that the spring maize produced by DuPont Pioneer had a yield of 1,250kg per mu (18.75t/ha). He was determined to create China's own maize seeds with a higher yield than American maize. In 1974, he was recommended to Laiyang Agricultural College (now Qingdao Agricultural University) for special training. Liu Enxun, the college teacher, gave him 20 valuable hybrid maize seeds named XL80. Yu Yi, an expert in maize cultivation, suggested that he try an upright-leaf maize type that could be thickly planted and with the potential to produce a higher yield than conventional spreading-leaf maize.

In 1979, Li separated a new variety Ye 107 from XL80 and used it as the parent plant to produce 7.2kg of hybrid maize seeds in Hainan. These seeds, known as Yedan 2, produced a record yield of 776.6kg per mu (11.65t/ha). Since then, Li has developed a series of new varieties from Yedan 6 to Yedan 12 with a yield per mu ranging from 824.9kg (12.373t/ha) to 953kg (14.295t/ha) and

ultimately to 962 kg (14.45t/ha). In October 1989, Li set a new world record with Yedan 13 that produced 1,096.29kg per mu (16.444t/ha). Therefore in 2004, he won the first prize of the National Science and Technology Progress Award. Some 16 years later, on October 17, 2005, a super maize DH3719 was created with a yield of 1,402.86 kg per mu (21.043t/ha). He had broken the world record again.

In his 38-year experience with maize cultivation, Li Denghai has broken China's record of summer maize production 7 times, and broke the world record 2 times. He has led the development of China's compact hybrid maize, hence he came to be called 'father of China's compact hybrid maize'.

4. Promoting the popularization of agricultural technological capability. To make agricultural technologies more accessible in rural areas, we will establish county and town-level and regional public service organizations dedicated to agricultural technology promotion, animal and plant disease control and agricultural products quality control. Systems of management, recruitment and evaluation will also be established. China will also raise the pay of workers to promote agricultural technology in rural areas to the salary level of rural public servants; while financial support should be given to build a top-down agricultural technology promotion system in all agricultural counties and to ensure that every county or town is accessible to agricultural tech programs. We should implement a market-based mechanism for the public-oriented functions of the agricultural promotion institutions and explore multiple channels to achieve public support for agricultural development. Cooperation will be enhanced between universities and research institutions on one hand and the agricultural promotion institutions and farmers' professional cooperatives at the grassroots level on the other, as well as between leading agricultural enterprises and individual farmers, to achieve an effective integration between technological innovation and agricultural production and operation. Colleges, universities and research institutions will be encouraged to set up agricultural demonstration bases to facilitate the integration, development and commercialization of agricultural technologies. China aims to establish a well-functioning agricultural technology market by fostering the diversity of competitors, improving regulations for trading and operation, and enhancing agricultural IPR protection.

IV. Improving Agricultural Facilities and Equipment

1. Carrying out more water conservancy projects. China will continue to build infrastructure to support large and major mid-sized irrigation areas and upgrade their water conservancy facilities. New irrigation areas will be established in areas with abundant water and land resources to increase effective irrigation of arable land. To improve the irrigation and drainage system, we will upgrade large and medium-sized irrigation and drainage pumping stations and the transformation of flooded areas. The existing irrigation facilities will be given full play, and for this purpose the major infrastructure to support construction and water conservancy upgrading projects for 70% of irrigation areas and 50% of medium irrigation areas will be completed. The construction of water conservancy projects will be accelerated in key counties and the supporting facilities among irrigation fields will be strengthened. Based on the local geographical environment, one or more choices of five small-scale water conservancy projects will be implemented: small water cellars, small ponds, small reservoirs, small pumping stations, and small canals leading to mountainous and hilly areas. Efforts will also be made to develop water conservancy facilities in pastoral areas with the construction of water-efficient irrigation facilities for forage land.

2. Expanding the construction of high-standard farmland that produces good yields in times of drought or excessive rain. We will speed up the transformation of at least 400m *mu* (27m hectares) of medium and low-yielding farmland into high-standard farmland that produces good yields in times of drought or excessive rain. A system of measures will be taken, with clear focus on key areas and key measures including land leveling, soil improvement, raising soil fertility, building tractor roads and forest planting amid fields according to the corresponding requirements and standards. We will establish and improve mechanisms for the management and protection of farmland and agricultural facilities to ensure the long-term yield benefits. A sound management system for farming facilities will be set up to ensure their long-term functionality.

3. Accelerating agricultural mechanization. Support will be given to upgrading the agricultural machinery industry, especially the research and development of critical components and products to improve their applicability, convenience and safety. Efforts will be made to address the particular challenges in mechanical transplanting of rice and mechanical harvesting of corn, oilseed rape, sugarcane and cotton. We will try to increase the penetration of mechanized production of grain and commercial crops such as cotton, oil-bearing and sugar-bearing plants while increasing mechanization in animal husbandry, forestry, fruit planting and primary processing of agricultural products. We will facilitate the development of agricultural and mechanical facilities for animal husbandry and aquaculture. We will extend the application of mechanical technologies for subsoiling, precise sowing, deep fertilizing, conservation ploughing and recycling of crop waste. By integrating agricultural machinery and processes, we will try to get more farmers to implement mechanized planting. Agro-industry will be encouraged to increase the productivity of fertilizers, pesticides and plastic mulches.

4. Building stronger disaster prevention and reduction capability. We will continue to improve the management and rehabilitation of major rivers, lakes, and medium and small-sized rivers; to consolidate reservoirs with potential risks; to enhance the comprehensive management and conservation of ecologically vulnerable areas; and to increase the capabilities of rivers to withstand floods, mountain torrents and geological disasters. On this basis, we will establish a flood-related disaster prevention and relief system for major rivers by combining engineering and non-engineering measures and to soundly bring under control major, medium and small-sized rivers, including tributaries of major rivers, rivers without tributaries rushing into the sea and inland waterways. We will carry out water source projects to address water shortages due to engineering factors. The meteorological infrastructure and service system will be strengthened to improve agro-meteorological disaster forecasting. To respond more actively to climate change, we will improve: the accuracy and precision of agro-meteorological disaster monitoring and pre-warning systems; the infrastructure of weather modification and research capacity; and the scientific exploitation and utilization of cloud-water resources. To act more efficiently in agricultural emergencies and minimize losses from disasters, we will strengthen disaster monitoring, pre-warning and response coordination. We will secure relief supply reserves, and upgrade emergency reporting and disclosure. We will improve the surveillance and control systems of animal and plant pathogens and their development by carrying out specialized prevention and control methods against forest pests and grassland rodent pests. A sound forage reserve system must be established to increase the capability for disaster prevention and mitigation in pastoral areas. Fishing port construction and fishing boat standardization will be expedited to increase the safety of fishery production.

V. Strengthening the Organization of Agricultural Production and Operation

1. Promote the industrialization of agricultural operations. Policies and measures for agricultural industrialization will be renewed while support in terms of finance, tax and information will be enhanced to build an integrated agricultural system encompassing an extended industrial chain with the functions of production, processing and sales. China will support agricultural leaders with great potential, influence and driving force to engage in technological innovation, production upgrading and brand building. Depending on the leading enterprises, we will establish professional, standard and large-scale production bases and promote the partnership between leading enterprises and farmers' professional cooperatives to organize and motivate farmers.

Jiangsu Province nurtures 'dragon's head' (leading) enterprises to boost new agricultural model

A policy paper was recently released by the general office of Jiangsu Provincial Government to organize a joint conference on agricultural industrialization work, including the provincial agriculture committee, the provincial development and reform commission, the provincial finance department and eight other departments. This was the third official order on boosting agricultural industrialization to foster a new breed of leading enterprises.

In recent years, Jiangsu's agricultural industrialization level has continuously improved and clusters of leading agricultural enterprises have continuously emerged to play an increasingly important role in the agricultural modernization process. According to the provincial agriculture committee, in January 2013 there were 5,447 leading agricultural enterprises at or above provincial level, 470 more than the previous year. The operatonal quality of these leading enterprises registered steady improvement. By the end of 2012, 443 of them had reached a sales turnover of more than Rmb495.5bn (US$80bn), and realized a net profit of Rmb15.257bn (US$2.46bn), representing increases of 25.86% and 10.17% respectively, with 11 of the enterprises achieving a sales turnover of more than Rmb10bn (US$1.611bn), This gave the impetus for 9.53m households to be involved in agricultural industrialization, which was 10.22% up over the previous year, accounting for 1/3 of China's total. In 2012, 443 leading agricultural enterprises at or above the provincial level gave the impetus for 9.53m households.

"*Improving the operating performance of leading agricultural enterprises is the key to promoting agricultural industrialization and to boosting a new breed of agricultural business,*" *said Xu Huizhong, Deputy Director of Jiangsu Agriculture Committee. In recent years, Jiangsu has become the first province in the country to organize activities 'to promote a year marking the improvement leading agricultural enterprises' operating performance' to encourage its enterprises to establish a steady purchase-sale chain and raw material production bases via independent operations, partnerships and outsourcing to specialized suppliers, in order to increase farmers' incomes. Meanwhile, Jiangsu issued 'Suggestions on Supporting Leading Enterprises in Agricultural Industrialization', offering official assistance for financial services and enterprise competitiveness.*

To support the provincial agricultural leaders and potential leaders, Jiangsu has set up a special fund for provincial agricultural industrialization. In 2012, Jiangsu spent a total of Rmb230m (US\$37m) for this purpose, benefiting 240 leading enterprises. It has signed a strategic cooperation agreement with the Jiangsu branch of the Agriculture Bank of China (ABC), committing Rmb132m (US\$21.3m) credit in total. The Jiangsu government, the provincial agriculture bank, the Nanjing Yurun Group and four other enterprises pledged a total contribution of Rmb100m (US\$16.11m) to establish Jiangsu Huilong Investment Guarantee Corporation to provide financing guarantees for agricultural enterprises. City and county-level competent authorities have implemented five effective measures to promote agricultural industrialization with clear requirements, plans, goals and responsibilities: to establish a local agricultural industrialization base; to make local farmers rich; to revitalize agricultural industry; to cooperate with farmers' cooperative organizations and to create a competent agricultural brand. On the other hand, the leading agricultural enterprises, equipped with technology, market resources and information, have actively engaged themselves in these activities, playing an important role in establishing farmers' professional cooperatives, enhancing partnerships with leading growers and breeders, and farmers' organizations. They have worked to strengthen their competence by building their own brands supported by organic, ecological and original products.

This year, a new challenge has arisen: how to lift agricultural industrialization to a new level? Pan Changsheng, chief of the agriculture industrialization guidance office, has proposed five initiatives: 1. Continue the development of model agricultural leaders to ensure growth of 10% and 8% respectively in annual sales and the number of farmers' households involved; 2. Accelerate the construction of local original industrial base, encouraging local competitive industries to develop *in favorable areas to form a multi-functional and coordinated modern agricultural industry system; 3. Support the construction of agicultural processing clusters and attract agricultural leaders to start up businesses there to promote industrial clustering; 4. Make efforts to build a modern circulation system for agricultural products with the aim that 10% of agricultural enterprises should achieve over Rmb10bn (US$1.611bn) in annual sales; 5. Improve administrative services, and support enterprises or bases (parks) to develop their research and development (R&D) capability, product inspection and testing, and information network construction. Besides these measures, the 382 provincial leadeing agricultural enterprises in late 2012 should be monitored on an ongoing basis and only the fittest should be able to keep this title.*

Source: *Farmers' Daily,* February 28, 2013

http://www.farmer.com.cn/xwpd/jjsn/201302/t20130228_813663.htm

The development of a leading industrialized agricultural enterprise

In 2003, Chen Shigui, a farmer in Wangjiafan Village, Yidu City, Hubei Province, founded the 'Tulaohan' (Local Old Fogey) Ecological Agriculture Development Company. He bought agricultural sideline products, which were regarded as weeds by most farmers, and processed and packaged them elaborately. Then these products were sold in supermarkets in cities and became very popular. In just a few short years, 'Tulaohan' has developed from a small rural workshop to become an important provincial-level leading enterprise. 'Tulaohan' has created an iconic agricultural brand renowned in Yichang, the province of Hubei and even throughout China.

'Tulaohan' focuses on traditional household foods in rural and mountainous areas, and develops them based on market demand. It insists on strict quality control in each production step, to ensure every product is pollution-free and all natural. Soon after its incorporation, it has developed 14 product categories with 35 varieties.

In April 2006, Chen Shigui's Hubei Tulaohan Ecological Agriculture Development Company merged with Yidu Municipality's Honghuatao (Safflower Set) Town Tangerine Cooperative, another agricultural giant in Yidu, to integrate their resources and advantages. After sufficient negotiation, Chen Shigui agreed to start up Yidu Tangerine Group Cooperative based on Honghuatao Town Tangerine Cooperative and 10 other tangerine cooperatives in Yidu. He implemented standardized production and strict quality control as well as emphasizing marketing strategy and R&D. With the brand strength of 'Tulaohan', his tangerine business has been expanding further and further.

Site of Tulaohan Ecological Agriculture Development Company factory

Now the enterprise has already developed three major product categories: 1. Selected Yidu tangerine and deep-processed tangerine products; 2. Seasonings (tangerine-flavored vinegar, soy sauce for cooking fish and black bean sauce); and 3. Snacks (dried fish, dried tangerine peel and preserves). Its products have won accolades such as 'Top 10 Specialties of Three Gorges Region', 'Most Popular Products of Hubei Province' and 'Famous Brand Products of Hubei Province'. They are also one of the best sellers in agricultural markets, branded supermarkets including Walmart and Carrefour, Zhongbai Holdings Group Co Ltd and Wuhan Department Store Group Co Ltd and in more than 20 large and mid-sized cities like Beijing, Shanghai, Wuhan and Yichang. Selected Yidu tangerines have been supplied for four consecutive years to Zhongnanhai in Beijing where the central government is located. The tangerines have also been exported to Russia, Central and Eastern Europe, Hong Kong and other countries and regions. In 2012, the group produced a sales income of Rmb1.5bn (US$240m) and paid a total tax of Rmb78m (US$12.6 m).

The group is located in Yidu Green Product Innovation Park in Honghuatao Town, covering 700 mu (some 47 hectares). It has a 23,350sqm agricultural and sideline products market, 55,000sqm of standard plants, and an 11,000sqm tangerine production center. Now there are more than 2,000 employees, including 105 professional technicians, 186 people with bachelor's degrees, 9 with master's degrees and 2 with doctoral degrees.

2. Developing farmers' cooperatives. China will fully implement *The Law of the PRC on Farmers' Professional Cooperatives* to accelerate the development of farmers' cooperatives and to support their growth with increasing market competitiveness. Innovation is encouraged to develop diversified cooperative forms, especially to establish specialized cooperatives for production and operation. We will extend the areas and functions of cooperative services and support qualified cooperatives to carry out cooperation in credit, land transfer and other fields. The supply and marketing cooperatives will provide more support to farmers' cooperatives. Farmers' cooperatives will be encouraged to set up agricultural product enterprises or to acquire equity in leading agricultural enterprises. Agricultural product associations will also be encouraged in areas with appropriate conditions.

Whether or not farmers' specialized cooperatives can overcome the dilemma faced by rural products of 'small producers in a big market'

Farmers' professional cooperatives have become China's fourth-largest market players after individual businesses, private enterprises and limited liability companies. According to the recently published report on the 'Development of Farmers' Professional Cooperatives in China 2006-2010', the average income of farmers working for cooperatives was 20% higher than non-cooperative farmers. However, farmers' professional cooperatives are still in the initial stage and have to tackle many challenges in building modern agri-businesses that will enable farmers to compete domestically and internationally.

"Farmers like me want to learn e-commerce so we can sell vegetables on the internet simply with the click of a mouse. But the fact is that we have no time until we get home from the fields in the evening. I only have some basic knowledge," said Zhou Zhongchao, a 55-year-old farmer in Dali County, Shaanxi Province. Since 2007, he has had his own vegetable business: the Zhongchao Vegetable Farmers' Cooperative, together with other vegetable growers in the village. All growers here are required to obey a system of rules concerning variety selection, management and sales. Through sustained development, the cooperative now has more than 800 farmer members. "Before the founding of the cooperative, the price of chilies was Rmb10 (US$1.6) per kilo. Thanks to our systematic management, our chilies have won more popularity because of their better quality, and the price has doubled now." Zhou said that the growers in his cooperative could now earn Rmb7,000–8,000 (US$1,130–1,290) per mu.

Zhao Tieqiao, Deputy Chief of the General Branch of Rural Cooperative Economic Operation Management of the Ministry of Agriculture (MOA), said that 'lack of people' and 'lack of money' are two major obstacles holding back the development of farmers' professional cooperatives. Most migrant workers from rural areas are young adults, among whom few have any sense of a market-oriented economy and management capabilities. Therefore MOA will train 190,000 cooperative directors this year and 15,000 more cooperative professionals in the next decade. Meanwhile, the MOA is encouraging young people in rural areas and village officials who are new college graduates to lead and engage in the development of cooperatives.

In terms of financial support, favorable policies have been jointly issued by the MOA with other relevant authorities. One of the policies is that farmer members should not be charged for selling their agricultural products through the cooperative, and should be exempted from value added tax. A system of credit rating, grants and application will be introduced for cooperatives.

Sales represent one of the biggest challenges for future development. According to experts and professionals in agricultural product marketing, the supply chains from farmers to supermarkets and from farmers' cooperatives to college dining halls will be encouraged, while various marketing activities such as exhibitions, trade fairs and agricultural trade fairs will also be encouraged. "Compared with other market players, small cooperatives may not be competitive. Therefore, effective forms of cooperation are needed to lead farmers and cooperatives to participate in market competition on a larger scale and at a higher level. For instance they could compete via specialized and associated cooperatives," said Zhao Tieqiao.

At the same time, cooperatives are encouraged to establish direct-sales stores, chain stores and retail agencies in residential communities and agricultural product markets in cities to realize a seamless transfer of agricultural products from farmers' land to consumers' tables.

In Zhao's view, farmers' professional cooperatives connect agriculture, farmers and rural areas. Supporting policies are needed in the future. Government support, however, serving as the guiding power, cannot decide the development of the cooperatives. It is important for them to build and increase their cohesion by implementing standard and democratic management, and establishing a system of governance including general meetings, council groups, supervisory boards and distribution channels.

Source: Xinhua News Agency, October 30, 2011

http://news.xinhuanet.com/fortune/2011-10/30/c_111133437.htm

3. Establishing a new non-government agriculture service system. China will accelerate institutional construction based on public service agencies and cooperative economic organizations, with the support of leading enterprises, and non-government participants will be encouraged to be part of this system. This system will combine public service and commercial functions, providing both specialized and comprehensive services. We will nurture and develop a wide range of socialized agricultural service organizations and lead farmers' professional cooperatives, supply and marketing cooperatives, special technology associations, rural water cooperative organizations, agriculture-related enterprises and other non-government participants to provide agricultural services before, during and after production. We will ensure that rural collective organizations will provide better services for farmers' production and operation.

4. Developing a modern agricultural products circulation system. To improve the agricultural products market system, we will build up and upgrade wholesale markets for agricultural products; and speed up the establishment of a wholesale market network with a scientific design, advanced facilities, all-round functions and a well regulated trading environment. We will upgrade trading services, support facilities and the management of agricultural products markets; develop a well regulated trading environment; and reduce operating costs. We will promote an agricultural futures market which will provide orientation for production, stabilize the market and hedge against risks. A modern circulation system for agricultural products will be established via the construction of infrastructure such as large logistics centers, cold chains for agricultural products and distribution centers for fresh agricultural products. Comprehensive pilot programs for modern circulation will be implemented for south-north vegetable transportation and west-east fruit transportation. Efforts will be made to develop the farmer-supermarket supply chain and healthy e-commerce for agricultural products, and ultimately to build up an efficient circulation network. We will foster and train rural brokers, agricultural product marketing specialists, agricultural products circulation enterprises and other market players to create an organized and industrialized circulation system for agricultural products.

Table 2-3: Key indicators of modern agricultural development during the 12th Five-Year Plan period (2011-2015)

Categories	Indicators	2010	2015	Average Annual Growth (%)
Supply of agricultural products	Overall grain production capacity (million tonnes)	>500	>540	
	Grain cultivation area (million hectares)	110	>107	
	Total cotton output (million tonnes)	5.96	>7.00	>3.27
	Total output of oil-bearing crops (million tonnes)	32.30	35.00	1.62
	Total output of sugar crops (billion tonnes)	120.08	>140.00	>3.12
	Total meat output (million tonnes)	79.26	85.00	1.41
	Total egg output (million tonnes)	27.63	29.00	0.97
	Total milk output (million tonnes)	37.48	50.00	5.93
	Total output of aquatic products (million tonnes)	53.73	>60.00	>2.23
	Overall pass rate in routine monitoring program for quality and safety of agricultural products (%)	94.8	>96.0	>[1.2]
Agricultural mix	Animal husbandry share of total agricultural production value (%)	30	36	[6]
	Fisheries share of total agricultural production value (%)	9.3	10	[0.7]
	Agro-processing share of total agricultural production value (%)	1.7	2.2	[0.5]
Agricultural infrastructure	Newly increased farmland with effective irrigation (million hectares)			[2.67]
	Effective utilization coefficient of water for farmland irrigation	0.50	0.53	[0.03]
	Total power of farm machinery (GW)	920	100	1.68
	Comprehensive mechanization level of ploughing, sowing and harvesting (%)	52	60	[8]
Agricultural technology	Contribution of advanced science and technology (%)	52	>55	?[3]
	Rural population with practical skills (million)	8.2	13.0	6.8
Organization of agricultural production and operation	Number of farmers' households benefiting from vertically integrated agriculture (million)	107	130	3.97
	Proportion of large-scale dairy cattle farming (herds of 100 or more) (%)	28	>38	>[10]
	Proportion of large-scale pig farming (units of 500 or more) (%)	35	50	[15]

Agricultural ecological environment	Penetration of appropriate household biogas digesters (%)	33	>50	>[17]
	Comprehensive utilization rate of straw (%)	70.2	>80.0	>[9.8]
Agricultural output value and farmers' incomes	Annual growth rate of added value of crop production, forestry, animal husbandry and fisheries (%)			5
	Agricultural migrant labor force (million)			[40]
	Per capita net income of rural residents (Rmb)	5,919	>8,310	>7

Notes: 1. [ ] indicates cumulative number over five-year period;
2. By the end of 2008, there were 8.2 million rural residents with practical skills;
3. The per capita net income of rural residents is calculated at 2010 prices and the growth rate is calculated at comparable prices.

Source: *National Plan for the Development of Modern Agriculture (2010-2015)* **issued by the State Council on January 13, 2012.**

Chapter 3

How to Carry Out Construction of a New Countryside in China

China is experiencing the largest ever scale of urbanization. It is expected that by 2030 China's population will peak at 1.5bn and that the urbanization rate will reach 70% under the most optimistic estimate. It means that in 20 years, more than 300m people will move into cities and towns from the countryside. This will be an unimaginably tough challenge. Even so, there will still be 400m to 500m farmers living in rural areas. Therefore, urbanization will be promoted in an active and steady manner while a new countryside must be constructed. Both tracks must be pursued in parallel.

In October 2005, the CPC Central Committee's *Proposal for Formulating the 12th Five-Year Plan for China's Economic and Social Development (2011-2015)* was issued at the 5th plenary session of the 11th Central Committee of the CPC. As part of the proposal, the CPC pointed out that a new socialist countryside will be one of China's major historic missions in modernization. Aiming at advanced production, affluent living, civilized rural communities, a clean and tidy village environment and democratic administration, steady progress will be made in building a new socialist countryside in accordance with local conditions, reality and farmers' wishes.

This begs the question: how to build such a new countryside? At the 4th plenary session of the 16th Central Committee of the CPC in 2004, 'two trends' were raised based on an analysis of the development experience of industrialized countries. In the initial stage of industrialization, agriculture serves as a supporting force for the growth of industry (manufacturing) while, when the country has become industrialized, manufacturing begins to 'reciprocate', or boost, agriculture, and cities support rural areas, resulting in balanced development between urban and rural areas. In December 2012 the Central Economic Work Conference asserted that China had entered the development stage when manufacturing would boost agriculture and cities drive the development of rural areas. In November 2012 the 18th CPC National Congress report stated that urban and rural integration would be the fundamental solution for solving issues relating to agriculture, farmers and the rural areas. China will further promote urban and rural integration, boost rural development, narrow the gap between urban and rural areas, and promote their common prosperity.

China's industrialization started with heavy industry which was taken as the first step to get rid of economic backwardness right after the founding of the PRC. At that time, the socio-economic development level was very low. In 1952, China's GDP per capita was just over US$50; the agricultural labor force accounted for 83.5% of the total labor force and the net agricultural output was 70% of the country's total. Therefore, agriculture was the major source of income to fund industrialization. It is estimated that in the 29 years leading up to 1979, the agricultural sector had provided Rmb450bn (US$72bn) for industrialization. This policy was necessary and effective overall, but the backward technologies of agricultural production would not have been developed if this long process had lasted any longer. Moreover, the longstanding separation between urban and rural areas hindered the free exchange of production factors. The huge rural labor force was confined to rural areas, and farmers were in fact excluded from China's industrialization. As a result of separate household registration systems, the rights and opportunities were imbalanced and the urban-rural gap was widening. Although the relationship between urban and rural areas has gradually improved since reform and opening up started in 1978, agriculture and the rural areas have remained underprivileged in terms of resource allocation and income distribution as well as development opportunities. The urban-rural separation as a byproduct of a planned economy has remained unchanged. Therefore, the imbalances between agriculture and industry and between urban and rural development have kept the urban-rural gap very wide.

Since the early 21st century, China has made great achievements in industrialization. China's GDP per capita has reached more than US$1,000; the output value of agriculture to non-agriculture is about 15:85; employment in the agricultural and non-agricultural sectors is about 50:50; and the urbanization level has reached 40%. These four indicators show that China has entered the middle stage of industrialization when the non-agricultural industries have taken the place of the agriculture sector as the leading segment in the national economy mix and serve as the driving force for national economic growth. According to international experience, this is the right time to implement a policy for industry to support agriculture. For example, before the Second World War, agriculture provided a strong support to industrial development in Japan. Since the late 1950s and the early 1960s, industry began to fuel the agriculture sector. In the mid-1960s, Korea depended on the agricultural sector to support industry. Since the late 1960s, the tables have turned.

The implementation of a policy for industry to support agriculture depends, on the one hand, on the level of China's industrialization, and on the other hand, on the uniqueness and complexity of China's agriculture and rural areas. Agriculture remains a weak link in the national economy due to its low productivity. More than 60% of China's population live in rural areas where the living standards and the development of education, science and technology, culture and health lag far behind the urban areas. Besides these disparities, the rural areas are faced with tougher challenges to build an affluent society. According to historical experience, farmers' wellbeing determines whether China will have sound development. Only by accelerating the economic development of agriculture and rural areas, especially by increasing farmers' incomes, strengthening grassroots democracy in rural areas, and building a harmonious and healthy countryside to ensure the majority of farmers live a sound life, can China achieve a stable rural society and long-term national stability.

In *Opinions of the CPC Central Committee and the State Council on Promoting the Construction of a New Socialist Countryside* issued in February 2012, together with other official documents, a number of significant measures and solutions were proposed to solve the underlying problems concerning the construction of the new countryside.[1]

The key concept of building a new countryside is to balance urban and rural development and to integrate the separate urban and rural systems by breaking down the institutional barriers. Agricultural development should be considered within the context of the entire national economy, rural advancement should be considered as an important part of national progress, and the increase of farmers' incomes should be given more weight within the distribution and redistribution system of national income while the country formulates plans on development policies, public resources, infrastructure and the industrial mix.

---

[1] See Appendix 1 to Chapter Three: The 11th Five-Year Plan: The Key Project of Building a New Socialist Countryside

The new countryside will be built according to local demand and the wishes of the public, while equal importance will be given to the rural areas both near and remote, and the local features will be highlighted. Efforts must be made to systematically plan counties, towns and villages, while rural infrastructure construction and social development should be balanced to create better and happier living conditions in rural areas.

I. Strengthening the Construction of Rural Infrastructure

By the end of 2005, there were still 50,000 villages without road access in China, half of villages nationwide had no access to tap water (centralized water supply), 300m rural residents had no safe drinking water, more than 60% of rural households had no access to sanitary toilets, and 2% of villages had no electric power supply. Therefore, in building a new countryside, particular importance was attached to building infrastructure.

Since 2006, the central government has substantially increased the investment in rural biogas and provided funding for village development planning and pilot villages. A guiding catalog has been formulated based on local circumstances for village development and environmental rehabilitation, especially for providing access to drinking water, roads, power and fuel. The government has helped farmers to separate residential and livestock living areas. Safe drinking water projects have been accelerated. The construction of the rural road network is being strengthened with the aim of making all towns and villages nationwide accessible by tarmac (cement roads), making all villages in eastern and central China accessible by tarmac (cement) roads, and making all villages in western China accessible by road, and a system of rural road management and protection is being established. Efforts are being made to promote renewable energy, including farmer household biogas, straw-fired biomass power generation, small hydro power stations, solar panels and wind turbines as well as the construction of rural power grids. A universal service fund has been established to enhance the construction of rural data networks, the development of rural post and telecommunications with the aim of making every village accessible by telephone and every town accessible by internet. In accordance with the requirements of land efficiency, complete facilities, environmental protection, energy efficiency and outstanding features, the government is making scientific plans for rural construction, guiding farmers to build their own houses on an appropriate basis and to maintain the original rural landscape.

By the end of 2010, safe drinking water had been made available for 210m rural people; electricity supply with urban standards had been made available to most rural areas; newly built and rebuilt roads reached more than 1.86m km in total; biogas use reached 40m households; and rural housing projects had been successfully promoted.

According to the 12th Five-Year Plan, the central government is committed to building a new countryside which has: safe drinking water, clean energy, convenient transport, comfortable housing and a clean environment. Basic rural infrastructure construction is being strengthened accordingly, as are rural living and production conditions.

1. Improving rural drinking water safety. Great importance must be attached to the water supply and safety in the construction of drinking water facilities including centralized, non-centralized and urbanized water supply systems in rural areas. By 2015, the proportion of rural population with access to centralized water supply will be about 80%. Efforts will also be made to strengthen the operation and management of drinking water projects, to identify people responsible for its management and protection, and to enhance water conservation and quality monitoring to ensure farmers will enjoy long-term benefit from these drinking water projects.

2. Strengthening rural electric power construction. The rural power grid will be upgraded to improve power supply reliability and capacity in rural areas. The equalization of public power services will be accelerated between urban and rural areas with the aim of eliminating gaps in power prices and power supply. To provide nationwide public power services, power facilities will be constructed in areas where people have no access to electric power. On the premise of protecting the ecology and the interests of farmers, small hydro power projects will be carried out with scientific planning and orderly development; counties fully equipped with electric power (electrified, so to speak) will be established; small hydro power facilities will be built to take the place of fuel facilities based on the local conditions; power grids will be built to support rural hydro power facilities.

3. Promoting biogas-focused clean energy in rural areas. To increase biogas penetration in rural areas, household biogas use and development will be promoted, and management and service systems for biogas facilities will be improved. Clean energy will match the rapid development of large-scale animal husbandry. Small and large-scale biogas projects will be pushed forward. Efforts will be made in the research and development of key biogas technologies and efficient use of biogas residue and slurry. To establish a clean, economical and convenient energy system in the rural areas, traditional wood and coal-fired brick beds will be transformed to increase energy efficiency; large straw-based energy projects will be promoted; and newly-built houses will use solar water heating and solar cookers.

4. Enhancing rural road construction. Road construction projects will be continued to make all villages in eastern and central China and 80% of the villages in the western area accessible to tarmac (cement) roads. County and town-level roads will be rebuilt and connected to each other to form a rural road network and increase mobility. Rural and urban transport systems will be integrated to achieve 100% effective reach of buses between villages and towns, and to make 92% of villages accessible by bus. Efforts will be made in bridge and culvert construction, bridge renovation, bus station development and other projects supporting public transportation. Rural road safety, maintenance and management will be enhanced.

5. Enhancing rural housing construction. Local farmers are encouraged to build their own houses through various forms under legal provisions in qualified rural areas. A rural housing security system will be established to renovate more than 8m rundown buildings; to confirm targets and standards of subsidy for housing renovation; to strengthen project quality, safety control, archive management and registration of property rights. Housing shortfalls in state-owned reclamation areas, forest regions and forest farms shall be made up by upgrading shantytowns in the forest regions, and farms and rundown buildings in reclamation areas. The herdsmen settlement project will be continued, which aims to make adequate provisions to settle all herdsmen, including 246,000 homes for nomads. The fishermen settlement project will also be speeded up to provide homes ashore to fishermen who have lived on boats.

6. Continuing the support for rural poverty alleviation and immigrants from reservoir construction regions. According to the *China Poverty Alleviation and Development Program (2011-2020)*, investment will be increased in poverty alleviation and development, especially in large poverty-stricken areas; more support will be provided in old revolutionary base areas, regions inhabited by ethnic groups and border areas; development-oriented poverty alleviation policy will be implemented focused on integrating the development of poverty-stricken areas and the rural minimum living standard security system; subsistence will be made available to the impoverished and measures will be taken to help them get rich as soon as possible. Policies to support the resettlement of immigrants from reservoir building regions will be implemented by increasing financial integration and investment, developing infrastructure and public services in reservoir and resettlement areas, and continuously improving living conditions and developing social facilities in resettlement areas. Pilot projects will be carried out to address the challenges of the poorest immigrants and to give them secure housing and development opportunities.

Wenchuan County, Sichuan: new rural transformation for a new life

Wenchuan County is located in southeast Aba Prefecture in the northwest of Sichuan Province. Breathtaking natural scenic sites in Sichuan, such as Jiuzhaigou Valley, Huanglong Scenic and Historic Interest Area, Mount Siguniang, and prairies are all within easy reach of Wenchuan County. Before it was hit by the earthquake in May 2008, Wenchuan housed 105,436 inhabitants, including 67,438 rural inhabitants and 36,705 people of Qiang minority in 6 towns, 7 villages, and 118 administrative villages within its 4,084sq km administrative area. Acclaimed as the 'hometown of Yu the Great, home of the giant panda, and the place of origin of Qiang ethnic embroidery', Wenchuan is the industrial base of Aba Prefecture and one of the four regions in China in which Qiang people live in tightly-knit communities.

On May 12, 2008, however, a major earthquake struck Wenchuan County, causing catastrophic damage with direct economic losses amounting to Rmb64.3bn (US$9.2bn). Under the firm leadership of the CPC Central Committee and the State Council and the government and party committees of Sichuan Province and Aba Prefecture, the rescue work achieved positive results and the post-disaster reconstruction was carried out smoothly and fruitfully. Economic recovery has been achieved and social stability has been maintained.

Aiming at developing agritourism and rural tourism, during its reconstruction after the earthquake, Wenchuan is committed to developing specialized farming, modern animal husbandry, forestry, and farm products processing, trying to establish a new type of villages and agriculture, which means 'every village has a specialty' and 'every county has a key economic driver'. At the same time, efforts have been made to develop major industries, mobilize major enterprises and establish local brands. Wenchuan aims to build up a modern farming system. Plantations of cherries, kiwi fruit and flowers have been built, which in turn have driven the planting of tea, traditional Chinese medical plants and the development of aquaculture. Efforts have also been made to establish a demonstration area of modern agriculture on the Min River. Within the next five years, unremitting efforts will be made to establish a 50,000 mu (3,333 hectares) kiwi fruit production base with a production capacity of over 10,000 tonnes, a 30,000-mu (2,000 hectares) cherry production base with a production capacity

Wenchuan, rebuilt after the earthquake

of over 10,000 tonnes, a modern animal husbandry base housing about 10m chickens, ducks, pigs, and goats a year, and a flower base along the arid valley area producing about 10m flowers and plants.

By June 2011, in Wenchuan, there were already 20,000 mu (1,333 hectares) of cherry plantations, 30,000 mu (2,000 hectares) of kiwi fruit plantations, 5,000 mu (333 hectares) of flower gardens, 5,000 mu (333 hectares) of tea fields, 15,000 mu (1,000 hectares) of pollution-free vegetable fields, and 40,000 mu (2,667 hectares) of improved hybrid corn fields. Four types of food produced in Wenchuan are certified as green foods; 384 families are raising poultry and livestock on a large scale, each having pens and coops totaling an area of 23.25sq km, earning about Rmb16,000 (US$2,578) annually. There are two newly established bacon processing factories, four large farms, two communities raising poultry and livestock on a large scale, 70 main roads in rural areas stretching 400km, and 112 water projects have been completed to provide drinking water to about 66,500 people in the countryside.

The 12th Five-Year Plan: construction of key rural infrastructure projects

Drinking Water

Safe drinking water will be supplied through centralized and local drinking water distribution systems and by extending urban water pipes to 30m rural residents (including teachers and students in rural schools and people in state-owned farm and forestry stations).

Power Supply

The rural power grids will be renovated and those that cannot meet the increasing electricity demand will be upgraded. Some 1,000 model solar-powered villages will be built, 200 green-energy counties will be established, 300 counties will be electrified with new villages powered by hydro-electricity, and the installed generating capacity of hydropower stations will be increased by 10GW.

Road construction

A total of 1m km of roads will be built or renovated in rural areas, making all administrative villages in eastern and central China and 80% of administrative villages in western China accessible via tarmac or concrete roads.

Biogas Engineering

Household biogas, small biogas projects, large biogas projects and related service systems will be built, making biogas available to more than half of the households in rural areas.

Housing

Some 8m rundown homes in rural areas will be renovated. Accommodation will be provided for employees of state-owned reclamation areas, forest regions and forestry stations. Also 246,000 apartments will be provided for the settlement of nomads and the final aim is for all nomads in China to have a permanent home.

Clean Countryside

Organic waste will be disposed of and recycled properly, while non-organic waste will be collected and transported in a centralized manner. At the same time, rural area afforestation and ground hardening will also be carried out.

Source: China's 12th Five-Year Plan for Rural Economic Development, NDRC, June 2012

II. Accelerating the Development of Social Undertakings in Rural Areas

During the 11th Five-Year Plan period (2006-2010), China strengthened universal compulsory education. No tuition fees are charged for rural students receiving compulsory education, and free books and boarding subsidies are provided for impoverished ones. Compulsory education in rural areas falls into the public finance security system, and a system has been established to ensure that education funds are secure. The central and local governments are all responsible for implementing such a system. The responsibilities of governments at all levels are specified, finance spending on this matter has been expanded, and related procedures have been carried out step by step to better ensure its security. Rural teacher training programs have been carried out, and 50% of teachers in rural areas have attended a professional training program. Related institutions in cities have been encouraged to help farmers by teaching them relevant knowledge, and sending more teachers from cities to teach in rural areas. Distance learning has been introduced in rural primary and middle schools.

We will continue to improve the healthcare infrastructure in rural areas, especially in the township hospitals and clinics, and develop the health service and medical aid systems in villages, townships and counties. Medical workers in rural areas have been trained, and doctors in cities have been encouraged to provide medical services in rural areas. Systems providing medicine and monitoring the sales of medicine have been established. Illnesses such as avian influenza have been guarded against and properly treated. Family planning management and service systems in rural areas have been improved and rural families are taught that 'having fewer children means getting rich faster' and those who comply with family planning are awarded.

We will enhance the setup of cultural centers, libraries and reading rooms in townships and counties. Projects to extend radio and television coverage to every village and to play movies in villages will be carried out. By 2010, all villages with more than 20 families had access to radio and television. Every month, one movie is screened in every village. Fitness programs encouraging farmers to exercise will be conducted. Farmers' lives have been greatly enriched now that there are cinemas, cultural centers and libraries in their neighborhood. Village affairs are publicized and public opinion is solicited in policy-making processes, so that villagers can exercise their rights to be informed, participate, administer and monitor.

We will carry out more training programs to produce more well educated farmers with professional skills and management competence. Technology courses will also be provided to farmers to enhance their skills and knowledge. Professional training will be made available to farmers so that farmers can find other employment opportunities. A host of new farmers who have outstanding farming, craftsmanship, business operation, and technical knowledge will be cultivated through various training programs.

In the 12th Five-Year Plan period (2011-2015), the construction of a new socialist countryside has made remarkable achievements in improving educational standards, making the countryside cleaner, enriching the life of villagers, and providing equal opportunities to farmers in finding jobs, so as to promote social undertakings in rural areas, lift the moral standards of the rural population and achieve comprehensive rural development.

1. Improving education in rural areas. We have allocated more public educational resources to rural areas, border areas, poor areas, ethnic minority areas and revolutionary base areas. Necessary primary schools and the like will be maintained. Facilities in rural schools have been upgraded to improve teaching expertise and accommodate more boarding students, and teachers there are carefully chosen and trained to improve educational results and to realize more balanced educational development across a whole county. Meals contain better nutrition and free books and boarding are provided for rural students receiving compulsory education, and impoverished ones receive boarding subsidies. We will accelerate promotion of universal high school education in rural areas and implement the policy of providing secondary vocational education to rural students free of charge. We will develop pre-school education in rural areas, building more kindergartens so that universal pre-school education can be realized and children can be taken care of in kindergartens. Professional training will be carried out on a large scale in rural areas so that by 2015, we will have produced 13m farmers who excel at farming, business operation and technical knowledge.

2. Improving medical and health systems. We will bring more medical and health resources to the rural areas. Medical and health service systems consisting of county and town-level hospitals and clinics will be improved. In such systems, county hospitals form the core, which will be responsible for disease prevention and control, and health monitoring. Basic centralized medical services will be provided to rural areas free of charge. A rural women's hospital childbirth subsidy will be implemented. Major infectious diseases, chronic diseases, occupational diseases, endemic diseases and mental illness will be brought under control. An emergency system will be built in the rural areas to better cope with health-related crises.

3. Promoting cultural activities and sports. China will adopt related policies and establish agencies to promote the development of cultural activities and sports in rural areas. Cultural infrastructure will be upgraded so as to offer movies, books, papers and plays to rural residents free of charge. More radio and television stations will be built to extend coverage to villages with fewer than 20 families and that have electricity but no television, and to bring satellite TV to rural areas with no broadband access. More village bookstores and bulletin boards will be built and more activities with local characteristics will be carried out. We will promote fitness, exercize and and improve sports facilities.

4. Providing employment services. We will improve employment services in both urban and rural areas, develop a platform where labor in rural areas can get help in finding employment. Services such as advice regarding job hunting and career development, and employment and unemployment registration will be provided to farmers who want to find non-farming jobs. An employment network that is multi-functional, inclusive, and easily available to farmers will be established.

Haidong, Qinghai, offers training programs for job hunters

Haidong district in Qinghai Province, western China, lies to the east of Qinghai Lake. With a population of 1.62m, Haidong covers an area of 13,200sq km, including Ping'an District, Ledu District, Minhe-Hui Ethnic and Tu Ethinic Autonomous County, Hualong-Hui Ethnic Autonomous County, and Xunhua-Salar Ethnic Autonomous County. Its GDP in 2011 reached Rmb21.937bn (US$3.33bn), and the average annual net per capita income of rural residents was Rmb4,599.83 (US$708).

In recent years, governments in Haidong have put employment high on their agenda, and have been committed to promoting training programs to raise the qualifications of the labor force in both urban and rural areas so they can find suitable jobs or start their own businesses.

Professional training projects are conducted to develop talented people. In conducting professional training, which includes programs such as the 'sunshine project' and the 'rainfall project', rural laborers have received training so that they can do non-farming jobs, and migrant workers can receive training for employment and business start-ups. About 184,000 rural workers, 79,000 migrant workers, 76,000 laid-off workers, and 3,068 people who want to start their own businesses have taken part in such training programs.

In the past, farmers mainly went from one place to another within the district to find short-term or part-time manual jobs that required a physically strong body. Now, they have been turned into well qualified workers who are fit for long-term jobs where they can make use of their skills. Labor transfer has become well organized and many people have started their own businesses. The aim of making workers mobile and helping them find jobs, settle down, and become well-off is being realized. The economy has been stimulated and poverty has been reduced. Local brands such as 'Hualong Beef Noodle' and 'Xunhua Salar Resturant' have gained an increasing reputation. Over the past years, more and more people have discovered other ways than farming to make a living, and their income has been getting higher as they become more skilled, representing a good momentum for economic growth. In 2012, making beef noodles and picking cotton and wolfberries were major sources of demand for labor, so Haidong government organized migrant workers and sent 61,111 of them to pick cotton in Xinjiang Province and 24,758 to pick wolfberries in Haixi City while providing necessary assistance to them. This employment produced a total income of Rmb420m (US$66.7m).

It is estimated that by the end of the 12th Five-Year Plan period, 60,000 people will have found new jobs and three million jobs will have been created for migrant workers, bringing services income to Rmb5bn (US$800m). The unemployment rate is under 3.5%. In all, 240,000 people will have received professional training, including 40,000 laid-off workers, 160,000 farmers and 15,000 people who want to start their own business.

III. Raising the Rural Social Security Level

In the 11th Five-Year Plan period (2006-2010), China established a pension insurance system in rural areas to align the level of development in rural areas with social security elsewhere. A new rural cooperative healthcare system has been established in the rural areas. A basic living allowance has been allocated to people living below the poverty line in some areas. Social assistance systems have been set up to provide a living allowance, aid relief or assistance in the form of food, clothing, medical care, housing and burial subsidies.

By the end of 2010, social welfare in rural areas had been improved, basic living allowance systems had been set up, 96.3% of rural residents were covered by the new rural cooperative medical care system, pilot programs to explore new pension insurance systems had been carried out in 24% of rural areas, and more than 50m rural residents had been included in a basic living allowance. Poverty alleviation and economic development in poverty-stricken areas have produced obvious effects.

During the 12th Five-Year Plan period (2011-2015), we will further expand social security in rural areas to meet people's basic needs and cover more people while making it more flexible and sustainable so that rural residents can enjoy medical and old-age care and get access to necessary aid in difficult times.

1. Establishing and upgrading the old-age insurance system in rural areas and making sure that every rural resident is covered by such insurance. Farmers' land can only be expropriated after basic living allowances have been provided to them. China will establish new old-age as well as healthcare insurance systems for rural areas and urban areas, and come up with a way to transfer insurance between the insurance systems in urban and rural areas so that both systems can develop at the same pace and eventually be integrated.

2. Perfecting a new type of cooperative health care insurance system. The per capita contribution and fiscal allowance rate will be gradually increased, and the average reimbursement rate and maximum amounts will be increased accordingly. We will improve the medical aid systems in rural areas, scaling up the amount and coverage of aid and grants. We will enhance the connection and integration of the urban and rural medical insurance systems, and encourage areas with appropriate conditions to build up an integrated medical insurance system.

3. Consolidating construction of the social aid system. China will enhance the basic living allowance system, giving all eligible rural senior residents access to assistance in the form of food, clothing, medical care, housing and burial subsidies. These senior residents can choose to stay at home or in a government nursing home. The amount of basic living allowance will be raised in accordance with price trends, and the average annual increase will reach 10%. The system of aid and relief will also be upgraded to provide disabled people in rural areas with more assistance and subsidies to help them live a better life. China will move faster to establish systems to offer help to rural residents in reproduction and child-raising, and provide related assistance to accident victims.

IV. Improving Rural Environment Conservation and Rehabilitation

During the 11th Five-Year Plan period, China made progress in ecological conservation and environmental protection. We have afforested 25.27m hectares of land, raising the forest coverage to 20.36%. Desertification was halted on 230,000 sq km of land. Soil erosion was basically brought under control with 0.817m more sq km of land eroded. A total of 80.17m sq km of grassland that showed symptoms of degeneration, desertification and salinization have been improved. Some 32.4m more sq km of grazing land have been returned to grassland. There are 2,588 nature reserves across the country and 50% of wetlands are under protection. Major progress has been made in ecological rehabilitation of rivers and lakes. Pollution prevention and control, and environment improvement in rural areas are being carried out.

During the 12th Five-Year Plan period, China will make vigorous efforts in developing circular agriculture, promoting clean agriculture and the reuse of agricultural waste. We will promote soil testing so as to determine appropriate fertilizers and encourage farmers to use green fertilizers and to use fertilizers more reasonably. We will promote pest control and recommend the use of biological pesticides and effective, low-toxicity pesticides with low residues. We will recycle agricultural plastic film and packaging, promote the reuse of straw, design farms scientifically, strengthen the prevention and treatment of pollution from animal and poultry farming and aquaculture, monitor soil pollution and treat it effectively to prevent environmental pollution in rural areas.

In places where garbage can be collected and disposed of in a centralized manner, every family will divide their garbage into different categories before dumping it into trash cans, and the village will collect the garbage which will be transported by related township agencies to the county where garbage is disposed of. In other places, garbage will be classified at the point of origin, minimized on the spot and eventually recycled. We will improve the treatment of polluted water in rural areas, and water pollution in big villages or areas near cities will be treated in a centralized way. We will promote the Clean Countryside Project, improving the sanitation and living environment of rural residents. By 2015, 60,000 administrative villages will have completed environmental rehabilitation. Industrial pollution from rural factories will be monitored more rigorously, and urban industrial pollution and other types of pollution will not be spread to rural areas.

Anji: building a new ecological, cultural, beautiful countryside

Anji County is located in northwestern Zhejiang Province 223km from Shanghai and 65km from Hangzhou. The county covers an area of 1,886sq km with a population of 460,000, of which 76% live in rural areas. It consists of 10 towns, 5 villages, 1 subdistrict and 1 provincial economic development zone. Anji is famous for white tea, chair production and bamboo flooring. It was China's first national ecologically advanced county. A number of ecological projects and a pilot program of sustainable development have been carried out, and a national model of beautiful villages and a national model of agritourism and rural tourism have been built there. It is also hailed as one of China's civil counties, clean counties, green counties, and one of Zhejiang's forest counties. It was the first county in China to be granted the 'China Human Habitat Award' and the 'UN Habitat Scroll of Honour Award'. It has been awarded the 'Yangtse Delta Investment Hotspot (Special Prize)' for two consecutive years.

Since 2008, Anji has been implementing the 'Beautiful Countryside Project', trying to make at least 85% of its villages beautiful with the aim of becoming model new socialist villages with a clean environment, affluent life and harmonious communities.

Anji has focused on the following elements: first, beautiful scenery as an advantage to make all villages sightseeing attractions; second, industrial development to modernize villages and improve people's living conditions, which in turn will benefit the conservation of scenery; third, making each village unique; fourth, overall development and planning of the county to make every village and every family part of a bigger transformation plan. In making villages beautiful, every town and village will do its part in accordance with the overall plan while their unique conditions are taken into consideration to meet the goal of development and making ecological improvements.

Anji's GDP in 2011 reached Rmb22.2bn (US$3.4bn). Government revenues amounted to Rmb2.91bn (US$448m) including Rmb1.67bn (US$257m) of local government revenues, ranking ahead of Huzhou City, and at the forefront of Zhejiang Province. The average disposable income of urban residents reached Rmb280,000 (US$43,077), while that of rural residents reached Rmb140,000

Scenic Majianong village in Anji attracts lots of visitors

(US$21,538), which are well above the average of Zhejiang Province. Its environmental conditions are getting better and better as a result of its ecological efforts. Aiming at a better environment, a higher industrialized level, higher civilization and better services, Anji has built a number of infrastructure facilities that benefit local residents, and has made significant progress with a characteristic rural economy, rural professional cooperatives, modern household industry and rural tourism. In addition to its titles as China's bamboo county and ecological county, Anji is starting to be famous for its beautiful villages since carrying out the 'Beautiful Countryside Project' which has brought enormous benefits to its people, and it has become a model for other counties.

Kang Hongliang, the secretary of the CPC's Yutiao Branch, said that Yutiao village has undergone great changes since people started the beautiful village construction. The environment is clean now that everyone knows the importance of good sanitation. In the past, few people would choose remote villages like Yutiao as a travel destination, but now on weekends and holidays, every farmhouse is full of tourists. Beautiful villages have made them rich.

V. Improving Rural Development System Mechanisms

During the 11ᵗʰ Five-Year Plan period, China made breakthroughs with
the reform program in rural areas. The agricultural tax has been abolished,
investment in agriculture, rural development and the well-being of farmers
have been increased significantly, the coverage and size of agricultural
subsidies has been expanded, the mechanism for protecting the prices of
major agricultural products has been improved, and the policies supporting
and protecting agriculture have been upgraded. Reform of collective forest
property rights has been advanced, 3.3bn *mu* (220m hectares) of grassland has
been contracted to non-government operators, there has been comprehensive
reform in rural areas and the reform of the rural financial system has been
intensified.

Meanwhile, new steps have been taken to balance urban and rural
development. Some institutional barriers separating urban and rural areas
have been eliminated. Migrant workers can find better jobs now. In China,
there are 242m migrant workers, 153m of whom are working outside their
hometowns. Migrant workers have become an important force driving
urbanization which is now accelerating. The integration of urban and rural
planning, industry layout, infrastructure development, public services,
employment and social administration has also accelerated. Rural-urban
integration is a clear trend.

However, essential reform goals in rural areas have not been completely
realized and the systemic separation between rural and urban areas still exists.
Certain policies are still obstructing the balanced distribution of resources
between rural and urban areas. So, during the 12ᵗʰ Five-Year Plan period,
China will make unremitting efforts to carry out reforms in the rural areas and
adopt innovative policies so as to sustain and upgrade the current operational
systems in the countryside, let the market play a basic role in distributing
resources and strengthen the macroscopic readjustment and control of rural
development. An economic system will be built up in the rural areas that
meets the demand of the socialist market economy to revitalize the rural
economy.

**1. Establishing a mechanism to ensure investment in agriculture, rural
areas and farmers continues to increase.** The central government has
stipulated that the increase of investment in agriculture will surpass the rate
of increase in regular government revenues. The government's budget for
infrastructure investment will prioritize agricultural and rural infrastructure

development. The revenues from land leasing will be used for the development of agricultural land and the construction of infrastructure in rural areas. The increase of investment in agricultural technology will also surpass the increase of regular government revenues, so the agricultural R&D investment as a percentage of added value from agriculture will increase. From 2003 to 2012, the central government invested more than Rmb6 trillion (US$1 trillion) in agriculture, rural areas and farmers, which played a big role in boosting agriculture, rural areas and farmers during the golden period of development. The central government's investment in agriculture, rural areas, and farmers has increased from Rmb214.4bn (US$35bn) in 2003, accounting for 13.7% of fiscal expenditure, to Rmb1.228 trillion (US$190bn) in 2012, accounting for 19.2% of fiscal expenditure, representing an annual increase of 21%, 4.5 percentage points higher than the increase of regular fiscal expenditure.

Figure 3-1: Central Government expenditure on agriculture, rural areas and farmers from 2005 to 2012 (Rmb x billion)

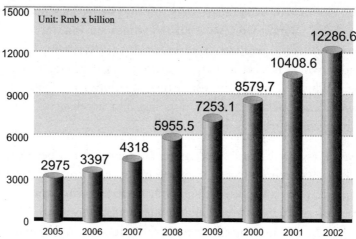

Source: People's Daily, January 22, 2013

(Unit: Rmb x billion

Vertical axis figures: 300, 600, 1,200, 1,500

Graph figures: 297.5, 339.7, 431.8, 595.55, 725.31, 857.97, 1,040.86, 1,228.66)

We will strictly implement the policy that the extra revenue gained from increased taxes on land use will be used solely for agricultural development. We will comply with relevant policy on accounting, withdrawal and use of land leasing income for the development of agricultural land and the construction of irrigation and water conservancy facilities. We will strictly implement the policy that the land use fee of increased building sites will be used solely for the development of farmland and land consolidation. We will try to expand the investment in agriculture by encouraging and guiding private investment in agriculture and rural areas.

2. Continuing and improving the basic rural operation system. We will continue the dual system in which the household contract responsibility system will be the foundation and unified operation coexists with individual operation. We will improve the legal and policy framework for rural land contracts, advance reform of the collective forest ownership system, improve the system of grassland contracts, and improve the household contract responsibility system covering farmland, forest and grassland. We will maintain the current land contracts, make sure that farmers have contracts and certificates in their hands, and that farmers have full operating rights over contracted farmland. We will make sure that farmers have the right to use and benefit from contracted land. We will improve the market for transferring contracted land on the basis of voluntary participation and better service, allowing farmers to subcontract, rent out, exchange, transfer or form partnerships on contracted land to form appropriate scale operations. We will support the development of farmers' professional cooperatives and leading agricultural enterprises. We will strengthen the system of social services and make farmers' operations more organized.

3. Improving farmland management reform. We will promote the confirmation, registration and certificate issuance concerning the ownership of collective rural land, the use right of house-building sites and the use right of collective construction sites. We will improve the administration system for the use of rural house-building land, strictly forbidding the excessive use of land for house building. We will make good use of the current plots of house-building land on the basis that farmers' rights are protected. We will establish mechanisms for compensating farmers once they give up their extra house-building plots. The extra house-building plots and other extra land will be reconverted to farmland and those being turned into collective construction land will be developed in accordance with the overall plan and be subject to the annual construction land quota. Moreover, the need for collective construction will be met in the first place. Pilot projects linking urban and rural construction land will be better regulated and strictly controlled regarding their coverage and size, and the added value of land used for collective construction will be invested in the development of rural areas.

We will establish a unified market for urban and rural construction land plots. We will reform policies on land expropriation, non-profit construction and for-profit construction will be strictly defined and separated, the scope of land expropriation will be reduced, land expropriation will be conducted in compliance with legal procedures, and the compensation system for land expropriation will be improved to increase the amount of compensation under a unified pricing system and make sure the compensation is delivered quickly and in the full amount to village collectives and individual farmers. If, other than planned urban construction, there are for-profit construction projects using collective rural land with approval, farmers will be allowed to participate in the operation of such projects in various legal ways and their legal rights will be protected. The use right of rural collective land for for-profit construction projects will be transferred in the unified urban market of state-owned land. Collective land that is legally obtained for for-profit construction in rural areas will be transferred through the unified land market in an open way and enjoy the same status as state-owned land provided that the land use is compliant with planning.

4. Renovating financial systems to assist rural development. We will stipulate more financial policies in favor of rural development. We will come up with more financing tools and accelerate the combined use of commercial financing, cooperative financing and policy-based financing. We will establish a safe adequately funded rural finance system and provide a multitude of good services. Savings in rural areas will be guided toward investment in the development of agriculture and the rural areas. Loans will be given mainly to local borrowers and the Agricultural Development Bank of China and Postal Savings Bank of China will expand their agriculture-related business. These banks will provide services to farmers, agriculture and rural areas, and their scope of services will be stabilized and expanded. We will deepen the reform of Rural Credit Cooperatives, making full use of their role as the main service providers for farmers, agriculture and rural areas. We will ease access for rural finance service providers, and encourage financial institutions to provide services to rural areas. We will accelerate the establishment of township banks, loan companies, and rural mutual cooperatives, and encourage the establishment of community banks at the county level in certain areas. We will develop small-loan institutions in rural areas. We will strengthen the credit system in rural areas, and allow more warrants. We will develop insurance systems in rural areas and improve related regulations. We will support eligible enterprises with business in rural areas and related fields to go public.

5. Deepening comprehensive reform of the rural areas. We will press ahead with reform of the collective forest ownership system and the stated-owned forest ownership system, and improve the grassland contract system. We will draw experience from pilot projects for comprehensive reforms in both rural and urban areas, and actively explore new ways for addressing issues regarding agriculture, rural areas and farmers.

6. Institutional innovation to promote urbanization development. We will intensify reform of the household registration system, and gradually give citizenship status to migrant workers and their families who have been working and staying in urban areas for a long time. We will relax the restrictions on obtaining urban resident status in small and medium-sized cities to gradually meet the needs of rural residents to settle in urban areas. We will continue to experiment with the establishment of a unified urban-rural household registration system. We will provide better services to migrant workers who don't meet the requirements for obtaining citizenship, making sure that public services are provided to all residents instead of just to registered citizens there. We will make sure that the children of migrant workers have equal access to compulsory education, and come up with a way for them to further their education. We will include migrant workers that have stable employment into the system of basic old-age insurance and medical insurance. We will expand the coverage of work-related injury insurance, unemployment insurance and maternity insurance particularly to include migrant workers and workers in private institutions. We will improve the housing conditions of migrant workers through various ways and encourage various possible means for eligible migrant workers to be included in urban housing insurance. We will take effective measures to solve issues involving second-generation migrant workers. We will push forward pilot projects giving greater autonomy to county governments, increasing the proportion of county-level finance schemes in regional (provincial) finance distribution. In certain areas, county governments may be directly supervised by provincial governments. We will give more rights to fast developing towns with large populations administrative rights to approve investment, business administration and social security.

Appendix I: The 11th Five-Year Plan; key projects in building a new socialist countryside:

The 11th Five-Year Plan (2006-2010): Key projects in building a new scialist countryside

Building grain, cotton and oil production bases and promoting high-quality food industry. *We will establish several large production bases in major grain-producing areas to continuously produce large amounts of good quality commodity grain. We will also continue to build cotton and oil production bases. We will build 10,000 mu (666.7 hectares) of standard farmland in the 13 major grain-producing areas and 484 main grain-producing counties, cultivating improved varieties, strengthening pest control and using advanced agricultural machinery.*

Fertile farmland. *We will make greater efforts to improve the quality of middle and low-yield farmland. We will establish model bases that use upgraded and innovative fertilizing technologies to increase yield.*

Vegetation protection. *We will establish county centers and provincial sub-centers of vegetation protection. We will set up several model bases that excel in preventing disasters, pesticide safety evaluation centers and regional centers for evaluating biotechnology.*

Upgrading facilities to support large irrigation areas and drainage pumping stations in Hunan, Hubei, Jiangxi and Anhui Provinces. *We will continue to build the supporting facilities in large irrigation areas and make them more water efficient. We will renovate and upgrade the drainage pumping stations in Hunan, Hubei, Jiangxi and Anhui Provinces.*

Planting and raising improved varieties. *We will establish a pool of crop varieties, crop variety transformation centers, new variety development bases, seed multiplication farms for livestock, poultry and aquatic products, aquatic breeding centers, and pools and centers of other products.*

Animal epidemic prevention. *We will establish systems for monitoring and early warning of epidemics, prevention and control, quarantine inspection, veterinary drugs quality and residue monitoring, technology support and material supply.*

Farm product quality evaluation system. *We will develop a national farm product quality standard and establish a testing and R&D center. We will establish regional, province-level and county-level farm products quality inspection centers.*

Safe drinking water. The existing problem whereby there are 100m rural residents drinking unsafe water that has excessive fluorine, arsenic or microbes, or that tastes bitter, or is polluted, and the problem that some areas are suffering from severe lack of water will be solved.

New roads. We will build and renovate 1.2m km of roads in rural areas with the aim of making all towns and administrative villages accessible by main roads.

Biogas in rural areas. We will transform the livestock pens, toilets and kitchens of rural households and build up biogas projects and biogas tanks. We will establish medium and large-scale biogas projects in some large-scale farms or communities.

Electricity supply and green energy. We will build 50 green-energy counties and make electricity generated by wind turbines, solar panels, small hydropower stations, or transferred via extending electricity networks, available to about 3.5m households and meet their demand for electric power supply.

Rural medical service system. We will build more county hospitals, maternity and child care institutions, county-level traditional Chinese medicine hospitals (or traditional ethnic hospitals), and especially more township clinics in central and western China.

Family planning system in rural areas. We will establish county-level family planning service centers, township family planning service centers and mobile service stations, especially in counties and towns in central and western China.

Transfer of surplus rural labor to other industries. We will provide more training programs and employment services to migrant workers and safeguard their legal rights. Migrant workers will have access to legal and policy inquiry services free of charge, job information, job advice and recommendations.

Chapter 4

How To Increase Chinese Farmers' Incomes and Make Them Rich

Ever since China introduced its policy of reform and opening up in 1978, Chinese rural residents have been enjoying a remarkable increase in income. From 2006 to 2010, their average annual income increased rapidly from less than Rmb3,000 (US$485) a year to Rmb5,919 (US$950), representing an average annual increase of 8.9% (adjusted for inflation) and the fastest growth since 1978. Their living standard has been improved too, spending on consumer durables has been growing exponentially and the consumption structure has upgraded. They also have better food, clothing, housing and transportation. Most impoverished people are sufficiently fed and clothed. However, the gap between the income of urban and rural residents has not been narrowed. In 2009, the absolute income disparity between urban and rural residents was Rmb12,000 (US$1,940); and the relative disparity rate has been expanded to 3.33 to 1. From 2010 to 2012, the income growth of rural residents has been growing faster than that of urban residents for three years in a row, by 10.9%, 11.4% and 10.7% respectively. And the income growth in the central and western regions is higher than that of the eastern region. The gap between the income of urban and rural residents has started to narrow since then. In 2012, the average annual net income of rural residents was Rmb7,917 (US$1,278).

In 2012, at the 18th National Party Congress, the goal was raised for GDP and the average income of both urban and rural areas to double by 2020 compared with 2010. In order to raise the income of Chinese people, the hard part is to raise the income of rural residents. Although, in recent years, rural residents' income has been rising rapidly for nine consecutive years, the growth is still lower than that of the national GDP and that of urban residents' income in the same period. Although in the last three years, the gap between the income of urban and rural residents has been narrowing, the gap is still wide. Besides, the standards and scope in accounting for the income of urban and rural residents are inconsistent. In terms of disposable income, the gap would be even wider. Even if the goal of doubling the income of Chinese people by 2020 is realized, the wide income gap would still exist. So in the future, the rural residents' income will have to grow at par with or even higher than that of urban residents in order to narrow the income gap.

To realize this goal, China will adopt proper policies to adjust the distribution system to put farmers in a favorable position in primary distribution and redistribution of wealth. We will also make sure that the price of farm products rises steadily and that the salaries of migrant workers are on the rise, too. We will increase agricultural investment and farmers' subsidies. We will find ways to help rural residents increase their incomes, in particular from non-farming jobs. We will improve economic development at the county level, and encourage rural residents to find jobs or start businesses outside their hometowns. We will also encourage migrant workers to go back to their hometowns where they can start a business. We will make great efforts to advance the property rights system reform in rural areas, safeguarding the rights of rural residents to benefit from collective resources and revenues.

I. Optimizing the Potential to Increase Rural Incomes

1. Raising the economic effects of agriculture through industrialization, guiding farmers to plant and breed scientifically, and developing high-quality and unique varieties.

Agricultural industrialization is a realistic path connecting 'small production' with 'big markets.' In many countries, there are fully-fledged agricultural cooperatives that provide various services to farmers before, during, and after the production of farm products. For example, in Japan, 90% of farmers are members of Japanese agricultural cooperatives. However, in China, such cooperatives are few. In developed countries, 90% of farm products are processed. In China, the percentage is only 30%. There are few large-scale industrialized agricultural companies, and there is no strong partnership between farmers and enterprises.

Therefore, we will strive to establish a complete industrialized agricultural system, covering all links in the production chain, in which cooperatives produce, process and sell farm products through big industrialized agricultural companies. Farmers can form contract-based partnerships with enterprises directly, or the collectives could buy, process and sell the products while farmers benefit from the revenues, so that the farmers could enjoy the added value from the processing and circulation of farm products.

Farmers' professional cooperatives can break through the difficult situation of 'small producers and big markets'

In 2007, Zhou Zhongchao, a farmer in Dali County, Shaanxi Province, set up a farmers' professional cooperative with other vegetable-growers in his village, and he named it after himself: 'Zhongchao Vegetable Cooperative'.

"There are many people in our village who plant onions, carrots, garlic, peppers and so on. But different people plant different varieties, and sell the plants on their own, making little revenue," Zhou said. For years, the failure in selling vegetables has gradually made people realize that the only way out is through cooperative production. For the last few years, those who joined the cooperative planted the same vegetables and sold these vegetables together. Now that is already a large-scale business. And more than 800 people have joined this cooperative.

Zhou said: "When there was no cooperative, 1kg of peppers could only sell for Rmb20 but now, since there is unified management, the peppers are branded and their quality is good, 1kg of peppers can generate Rmb40." Now farmers who join the cooperative can earn Rmb7,000 to Rmb8,000 per mu (0.067 hectare) of farmland.

In the past, every family worked on their own land so the quality and quantity of farm products varied. Now the production is organized through cooperatives, and the producing activities are adjusted in accordance with changes in the market. So the production could be increased to scale operation, and a standard is followed. At the same time, cooperatives can provide funds to farmers and supervise farmers, so the quality of farm products is guaranteed, and products gain credibility which brings more sales.

Experts believe that cooperatives can help famers gain more say in the market and extend the industrial chain. Relying more on market demand to decide what to produce, cooperatives can help farmers avoid producing blindly. Cooperatives can also help farmers form partnerships with supermarkets and schools, lowering the transportation cost and increasing farmers' incomes. According to the 'Report on the Development of China's Farmers' Professional Cooperatives 2006-2010', now farmers that join collectives earn 20% more than those who don't.

Source: http://news.xinhuanet.com/fortune/2011-10/30/c_111133437_3.htm

2. Diversifying agricultural business models, developing tourism, such as farm-stays, agritourism and handicrafts production, and utilizing beautiful scenery and unique customs in the countryside.

Chengdu develops agritourism to create 'Five Gold Flowers'

'Five Gold Flowers', an agritourism recreation area in Jinjiang District, Chengdu City, Sichuan Province, has become a model of agritourism. 'Five Gold Flowers', a 4-star tourist attraction, referring to five recreational farm stays named 'Flower Village', 'Forest of Plum Blossom', 'Jiang's Vegetable Garden', 'Chrysanthemum Village' and 'Moonlight Over the Lotus Pond', is located on the outskirts of Chengdu and includes six administrative villages: Hongsha, Xingfu, Wanfu, Fuma, Jiangjiayan and Da'anqiao, covering an area of 12sq km.

The reason why 'Five Gold Flowers' has developed so rapidly is because it forms a larg-scale coalition, avoiding the risks an individual farmer would face in the market. The five farm-stays have differentiated tourist attractions. Flower Village positions itself as an industrial base of flowers and holds various flower festivals to attract tourists. Moonlight Over the Lotus Pond has 1,074 mu (71.6 hectares) of water and the scenery here focuses on water, lotuses and frogs. Chrysanthemum Village, located in the hills, invites tourists to plant, enjoy chrysanthemum and eat related cuisine to ease their minds and spirits. Forest of Plum Blossom has 200,000 plum trees and attracts tourists to enjoy the beautiful plum blossom and learn more about plums in the plum blossom museum there. And Jiang's Vegetable Garden divides 500 mu (33.3 hectares) of farmland into small plots (0.1 mu each) and rents them to urban residents at Rmb800 (US$133) a year who want to plant things themselves or teach their children about agriculture but don't have the land.

Located at the buffer zone between urban and rural areas, the 'Five Gold Flowers' take advantage of tourism resources in the countryside and combine natural scenery with festivals, recreation, and cultural resources such as ancient towns, forming an agritourism zone that features farm stays, countryside hotels, national model agritourism spots, and ancient towns. It adds lustre to tourism in Chengdu City, shows there is a huge potential for agritourism and promotes the sustainable development of agritourism. The environment, folk customs and the ways of making a living in the countryside have seen changes. Agriculture is going along a path of large scale and industrialized development. The revenue *from farmland has increased remarkably. The annual income from growing grain was about Rmb200 to Rmb300 (US$33 to US$50) per mu (0.067 hectares), and the income from growing vegetables or flowers was Rmb2,000 to Rmb5,000 (US$333 to US$833) per mu, but now that figure has increased to more than Rmb10,000 (US$ 1,667).*

By developing tourism, more than 3,000 households (more than 11,500 people) are doing tourism-related jobs and have been registered as urban residents, and at the same time help 9,790 farmers to find non-farming jobs. This is conducive to advancing urban and rural integration, contributing to the development of commerce and services in this area. 'Five Gold Flowers' has generated nearly Rmb10m, giving a strong push to the economic development of this area.

New look of Hongsha Village of Sansheng Town, Jinjiang District, Chengdu City, Sichuan Province

3. Adjusting the agricultural structure, utilizing comparative advantages, encouraging 'one product per village', so as to build a number of villages and towns with distinctive features.

Shaanxi Province: 'One product per village' helps raise farmers' incomes

In April 2004, government leaders of Shaanxi Province signed contracts for economic cooperation and exchange with their Japanese counterpart Morihiko Hiramatsu from Oita City, introducing the concept of 'one product per village' to

Shaanxi. After a variety of investigations and research, the provincial government issued 'The Shaanxi Provincial Program To Establish Thousands More 'One Product Per Village' Model Villages'. Several years later, this movement has already made headway.

First, an industrial base has begun to take shape. By the end of 2010, 3,823 villages in Shaanxi Province had become 'one product per village' models, 186 villages had become 'one industry per village' models, and 20 provincial-level model villages featuring recreational attractions had been established. About 1.8m rural households and 5m people were involved in major agricultural undertakings, including growing grain, fruit or vegetables, raising livestock, handicrafts, processing farm products, and developing agritourism. About 6,250 farmers' professional cooperatives had been set up; 551 villages had become models in building effective partnerships with big enterprises; and 165 villages had a wholesale market.

Second, production clusters or belts have formed. Based on the advantages of different areas, scientific planning and more investment have been made in 11 counties to set up different industry belts or product clusters, including Luochuan (apples), Zhenping (pigs), Jingyang (vegetables), Shiquan (silkworms) and Wugong (handicrafts). Eighteen counties are accelerating the establishment of five product belts including kiwi fruit, melons, vegetables, tea, konjac (also known as devil's tongue or elephant yam) and Sichuan peppers. The 'one product per village' campaign is linking up different producing areas that complement each other to form synergistic belts and zones. The 'one product per village' model is transforming into 'multiple villages one product', 'one industry per township' and 'one industry per county'.

Third, more brands have been launched. Among the 'one product per village' model villages, 7.5% (288 villages) have developed brands recognized at or above provincial (municipal) level, 3.9% (148 villages) have obtained 'Products with Geographic Symbol of Origin Protection', 6.3% (239 villages) have products with registered trademarks, and 13.3% (471 villages) have pollution-free agricultural products, green food or organic farm products. Special local products are renowned around the world, such as apples from Luochuan, kiwi fruit from Zhouzhi, Sichuan peppers from Hancheng, red dates from Qingjian, green tea from southern Shaanxi, beef from Qinchuan, and clay sculptures from Fengxiang. Those products have become drivers of the local economy and increased people's incomes.

Fourth, many villages have become 'one product per village' model villages.

> *Yusheng Village in Zhouzhi County is a model of developing leading enterprises, Di'erpo Village in Meixian County is a model of service driving production, Huama Village in Jingyang County is a model of production driven by professional markets, Huangying Village in Dali County is a model of stimulating production via leading farmers, Longtou Village in Pingli County is a model of advancing the economy through local specialties, Yuanjia Village in Liquan County is a model of exploiting local customs, and the list goes on. Such models have driven the local rural economy and encouraged other farmers to find more ways to become rich.*
>
> *Fifth, farmers' incomes have increased markedly. In 2010, the average net annual income of residents of 'one product per village' model villages was Rmb5,800 (US$853), an increase of 97.3% from Rmb2,860 in 2006 representing an annual increase of 18.5%, and was 41.3% higher than the average for the whole province, which was Rmb4,105 (US$604). More than 70% of their income comes from leading industries or products.*

Source: Shaanxi: 'One product per village' stimulates agricultural development', February 15, 2013. http://gb.cri.cn/27824/2011/10/27/498 5s3416208.htm

II. Actively Develop Secondary and Tertiary Industries in Agriculture

In 2003, among 490m rural workers, 135m transferred from rural areas to work for TVEs. However, in the foreseeable future, despite the fact that an increasing number of rural workers will enter cities, the problem of surplus labor and underemployment in rural areas will remain. Therefore, we must expand their employment in an all-round way. Job opportunities can be created in rural areas by developing secondary and tertiary industries.

1. Strenuously develop the agricultural product processing industry. China will accelerate the development of preliminary processing of agricultural products by improving facilities, thus reducing post-harvest losses and upgrading the market competitiveness of products. Following market orientation, China will try to improve intensive processing of agricultural products, develop processed products based on grain and oil, sugar, fruit, vegetables, meat, aquatic products, dairy products and the processing of characteristic agricultural resources, and turn out safe and nutritious products with high-added value and high quality. Optimize the arrangements of the agricultural product processing industry by encouraging enterprises to consolidate in advantageous regions. Agricultural product processing enterprises will be supported to undergo technological transformation, improve facilities and upgrade technologies, thus enhancing the product quality and creating famous-brand products with high market share.

2. Promote the development level of TVEs. We will urge TVEs to upgrade themselves, step up technological innovation, promote industrial restructuring, improve operating and managing mechanisms, and enhance employee competence and enterprises' core competitiveness. We will promote rural enterprises to conserve energy and reduce emissions, carry out cleaner production and develop a circular economy. We will encourage rural enterprises to establish conglomerates through mergers and acquisitions across regions and industries. Rural enterprises will be centralized or clustered in counties, small towns and parks to increase the clustering effect. We will adopt preferential fiscal policies and provide financial support to enterprises in terms of guarantees, loans and public offerings, thus creating a good environment for the development of rural enterprises. Township and village enterprises will be supported to participate in the development of modern agriculture, the construction of rural and agricultural infrastructure and the supply of public services.

3. Speed up the development of tertiary industries in rural areas. Producer services including finance, information and technology will be developed to meet the demand of rural economic development. We will support cooperative organizations such as commercial and trading cooperatives and farmers' professional cooperatives to develop chain operations and promote rural finance credit marketing. We will firmly implement the '10,000 villages and 1,000 townships' market program to encourage large trading enterprises to extend their services to rural areas, promote the construction of e-commerce systems in rural areas, and to improve logistical systems to increase logistics efficiency. In order to satisfy the needs of rural residents, we will develop consumer services including communication, culture, catering, tourism and entertainment, enrich the variety of service products, enlarge the supply of services and improve service quality. We will also develop services for the aged and community services to adapt to life-style changes brought about by the aging of the population.

New ways for farmers to start local businesses: a survey of e-commerce development in Shaji Town, Suining County, Jiangsu Province

As a symbolic marketing tool in the information age, e-commerce, without any geographical restrictions, is able to offer farmers opportunities to start local businesses because of its low trading costs, simple trading procedures, and unlimited market space. Farmers in Shaji Town, Suining County, Jiangsu Province, have extended their business nationwide and even to foreign countries like Singapore. Nongfeng Village in this town was given 'The Honor of Distinction for Starting E-commerce Business in China's Rural Areas' by the 13th International E-Commerce Conference and Shaji Town was heralded as 'the best place for e-business people' by the organizing committee of the E-Business People's Conference in 2010.

1) Main Methods of Doing Things

1. Supplying direction for the development of rural areas and promoting endogenous development. Because farmers are pragmatic and reluctant to try new things, e-commerce, the new mode of trading and production, needs to be promoted by able people (leaders) in rural areas.

In 2006, the 'three musketeers' Sun Han, Xia Kai and Chen Lei in Dongfeng village started their internet business. At first, they sold pendants and home accessories and later they turned to panel furniture. In order to increase the profitability, Sun Han first invested Rmb100,000 (US$16,110) to build a furniture workshop, using an integrated sales and production model. Their success motivated many rural residents to follow in their footsteps, including the aged, women, the disabled, farmers working away from home, and even middle-level managers of large enterprises. Hu Cuiying was a housewife and her husband and son worked away from home all year round. After noticing that internet commerce was profitable, she asked her family to return home. Later, their family workshop was started, with her son making designs and her daughter-in-law in charge of sales. Liu Xingli, a line manager from Xuzhou Dadi Group, went back home with his wife and set up Sanshi Furniture Company. The influence of the 'three musketeers' spread quickly throughout Dongfeng Village, and even extended to Shaji Town. Now the nearby towns of Lingcheng and Gaozuo, and even Gengche Town in Suqian and Shantou Town in Sichuan Province, have all been affected.

2. Consolidating and upgrading industries. E-commerce has boosted the expansion of furniture production and supporting industries and also the development of industry chains. The supporting industries such as panel processing, furniture accessories and logistics are developing very fast and the industrial chains are being extended. Up until now, there are being more than 200 furniture production plants, one professional service provider for e-commerce, two furniture accessory stores, six panel processing factories and 16 logistics enterprises. With the expansion of industries, industrial upgrading is a natural next step. At present, the furniture industry in Shaji Town is undergoing a big transformation. Family workshops are being replaced by modern companies, and low-end furniture is being replaced by high-end furniture. Instead of making the same products or imitating others, they offer customized services and make innovations. Besides, they develop their own brands and no longer imitate famous brand products. For example, in 2010, Shaji Town applied for 50 registered trademarks and more than 100 products are trademark-protected.

3. Self-regulating the industry and standardizing its development. In order to regulate the industry, promote its healthy development and gain a greater say in the material supply chain, the telecommunication network and logistics, Shaji Town has established an e-traders' association. Through experience sharing, joint purchasing and business training, the association has attracted a lot of members, set up rules applicable to all members and regulated the e-traders' management. Sun Han, the president of the association, said, "We have over 200 members. Through consultation, a system of rules and regulations have been established. Now we are formulating technical standards for furniture quality in Shaji Town and e-commerce customer service standards to better regulate the industry's production and services."

4. Services follow-up backed up by management. The development boom in newly emerging industries cannot be separated from the services and management provided by party committees and government. The Suining County and Shaji Town governments have offered high-quality services in finance, telecommunications, public security, training and legal affairs with the intention of creating a good atmosphere and favorable conditions for business start-ups. For instance, a project to bring broadband into households was implemented to encourage the opening of rural online stores; rural road and highway widening has been supported by the county's finance bureau; streetlights have been installed to facilitate the transport of goods at night; a fire brigade has been set up to eliminate any fire risk; a network training center has been established by the county's women's federation to educate rural women about e-commerce. The emergence of e-commerce in Shaji Town has come from farmers' spontaneous behavior, so in order to maintain the enthusiasm of farmers to run and start their own businesses and to give them plenty of room, the government has focused on offering services to them. As the county's party secretary Wang Tianqi puts it: "Our government can't intervene unless farmers request us to do so."

2) Achievements

1. *Economic prosperity has been promoted. Starting online businesses in Shaji Town is quite popular nowadays. There are over 1,000 e-traders and nearly 2,000 online stores in Shaji Town and the sales in 2010 exceeded Rmb300m (US$48m). Hu Cuiying's family used to be very poor, but their net income from online sales reached more than Rmb100,000 (US$16,110) last year. Wang Congzhang who previously collected and sold trash for a living in Anhui Province earned over Rmb200,000 (US$32,220) last year. Local residents said: "Opening an online store at home gives people a very good life."*

2. *Industrial transformation has been accelerated. The agricultural land per capita in Shaji Town is less than one mu, most of which is saline-alkali soil. Villagers used to work far away from home, recycle waste plastics, make tiles, or process flour and noodles. Although these means of subsistence have increased farmers' incomes to some extent, they have also caused various problems such as environmental pollution and waste of resources. The emergence of e-commerce in rural areas has promoted the development of other industries, boosted the expansion of industry chains and expedited the transformation and upgrading of the economic structure. From 2009, as an increasing number of farmers turned to e-commerce, the online business industry has surpassed other industries such as the recycling and processing of waste plastics in Dongfeng Village.*

3. *Rural growth momentum has been strengthened. Industrialization and urbanization have attracted many young people - especially outstanding people - to cities, while the old, the weak, women and children were left behind. As a result, new socialist countryside construction remained weak, which has perpetuated the wide gap between rich and poor and the evident urban-rural divide. Among 4,000 people in Dongfeng Village, over 1,000 people worked away from home before, and sometimes the number even reached over 2,000. The success of e-commerce in Dongfeng Village has acted like a magnet drawing more than 90% of the people who worked away from home to come back and start their own business. In the past, the village was desolate, but now it is becoming revitalized as a hot bed for start-ups.*

4. *Social harmony has been enhanced. In the past, there was a large number of 'empty-nest households' since young people were working away from home. Therefore, the old were not well supported, children lacked parental care, couples were separated for a long time and alienated from each other, and some people were idle all day long, which led to a series of social problems and disrupted social*

harmony and stability. Now, as many people have returned home, the empty-nest problem has basically been settled and thus people are enjoying a happy life. As party secretary Huang Hao puts it, each and every household is too busy to make trouble and disturb public security, so there has been a dramatic decline in the number of criminal cases and civil disputes.

Source: A case compiled by Wang Youming, China Executive Leadership Academy Pudong

A national model village: the development of Jiangxiang village, Changshu

Jiangxiang village is located in Shajiabang, a town which is crisscrossed by rivers and dotted by lakes in the Yangcheng water network, and borders on three cities in Jiangsu Province: Changshu, Kunshan and Taicang. Covering 3sq km, the village has 800 residents belonging to 186 families. The beautiful scenery is made up of rivers, weeping willows, well-proportioned gardens and winding paths that pleasantly surprise visitors. Just 40 years ago, Jiangxiang was an isolated and poverty-stricken village. Most residents lived in delapidated thatched cottages with clay walls and contracted schistosome. It used to be the poorest region in Changshu County (now known as Changshu Municipality). However, after 40 years have passed, Jiangxiang Village has become a national civilized village, a national model village of rural modernization construction and a China top 10 affluent construction beautiful red guard unit.

Jiangxiang village's development path has attracted people's attention. *In the late 1960s, under the leadership of the village's party secretary Chang Desheng, villagers strove to fight against poverty. They spent 20 years topping up 1,700 mu (113 hectares) of low, arid land, raising the ground level by an average of one meter. Meanwhile, they also cleared up ponds and used sludge to fertilize the soil. In the late 1970s, with the past barren land turned into mellow-soil fields, Jiangxiang village's rice and wheat per unit yield came to rank first in Changshu.*

While developing agriculture, Jiangxiang Village also made a foray into industrialization. In the mid-1980s, rural enterprises sprung up in the south of Jiangsu province, which promoted the development of modern agriculture and rural urbanization. Villagers built light building material factories which produced composite panels. Nowadays, Changsheng Group Co Ltd, which started from a light building material factory, has developed into the largest corporation manufacturing light and heavy steel structures and light building materials

95

in eastern China. It has become a national enterprise group, with its products becoming the only famous-brand product of the industry in Jiangsu province. Within a decade, the company has paid Rmb200m (US$32m) in national tax revenue, and invested over Rmb100m in new rural construction, which has laid a solid material foundation for transforming Jiangxiang village into an affluent community.

Jiangxiang village is also engaged in developing sightseeing agriculture. In 2003, the village received 50,000 domestic and international visitors. The National Tourism Administration has designated Jiangxiang village as a national demonstration site for agricultural tourism. Jiangxiang village, based on its beautiful scenery, perfect living environment and prosperous industries, is another resort and also a backyard garden of surrounding cities. Tourism is becoming Jiangxiang village's new economic growth node.

Currently, due to its structural adjustment of agriculture and planting industry, villagers are reallocating land and pond resources to build ecological plantations combining agricultural production, the natural environment and ecological benefits. It symbolizes that Jiangxiang village has started to farm in a scientific way.

In 2010, Jiangxiang village's total economic output reached Rmb1.2bn (US$193m), of which industrial output exceeded Rmb1bn and tourist income was more than Rmb12m (US$1.93m). Villagers' per capita income was more than Rmb25,000 (US$4,027) (excluding collective welfare and house purchase subsidies) and per capita dividends were Rmb6,000 (US$967).

From 1995, Jiangxiang village started building a farmers' concentrated residential quarter. After the project was finished, the houses were sold to villagers at half the market price. Some 100 apartments were specially designed and built for the elderly, each with an average of over 50sqm and equipped with standard three-star hotel facilities. The elderly are free to choose their houses, but they are encouraged to live with their children in the houses and can get Rmb2,000 to Rmb3,000 (US$322 to US$483) bonus per year. If they live in the apartments, they don't need to pay housing rent but don't get the bonus.

Since 2001, Jiangxiang village has bought the five 'insurances', including pensions, medical, work-related injury, unemployment and maternity insurance. Villagers' basic livelihood is guaranteed, they have jobs to support themselves, and the old, the weak, the sick and the disabled have something to rely on. In a word, they are marching toward an affluent society with no worries about the future.

Farmers' houses in Jiangxiang village

III. Developing Expansion of the County-Level Economy

The county-level economy connects the rural economy with the urban economy. Accelerating the development of the county-level economy can invigorate the rural economy, promote the transfer of surplus rural labor to non-agricultural industries and towns, speed up urban-rural integration and enhance the harmonious development of the urban and rural economy.

1. Accelerating the cultivation of county-level leading industries. By utilizing comparative advantages and improving the development environment, we will nurture key enterprises, accelerate the cultivation of county-level leading industries, drive the development of supporting and correlated industries, and facilitate the development of industrial clusters. We will make overall plans to construct county-level industrial parks, promote the parks' integrated development, improve the infrastructure, reinforce the parks' management and innovation, enhance the parks' services and strengthen their bearing capability and hub-and-spoke functions. We will lead corporations, resources, funds and talent to gather in parks and make industrial parks specialized and standardized to develop synergy there. We will encourage western regions to accept the transfer of industries from eastern regions.

Small commodities and large markets: China's small commodity city in Yiwu, Zhejiang

Yiwu is a county-level town in Zhejiang Province's Jinhua Municipality. Jinhua-

Yiwu (central Zhejiang), Hangzhou (northern Zhejiang), Ningbo (eastern Zhejiang) and Wenzhou (southern Zhejiang) together comprise the four key urban districts of Zhejiang Province. Located in the middle of Zhejiang Province, Yiwu is in the eastern part of the Jinqu basin and is surrounded by mountains on three sides. Some 58.15km long from north to south and 44.41km wide from east to west, it covers an area of 1,105sq km. Yiwu County was founded around 222 BC and in 1988 the former Yiwu County was turned into a municipality. By the end of 2012, Yiwu's registered population was 753,312, the registered migrant population was 1.595m and its total employed labor force was 1.377m mainly from Jiangxi, Henan, Anhui, Guizhou and Zhejiang provinces.

Yiwu has a long history of handicrafts. After the 3rd plenary session of the 11th Central Committee of the CPC in 1978, there was rapid growth in industrial enterprises owned by the whole people, collectives, and towns and villages. In 1984, industrial system reform was fully implemented, the autonomy of enterprises was expanded, and rural enterprises commonly adopted the household contract responsibility system. During the 11th Five-Year Plan period (2006-2010), Yiwu's total industrial output rose from Rmb59.3bn (US$9.55bn) in 2005 to Rmb97.2bn (US$15.66bn) in 2009 with an annual increase of 13.1%. It basically formed the development pattern of manufacturing small consumer goods, building a large market for small consumer goods, and the aggregation of small enterprises. The value of small commodity manufacturing accounted for 70% of Yiwu's industrial output.

Yiwu is one of the richest regions in China. According to Forbes, it ranked among the top 10 richest county-level cities in China in 2013. Yiwu is the world's biggest small commodity collection and distribution centre. China's small commodity city was established in Yiwu in central Zhejiang in 1982, and was one of the earliest specialized markets to be created in China. With an area of more than 4.7m sqm, it has 70,000 stores, over 210,000 sales people and 210,000 consumers per day. The small commodities there can be divided into 16 categories, 4,202 types, 33,217 subtypes, and 17m individual items. As the international center for the circulation, information and display of small commodities, Yiwu Market was honored by the UN, the World Bank, Morgan Stanley and other world authorities as the 'largest small commodities wholesale market in the world'. In 2013, the China Commodity City's transactions amounted to Rmb68.30bn (US$11bn) ranking top of the list of specialized markets nationwide for 23 consecutive years.

Comprising three markets, Yiwu International Trade Mart, Huangyuan Market and Binwang Market, Yiwu Market encompasses almost all manufactured goods for daily use, including handicrafts, accessories, daily necessities, electronics, toys, textiles and clothing, of which accessories, socks and toys account for 1/3 of the national market value. Yiwu Market, with a wide range of low-cost, high-quality products, is very competitive.

A flurry of activity in the accessories aisle of Yiwu's international trade and commerce city

Yiwu Market is also one of China's biggest small commodities exporting bases. Some 570,000 TEU of containerized goods have been exported to 219 countries and regions, of which foreign trade makes up for 65%. There are 3,059 offices of foreign companies in Yiwu, more than in any other county-level location in China, with more than 13,000 foreign people doing business there. Institutions such as the United Nations High Commission for Refugees (UNHCR) and the Ministry of Foreign Affairs have built purchasing information centers and 83 countries and regions have set up commodity import centers in Yiwu. A hub for the 'worldwide buying and selling of goods' is taking shape in Yiwu.

Since 2006, China's Ministry of Commerce has published annual indexes of China's Small Commodity City and the 'Classification and Codes for Small Commodities', which make 'the world's supermarket' in Yiwu the pace setter in setting prices and standards for the small commodities market worldwide. It was a great leap for Yiwu to export standards and regulations, not just commodities like before.

In 2012, Yiwu's total output reached Rmb80.3bn, an increase of 10.2% over the previous year. Its per capita output was Rmb107,009 ($16,952 at the 2012 exchange rate), an increase of 9.6%. The relative shares of Yiwu's three industries have been optimized at 2.6:41.6:55.8.

2. Actively promoting the development of small towns. Focusing on counties and central towns, China will develop a number of larger towns with strong influence. The overall plan for land utilization will be strengthened by reinforcing the planning of small towns and defining reasonable development boundaries. We will promote the intensive growth of towns, aligning the expansion of towns with the aggregation of industries and population. We will enhance infrastructure construction in small towns, improve comprehensive economic growth, improve public services and living conditions, and encourage rural surplus labor to find jobs in local or nearby towns, return home to start a business, or settle down in towns.

IV. Promoting the Employment of Rural Migrants

1. Expanding the employment channels for rural workers. We will make great efforts to support the training of rural workers, offer subsidies for occupational skills testing and initiate vocational training programs such as order-based training and targeted training to meet labor market demand and practically improve rural workers' skills. In order to encourage farmers to find non-agricultural jobs in their hometowns or nearby towns or cities, we will strengthen infrastructure construction in rural areas and focus on labor-intensive industries while developing the secondary and tertiary sector sin rural areas and counties. We will also provide employment information services and build labor outflow platforms to help farmers seek jobs in other areas. Via policies supporting farmers to start their own business, we will provide services for free such as counseling, training, project guidance, and provide small-sum loans at discounted interest rates or loan guarantees to encourage farmers to start their own business in their hometowns to create new jobs.

2. Enhancing the protection of rural workers' legitimate rights and interests. We will build up a unified, regulated and flexible labor market to promote equal employment opportunities for both rural and urban workers. We will carry out the labor contract system nationwide to promote the use of signed contracts among rural workers and to regulate the process of labor utilization and dismissal. We will enhance the wage-setting and wage-raising mechanisms, guarantee wage payment, and improve the minimum wage system and the wage guideline system, increasing the minimum wage gradually to achieve equal pay for rural and urban workers. We will also improve working conditions to ensure safety and provide healthcare services, especially the prevention and treatment of occupational diseases; set up a tripartite mechanism for labor relations involving government authorities, labor unions and employers; intensify labor security supervision and law enforcement efforts, develop labor dispute settlement mechanisms, and provide rural workers with free services, such as dispute mediation and arbitration.

Kunshan Municpality in Jiangsu Province establishes direct access to legal aid for rural workers

Kunshan is a city in southeastern Jiangsu Province. Located between Shanghai and Suzhou, it covers an area of 927.68sq km, of which 23.1% is water. Kunshan is also the cradle of Kun Opera, the oldest extant form of Chinese opera. Kunshan is also the best developed county-level city in China and has remained top of the 100 best county-level economies in China. In September 2010, Kunshan was one of five cities to win the UN-Habitat Scroll of Honour Award along with Singapore and Vienna.

In recent years, migrant workers have flooded into Kunshan, amounting to more than 1.3m now, which far exceeds the local population. As a result, more disputes related to rural workers have appeared, which require more legal assistance. In order to protect the rights and interests of migrant workers and maintain social stability, the Kunshan Legal Aid Center has taken five measures to ensure access to legal aid for migrant workers.

First, the center enhances legal aid team building for rural workers via: enlarging the team of lawyers available for legal aid; strengthening training; and intensifying performance evaluation to reward good behavior and punish bad behavior to strengthen the foundation for teams of lawyers.

Second, the center works on spreading knowledge about the law among rural workers by: initiating training programs on 'Law Lectures for New Citizens'. The lectures are delivered in villages, towns and enterprises where rural workers are gathered, with the aim of informing more workers about legal aid.

Third, the center provides timely services while handling cases by: completing the assignation and materials handover promptly; and making mediation the first choice to solve problems quickly, cheaply and efficiently.

Fourth, the center improves the legal assistance network for rural workers by: enhancing cross-departmental connections with trade unions, the Communist Youth League, All-China Women's Federation and the courts; conveying sound knowledge on rights protection to rural workers; helping to mediate in the process of rights protection to save time for rural workers and help lawyers to obtain evidence, examine records and file cases.

Fifth, the center further regulates the work of legal aid for rural workers. Teachers and students from Nanjing University Law School also provide specific legal aid to meet farmers' needs, making legal aid for rural workers a feature of the Kunshan Legal Aid Center.

Source: China Legal Aid website

http://www.chinalegalaid.gov.cn/China_legalaid/content/2011-02/15/content_2473224.htm?node=24963 (February 15, 2011)

V. Striving to Increase Transfer Income for Rural Workers

1. Abolishing agricultural taxes. Agricultural taxes (including the agricultural tax, slaughter tax, the animal husbandry tax and agricultural specialties tax), except for the tax on tobacco leaves, have been abolished in China since January 1, 2006, ending the 2,600-year-old agricultural taxes based on cropland acreage. Compared with 1999 when taxation reform had not begun, farmers in China have been able to save over Rmb100bn (US$16.1bn) in taxes (Rmb120 per capita) every year since 2006. The abolition of agricultural taxes is an indication that China's agriculture is starting to follow international practice. When a country's economy develops to some extent, the country eliminates agricultural taxes and provides subsidies for farmers. Therefore, it was a logical step for China to abolish agricultural taxes and to implement a policy of giving more, taking less and loosening control in the process of its development.

2. Providing agricultural subsidies. In 2002, China launched a pilot project to grant agricultural subsidies. Two years later, in 2004, the agricultural subsidies were given to all farmers (including subsidies given directly to grain growers, subsidies for purchasing quality seeds and agricultural machinery and tools, and general subsidies for purchasing agricultural supplies). Although the total subsidies are more than Rmb100bn (US$16.1bn), they are still very low on a per capita basis, around Rmb200 (US$32.20), less than 4% of a farmer's average annual net income. Therefore, with its financial strength increasing, China should upgrade its agricultural subsidies policy and increase the total amount of subsidies. China should also make good use of both existing and additional financial resources and improve the regulation of subsidy distribution. We will strengthen the mechanisms for granting subsidies in major grain-growing areas for farmland protection and ecological protection to accelerate the progress towards achieving reasonable profitability in agriculture and raising the financial strength of major grain-growing areas to the average level of the country or the provinces. The newly added subsidies will focus on major grain-growing areas and areas with advantageous conditions to grow grain, and will be directed mainly toward new production and management businesses, such as large specialized farming businesses, household farms, and farmers' cooperatives. We will ensure the subsidies are paid to farmers. We will increase the amount of subsidies for purchasing quality seeds, agricultural machinery and tools, and carry out a pilot project of 'trading in old machinery for new'. We will improve the dynamic adjustment mechanisms of rural infrastructure subsidies and gradually increase the range of subsidies for large farming businesses.

3. Other supporting policies. China will continue to help develop technologies for preventing and mitigating disasters, raising productivity and soil organic matter. We will also support comprehensive and professional prevention and control of plant diseases and pests, and launch pilot projects on using low-toxin and low-residue pesticides, and effective low-release fertilizers. We will improve the policy for supporting livestock industries including the beef cattle industry and the mutton sheep industry, and we also will implement the policies of subsidies and tax reduction for the ocean fishing industry. We will increase the financial rewards for major grain-producing counties to reward counties that provide large quantities of pigs and large quantities of grain seeds. The investment in comprehensive agricultural development will also be increased. And the investment in modern agriculture will focus on the development of the grain-growing industry and industries with local relative advantages or special industries. We will increase the agricultural categories eligible for insurance subsidies and expand the coverage of agricultural insurance. Pilot projects on agricultural insurance will be launched and expanded gradually.

4. Continuing to improve basic public services. We will set up a new old-age pension system for rural residents, and increase the contribution standard and the level of subsidies and reimbursement in the new rural cooperative medical system to achieve a 10% annual growth in rural minimum living standards.

5. Increasing investment in poverty alleviation. China is the most populous developing country in the world with a weak economic foundation and notably unbalanced development. In particular, it has a large population below the poverty line in rural areas, rendering the mission to alleviate poverty particularly difficult. For this reason, China's poverty alleviation program is mainly about solving the rural poverty problem.

In the mid-1980s, the Chinese government started the development-oriented poverty alleviation program in rural areas in an organized and planned way. It formulated and implemented the *Eighth Seven-Year Priority Poverty Alleviation Program (1994-2000)*, the *Outline for Poverty Alleviation and Development of China's Rural Areas (2001-2010)*, and the *Outline for Development-Oriented Poverty Alleviation for China's Rural Areas (2011-2020)*, and a few other poverty alleviation plans, making poverty alleviation a common aim and action of the whole society. China's development-oriented poverty alleviation program in rural areas has promoted social harmony and stability, fairness and justice, and made contributions to the development and progress of the country's human rights cause.

In 2001, the Chinese government issued a white paper entitled *Development-Oriented Poverty Alleviation Program for Rural China*. The past decade has witnessed China's stable and rapid economic growth and increasing national economic and social development. The Chinese government has incorporated development-oriented poverty alleviation into its overall development plan, formulated and implemented policies and measures conducive to the development of poverty-stricken rural areas, made poverty alleviation a priority in the public budget and identified poor areas as key recipients of public financial support. The country has continuously increased support for poor areas and earnestly enhanced its ability to implement poverty-alleviation policies.

(1) Rural policies. China is traditionally an agricultural country with a large rural population and a great number of people in poverty. The implementation of rural policies to reduce rural poverty is thus extremely important for the elimination of poverty in rural China. In the past decade, the Chinese government has carried out a strategy of coordinating urban and rural socio-economic development, and followed the principles of industry nurturing agriculture, urban areas supporting rural areas and 'giving more, taking less and loosening control' to promote comprehensive development of the rural economy and society to benefit all poor areas and all the rural poor. The government has successively abolished agricultural taxes, granted direct subsidies to grain growers and gradually established and improved the social security system for rural China and pushed forward the construction of infrastructure for safe drinking water, electricity, roads and biogas, along with the renovation of rundown rural houses. The system of collective forest rights has been reformed to make farmers real contractors of forested land and real owners of trees in the forests, and various preferential policies have been implemented to develop the forest economy and forest tourism to increase farmers' incomes. The government has kept increasing investment into measures that strengthen agriculture and measures that benefit farmers and increase their incomes, as well as the development-oriented poverty alleviation program. Central budget spending on agriculture, the countryside and farmers increased from Rmb214.42bn (US$35bn) in 2003 to Rmb857.97bn (US$138bn) in 2010, representing an annual increase of 21.9%, indicating that the country is quickening the pace of agricultural support. Some state policies that strengthen agriculture, benefit farmers and increase their incomes were first carried out in impoverished areas. Of them, some policies were first carried out in key counties in the national development-oriented poverty alleviation program, and these policies included the pilot project to abolish agricultural taxes, the policy to offer rural students free compulsory education, and to provide living subsides for boarding students, and the policy to reduce or cancel the required supporting funds to be supplied by local governments at and below the county level for the new public welfare infrastructure projects listed in national plans. Poor areas and poor people were made the top priority in the implementation of some policies that strengthen agriculture and benefit farmers. The central government has given considerable financial support to the central and western regions concerning subsistence allowances for rural residents, new cooperative medical care and new social endowment insurance for rural residents. In 2010, the civil affairs departments paid a total of Rmb1.4bn (US$225m) in subsidies to 46.154m people in the new rural cooperative medical care scheme, or an average of Rmb30.3 (US$4.90) per person.

(2) **Regional development policies.** At the end of the 20th century, the Chinese government started large-scale development of the western region. Compared with other regions of China, western China has rather adverse natural conditions, underdeveloped infrastructure and a larger poor population. In the last decade, water conservancy projects, projects for returning cultivated land to forests and projects of resource exploitation,

as planned in the strategy of developing the western region, were launched first in poverty-stricken areas; highways were extended to poor areas at a quicker pace to link up the county seats of poor areas with national and provincial highways; the labor force from poor areas was given preference in infrastructure construction projects to increase the cash income of the poor. The government has also worked out and implemented a series of policies for regional development to promote socio-economic development in Tibet and Tibetan-inhabited areas in Sichuan, Yunnan, Gansu and Qinghai provinces, as well as in Xinjiang, Guangxi, Chongqing, Ningxia, Gansu, Inner Mongolia and Yunnan, and pushed forward the development-oriented poverty-alleviation program as a policy priority.

(3) **Rural social security system.** To provide basic social security for the poverty-stricken population is the most fundamental way to steadily solve the problem of guaranteeing their basic livelihood. Ten years ago, the state decided to establish a rural subsidy system covering the rural areas including all rural residents with a per-capita annual net household income below the prescribed standard, so as to guarantee the basic livelihood of the rural poor in a stable, lasting and effective way. The standards of rural subsistence allowance were determined by local governments above the county level on the basis of the fees needed for such basic necessities as food, clothing, water, electricity and other things throughout the year. By the end of 2010, the system covered 25.287m rural households, totaling 52.14m people. In 2010, a total of Rmb44.5bn (US$7.2bn) of rural subsidies were granted, including Rmb26.9bn (US$4.3bn) of subsidies from the central government. The average standard for rural subsistence allowance was Rmb117 (US$18.80) per person per month, and the average subsidy was Rmb74 (US$11.90) per person per month. The state has provided five guaranteed forms of support (food, clothing, housing, medical care and burial expenses) for old, weak, orphaned, widowed or disabled rural residents who are unable to work and have no family support. During the past decade, the government has gradually turned these five forms of support from a collective welfare system into a modern social security system financed by the state instead of by the rural people themselves. By the end of 2010, the five forms of support had been extended to 5.34m rural households totaling 55.63m rural residents and basically covering almost all eligible rural residents. Public finance at all levels totaling Rmb9.64bn (US$1.5bn) was extended to eligible rural residents for such support. In 2009, the state launched a pilot scheme offering a new type of social endowment insurance for rural residents in some

places. By July 2011, the scheme had been extended to 60% of rural China, covering 493 key counties in the national development-oriented poverty-alleviation programs, accounting for 83% of such counties. Under this new social endowment insurance system for rural residents, the funds needed are pooled from personal contributions, collective grants and government subsidies, and pensions are paid from the basic funds and personal accounts; the central finance gives central and western China all the basic funds for old-age pensions in line with the standard set by the central government, and grants 50% of such funds for eastern China. In 2010, the central finance provided a total subsidy of Rmb11.1bn (US$1.8bn) for the basic old-age pension funds of the new social endowment insurance for rural residents, while local finances supplied Rmb11.6bn (US$1.8bn) for the same purpose. In 2004, the state introduced a standard minimum wage system, which has played a positive role in guaranteeing the rights and interests of laborers, mainly migrant workers from rural areas, with respect to remuneration for their labor.

(4) Improving the implementation of poverty-alleviation policies. The success of a policy lies to a large extent in its implementation. The Chinese government takes the establishment of a job-responsibility system, strengthening of the development of cadres and building of relevant institutions as the keys to implementing poverty-alleviation policies, and has taken effective measures to ensure the implementation of the policies. The central government has raised a requirement that 'provincial governments should take the overall responsibility and county governments are responsible for the implementation to ensure that poverty-alleviation staff go down to the villages and that the policies reach every household'. In accordance with this requirement, provincial governments assume the tasks, receive funds and exercise the power; governments of key counties covered in the national development-oriented poverty-alleviation programs take poverty alleviation as a central task, and are responsible for implementing the relevant policies and measures for every poor village and poor household. A responsibility system has been established for top leaders of local party committees and governments in the poverty-alleviation program, and their performance in this regard is taken as an important criterion for evaluating their official job performance. To strengthen the development of cadres in poor areas, the

Chinese government has incorporated the training of county-level cadres and cadres from poverty-alleviation departments above the county level in poor areas into the program of party and government cadre training, and strengthened and improved the contingents of cadres in poor areas by such means as appointing them to temporary posts or exchange posts. The government has strengthened statistics collection related to, and supervision over, poverty-alleviation work to provide reliable data for scientific decision-making. The state has strengthened organization building at the primary level in poor areas, worked hard to improve the ideology and work style of cadres at the primary level, and taken comprehensive measures to maintain law and order for the maintenance of social stability in these areas. The state has enhanced poverty-alleviation work organizations at all levels, ensured their personnel stability, improved their conditions and quality, and enhanced the organization, leadership, coordination and management of poverty-alleviation work. Relevant departments under the State Council regard poverty-alleviation as an important task and conscientiously implement poverty-alleviation policies in line with their corresponding functions and powers.

In 2012, the central government invested more on poverty alleviation, appropriating Rmb299.6bn (US$48.3bn) for poverty alleviation in 2014, an increase of 31.9% over the previous year. The total budget expenditure on poverty alleviation of 28 provinces, autonomous regions and municipalities was Rmb14.78bn (US$2.4bn). The central government invested Rmb1.898bn (US$306m) in designated poor areas in the form of direct aid, both in cash and in kind. The total investment also included various other support funds amounting to Rmb9.034bn (US$1.5bn).

By the end of 2012, the State Council had approved 11 programs for the development of contiguous poverty-stricken areas as well as the priority poverty-alleviation program which has been implemented throughout China. Some livelihood improvement projects and infrastructure construction projects have been carried out. Some 310 organizations have run poverty-alleviation projects in designated poor areas. This is the first time all the key poverty-stricken counties have been involved, leading to a reduction of people below the poverty line to less than 98.99m, which was 10.2% of the total rural population of China.

The emergence of three characteristics of 'Chinese-style poverty alleviation' programs
The State Council Information Office issued a white paper entitled 'Development-Oriented Poverty Alleviation for Rural China' on November 16, 2011. The white paper states that China has realized the goal of cutting the poverty-stricken population by half ahead of the United Nations Millennium Development Goals, thus making great contributions to the world's poverty-alleviation efforts. China's development-oriented poverty-alleviation policies display the following characteristics:

Combining development-oriented poverty alleviation with social security. *The state offers development guidance for poor areas and people in poverty, in line with market-oriented objectives, to improve their capability of self-accumulation and self-development. From 2001 to 2010, 592 key counties in the national development-oriented poverty-alleviation program have seen their per-capita gross regional product rising by an annual average of 17%, and the per-capita net income of farmers rising by 11%. Both growth rates are higher than the national average. By the end of 2010, the social security system, especially the provision of basic living allowances, covered 25.287m rural households, totaling 52.14m people. Old-age endowment insurance for rural residents is covering more and more areas.*

Combining special poverty-alleviation actions with industrial and social development efforts. *Special poverty-alleviation funds have been appropriated from the public budget as the main source to support special development programs which are carried out on a yearly basis. The Ministry of Water Conservancy and the Ministry of Transportation give top priority to the development of poor areas. Government departments, enterprises and public institutions give special support to designated poor areas, eastern and western regions of China cooperate to reduce poverty, the army and armed police give their support, and all sectors of society participate in this program. This is a poverty alleviation model with Chinese characteristics, which helps poor areas to develop and poor farmers to increase their income.*

Combining outside support with self-reliance. *Through the special poverty-alleviation funds, transfer payments from the central government budget, projects undertaken by various departments, social donations and foreign capital, the financial input into poor areas has been continuously increased. People in poor areas are also exerting themselves constantly and making every effort to lift their local areas and people out of poverty and backwardness. According to*

109

incomplete statistics, by 2010, US$1.4bn in foreign funds had been invested in poverty alleviation in China, and the total direct investment had reached nearly Rmb20bn (US$3.2bn) if supporting funds from the Chinese government are taken into account, benefiting nearly 20m impoverished people.

Source: *New Progress in Development-Oriented Poverty Alleviation Program for Rural China*, 2011. http://www.chinanews.com/cj/2011/11-16/3464376. shtml (November 16, 2011)

Chapter Follow-up Questions and References

Chapter 1

Questions:

1. Please briefly describe the basic rural operation system in China in your own words, including the land system and the two-tier operation system in rural areas based on the household contract responsibility system.

2. From the above analysis we can see the role of TVEs in promoting rural industrialization in China. Please give your comment on how to define the relationship between rural industrialization and agricultural modernization.

References:

1. Chen Xiwen, Zhao Yang, Chen Liubo and Luo Dan, *Transformation of China's Agriculture and Rural Areas (1949-2009)*, Beijing: People's Publishing House, October 2009

2. Chen Xiwen, Zhao Yang and Luo Dan, *Achievements and Outlook of China's Rural Reform (1978-2008)*, Beijing: People's Publishing House, December 2008

3. Song Hongyuan, *On China's Rural Reform (1978-2008)*, Beijing: China Agriculture Press, March 2008

4. Ministry of Agriculture Research Center for Rural Economics, *The Past and Future of China's Rural Reform*, Beijing: China Agriculture Press, September 2008

5. D. Gale Johnson, *Economic Development in Farming, Farmers and Agriculture*, translated by Justin Yifu Lin et al, Beijing: Commercial Press, September 2004

6. Justin Yifu Lin, *Institutions, Technologies and the Development of China's Agriculture*, Beijing: Truth & Wisdom Press, September 2014

Chapter 2

Questions:

1. Compared with its large population, China's land and water resources are inadequate. In this context, what measures could China take to ensure food security?

2. Where can efforts be made to increase food production?

3. What are the possible approaches and methods for increasing the efficiency of agricultural production and operation?

References:

1. *The 12th Five-Year Plan for the Development of the Rural Economy*, NDRC, June 2012

2. *The 12th Five-Year Plan for National Economic and Social Development of the PRC*, Xinhua News Agency, March 2011

3. *China Statistical Yearbook 2012*, China Statistics Press, 2012

4. Theodore Schultz, *Transforming Traditional Agriculture*, translated by Liang Xiaomin, Beijing: Commercial Press, November 2010

5. Pei-Kang Chang, *Agriculture and Industrialization*, Beijing: China Renmin University Press, November 2014

6. Yujiro Hayami and Vernon W. Ruttan, *Agriculture Development: An International Perspective*, translated by Wu Weidong, Beijing: Commercial Press, September 2014

Chapter 3

Questions:

1. What is the relationship between urbanization and the construction of a new socialist countryside?

2. To build a new socialist countryside, in what ways is the Chinese government directing its efforts? And what attempts have they made to improve the development mechanisms in rural areas?

3. What policies do you recommend for narrowing the gap between urban and rural areas?

References:

1. NDRC, T*he 12ᵗʰ Five-Year Plan for Rural Economic Development,* June 2012

2. Xinhua News Agency, *The 12th Five-Year Plan for National Economic and Social Development of the PRC,* March 2011

3. Wen Tiejun, *Report on Building a New Socialist Countryside,* Fujian People's Publishing House, April 2010

4. Song Hongyuan, Zhao Hai and Xu Xuegao, *From Poverty to Overall Affluence: Reviewing China's Agricultural and Rural Development During the 20th Century* [J], China Economist, May 2012

5. Han Jun, *Building a New Countryside: a Long-term Task in China's Modernization Drive* [J], China Economist, November 2007

   http://news.xinhuanet.com/ziliao/2011-03/28/c_121239866.htm

6. http://english.gov.cn/special/rd_index.htm

7. http://english.agri.gov.cn/

Chapter 4

Questions:

1. Apart from helping farmers find non-agricultural jobs in towns or cities, will local industrialization, urbanization and agricultural modernization help increase farmers' incomes? And what else can the government, market and society do to help increase their incomes?

2. What has China done to alleviate poverty?

3. What similarities and differences exist in terms of agricultural and rural development between your country and China? In which areas can the international community work together?

References:

1. Li Keqiang, *Public Products Supply and Development in Rural Areas,* Beijing: China Social Sciences Press, May 2013

2. Han Changbin, *The Development and Future of Rural Workers in China,* Beijing: China Renmin University Press, July 2007

3. Xie Chuntao, editor-in-chief, *China's Urbanization: the Story of Hundreds of Millions of Farmers Moving into Cities,* Beijing: New World Press, November 2014

4. Qin Hui, *China's Farmers: Reflection on History and Practical Choices*, Zhengzhou: Henan People Publishing House, June 2003

5. Zhu Ling, *Poverty Alleviation and Social Inclusiveness: Development Economics Research, Beijing*: China Social Sciences Press, January 2013

6. Xinhua broadcast, *The 12th Five-Year Plan for National Economic and Social Development*, March 2011

7. http://english.agri.gov.cn/

责任编辑:洪　琼
版式设计:顾杰珍

图书在版编目(CIP)数据

中国农业与农村发展/冯　俊　等著. —北京:人民出版社,2017.2
(中国故事丛书/冯俊主编)
ISBN 978－7－01－016474－8

Ⅰ.①中…　Ⅱ.①冯…　Ⅲ.①农业经济发展-研究-中国　②农村经济
发展-研究-中国　Ⅳ.①F323

中国版本图书馆 CIP 数据核字(2016)第 166844 号

中国农业与农村发展
ZHONGGUO NONGYE YU NONGCUN FAZHAN

冯　俊　王友明　胡云超　余　佶　著

人 民 出 版 社 出版发行
(100706　北京市东城区隆福寺街 99 号)

北京汇林印务有限公司印刷　新华书店经销

2017 年 2 月第 1 版　2017 年 2 月北京第 1 次印刷
开本:710 毫米×1000 毫米 1/16　印张:15.25
字数:250 千字　印数:0,001－5,000 册

ISBN 978－7－01－016474－8　定价:42.00 元

邮购地址 100706　北京市东城区隆福寺街 99 号
人民东方图书销售中心　电话 (010)65250042　65289539

《中国农业与农村发展》一书的英文部分由黄协安(Huang Xiean)翻译